500

COMMON

BIRD
CALLS

in Southern Africa

ree-oo-ree pi-ri-ri-ri tirup chip tink tseep zeeerrr
dzeei pee-ya zrik zeep-zeep-zeep chip-chip-chip churra-churra-churra witta-
-witta-witta deeu, chiru de-zip chree-chiu-chip-ch
dee-tir preeeuuuu sppree-reeu tututututututututu ti-t

Doug Newman

Published by Struik Nature
(an imprint of Random House Struik (Pty) Ltd)
Reg. No. 1966/003153/07
First Floor, Wembley Square, Solan Road, Gardens, Cape Town, 8001
PO Box 1144, Cape Town, 8000, South Africa

Visit www.randomstruik.co.za and join the Struik Nature Club
for updates, news, events and special offers

First published 2013

1 2 3 4 5 6 7 8 9 10

Publisher: Pippa Parker
Managing Editor: Helen de Villiers
Editor: Emily Bowles
Design Director: Janice Evans
Typesetter: Tessa Fortuin
Proofreader: Thea Grobbelaar

Reproduction by Hirt and Carter Cape (Pty) Ltd
Printed and bound by Toppan Leefung Packaging and Printing
(Dongguan) Co., Ltd, China

ISBN 978 143170 120 9

TRACK CREDITS

Cover: *Front:* *Cape Grassbird* (J. de Bruyn); *Red-capped Robin-Chat*
(Illustration by N. Arlott); *Back (clockwise from top right):* African
Harrier-Hawk (A. Froneman / Images of Africa); *Cape Spurfowl; Karoo
Long-billed Lark.*
Page 1: Top: Cape Bulbul (N. Dennis / Images of Africa); *Middle: Cape
Sparrow* (N. Dennis / Images of Africa); *Bottom: Tropical Boubou*
(A. Froneman / Images of Africa)
*This page: Birds that fall into the starling group, like this
Wattled Starling, give a wide range of different sounds.*
*Page 3: Surprisingly, the Pied Crow is considered to be a songbird,
although its call is harsh and unmusical.*

CONTENTS

INTRODUCTION

Recognising birds by their calls is a particularly rewarding activity in southern Africa, where we are blessed with almost 1 000 bird species. Bird calls are often the best route to identifying a shy bird or to telling similar-looking species apart. In fact, sometimes song provides scientists with their first clue that seemingly identical birds are, in fact, distinct species or subspecies.

Birdsong is a complex topic and many gaps remain in our understanding of why birds sing and call. Here we present a little guidance on how to use this book and a brief overview of some interesting aspects of bird vocalisation.

The audio tracks accompanying this book are a broad selection of those bird calls heard most often in our region. Included are the common, striking and interesting calls of indigenous species, naturalised aliens and a few rare or nomadic birds that are either well-known or worth listening out for.

If you're new to 'birding by ear', you may find it helpful to choose a bird or birds that you're familiar with and then to learn the calls of other members of that group.

If you're interested in how birdsong unlocks aspects of behaviour, then try listening to a particular species singing and calling at various times of the day, noting, for example, any differences in how it sounds at dawn or when settling down for the night.

You may even want to start by observing just one bird in your garden or neighbourhood and keeping a journal on it. For example, while regularly observing a Karoo Thrush family living in my garden, I soon noticed that the fledgling would give a particular call from a secluded shelter that would reliably draw the parents near. In a case like this, it is reasonble to conclude that the chick is using this call to beg for food.

A juvenile Karoo Thrush, photographed in the author's garden. Patient observation soon revealed which of its calls was the cue for the adults to arrive with food.

HOW TO USE THIS BOOK

The species accounts in this book follow the order of a conventional field guide, using the traditionally accepted taxonomy. This taxonomy has recently undergone substantial revisions, with some bird families being split in surprising ways, but the older order remains valuable to birders, since it lists species in a way that seems intuitively logical.

African Harrier-Hawk

A. Froneman / Images of Africa

Each species account is linked to an audio track – look for the numbered CD icons **1**. As far as possible, the sound supplied is that which you are most likely to hear in the field, whether it be a song, a call, a non-vocal sound or all of these. So even if a bird has a distinctive song, if you're most likely to hear its alarm call, then that is what is given on the CD.

The bulk of the book comprises species accounts with details of the main song and other sounds, a description of each species' habitat and a list of birds that sound similar.

Determining which birds sound similar is highly subjective and open to endless reinterpretation, but here we've tried to cross-reference sounds comprehensively, even where a given resemblance is tenuous or where habitat preferences render confusion unlikely (for example, the African Harrier-Hawk sounds a lot like a begging Red-knobbed Coot, although the former is not a water bird). The reason for doing so is that a good way to expand the number of songs and calls you know is to start with a bird whose sounds you already recognise, and then get familiar with those species that sound similar.

Rattling Cisticolas have highly varied repertoires. Even birds in fairly close proximity may sing quite different phrases. This variation serves a territorial function.

N. Dennis / Images of Africa

Above The African Red-eyed Bulbul gives a range of distinct sounds that illuminate its behaviour, such as resting chatter, anxious scolding and territorial advertisement songs.

Left A Red-knobbed Coot; juvenile coots begging for food sound very much like African Harrier-Hawks (top), but these birds occur in such different habitats that confusion is unlikely.

N. Dennis / Images of Africa

> **Note that unless otherwise indicated, the song is given by the male.**

BIRD ANATOMY

The human larynx (voice box) is made up of muscles and cartilage and is located fairly high up in the trachea (windpipe). We produce sound by expelling air from our lungs, while moving the muscles of the larynx back and forth, which generates sound waves. In contrast with humans, a bird's syrinx (equivalent to our larynx) is located lower, at the point where the windpipe splits into two bronchial tubes leading into the lungs. In humans the larynx is one organ, but in birds the syrinx comprises two halves. Indeed, many of the most sophisticated songs are produced by birds in which independent nerve systems connect each half of the syrinx to the brain. This is the reason why some of the so-called true songbirds (see 'Which are the true songbirds?' opposite) can produce two completely different sounds simultaneously. In a sense, they are able to duet with themselves!

A bird's brain has distinct song centres that may be highly developed to allow it to memorise new sounds.

Three brain centres are devoted to song: firstly, an area that instructs the syrinx to vibrate, producing sound; secondly, an area linked to the ears that enables the bird to hear itself sing (crucial to learning the songs of family members and neighbours and to mimicking other sounds) and, finally, a dedicated area of the brain that memorises songs.

In male birds the song control centres change size with the seasons, driven by alterations in levels of the hormone testosterone. These centres are larger in the breeding season, when birdsong plays a critical role in mate attraction. Outside of the breeding season, the song control centres shrink, reducing the desire to sing – and probably also a bird's ability to do so. In birds that are not true songbirds, however, these song control centres are far less highly developed and so seasonal variations in song are not as dramatic.

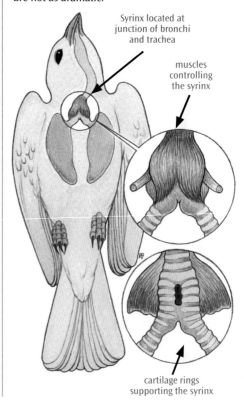

Syrinx located at junction of bronchi and trachea

muscles controlling the syrinx

cartilage rings supporting the syrinx

Some birds, like this Short-clawed Lark, are able to generate two distinct melodies at once. A bird's syrinx comprises two halves (see illustration), but not all species are able to use these halves independently as this lark does.

WHICH ARE THE TRUE SONGBIRDS?

What defines a true songbird? Contrary to what one might expect, they are not separated from other birds on the basis of the relative beauty of their songs. For example, a Pied Crow with is grating *kraaah* is considered a songbird, while the Diderik Cuckoo is not, despite its sweet musical *di-di-di-diderik* whistle.

The distinction is a simple one: *Songbirds learn their songs, while other species inherit their songs genetically.*

Technically, true songbirds belong to the order of birds known as oscines, while birds that do not learn songs may belong to the suboscines or another of the bird orders.

True songbirds, the oscines, fall into the following groups – listed here in roughly the order you'd find them in a standard bird field guide:

- bulbuls, brownbuls, greenbuls and nicators
- canaries, siskins, buntings, chaffinches and seedeaters
- cisticolas, prinias, apalises, wren-warblers, camaropteras
- creepers
- crested flycatchers
- crows, ravens
- cuckooshrikes
- drongos
- larks, sparrowlarks
- flycatchers, robin-chats, scrub robins, thrushes, akalats, wheatears
- orioles
- pipits, longclaws
- rockjumpers
- shrikes

- sparrows, petronias
- starlings, mynas, oxpeckers
- sugarbirds
- sunbirds
- swallows, martins
- tchagras, boubous, bushshrikes, brubrus, puffbacks, batises, wattle-eyes, helmetshrikes
- tits
- wagtails
- warblers, babblers, blackcaps, crombecs, hyliotas, eremomelas
- waxbills, finches, twinspots, mannikins,
- pytilias, crimsonwings
- weavers, bishops, queleas, widowbirds
- white-eyes
- whydahs, indigobirds, cuckoofinches

Rufous-naped Lark

Pied Crow

A. Froneman / Images of Africa

Marsh Warbler

P. & B. Pickford / Images of Africa

Rattling Cisticola

CALLS, SONGS, SUBSONGS AND NON-VOCAL SOUNDS

The terms *call*, *song* and *subsong* are often used interchangeably, but they actually describe quite different things:

- *A call* is a short, often sharp, sound given in a specific context, for example to establish and maintain group contact, to register distress or alarm or to beg for food (see 'Identifying and describing bird sounds' opposite). Sometimes given repeatedly, calls have simpler structures than songs.

- *A song* comprises longer, more complex sounds – both vocal and non-vocal – given to attract a mate in the breeding season. For this reason, most species have songs (although, as already mentioned, only true songbirds can learn songs).

- *A subsong* describes both the vocalisations of young birds when they're practising their songs (something like a human baby's early babbling) or the subdued singing of an adult songbird outside the breeding season, when its song control centres have shrunk. Adult subsong may bear only a slight resemblance to the full breeding song.

- *A non-vocal sound* may be given by many bird species, often as part of a mating display, and is thus considered to be a form of song. The African Snipe is a southern African species that exhibits this behaviour; its breeding display is distinguished by the vibrating hum of its tail feathers when it dives in the air. Woodpeckers are another good example. They proclaim their territory and attract mates by using their bills to drum rhythmical ringing phrases on hard branches, and each species has its own unique pattern. The bill-clicking of storks and the wing-rattling displays of clapper larks are other good examples of non-vocal sounds.

African Snipe

The male Pin-tailed Whydah shows off his long tail feathers during his display flight. He bobs up and down as he gives the ringing notes of his song.

IDENTIFYING AND DESCRIBING BIRD SOUNDS

When you start listening to and analysing songs and calls, try to bear in mind both their structure and their function.

Structure describes all aspects of how the song or call sounds, including the relationship between the parts. Are the notes long or short, clean and clear, or vibrating and trilled? Are the phrases simple or complex? Do they comprise jumbled notes or repetitive patterned groups of notes, or some combination of the two? Pitch and tone are equally important aspects of structure. Is the song sweet and musical, harsh and grating or a bit of both? Is it steady in pitch or does it ascend or descend, or does this vary?

Capped Wheatear males use song to defend their territory and guard their mates from would-be usurpers.

Function describes the purpose of the song or call. Bird sounds generally fall into one of the following categories:

● **Song or display song** A male ready to breed will generally sing loudly and clearly from a prominent position so that any potential mates can easily find him.

● **Territorial proclamation song** Once the male has paired up with a female he may call to announce to other males that his territory is occupied. This call is frequently very similar, or even identical, to the main song.

● **Territorial conflict** In some species, when competing males confront each other in a battle over territory or a female they give an agitated call that differs from the song. However, in many species the males simply compete by singing their display songs loudly.

● **Alarm or distress call** Alarm calls are often quite high pitched and have a ventriloquial quality. This enables an individual to warn other birds of potential danger, without giving away its own location.

● **Contact or group interaction call** Members of most bird species give rather quiet contact calls and chatter when they meet and interact, since loud calls could attract predators.

● **Settling call** Certain birds give a unique call as they settle down for the night. It is heard just before complete darkness sets in, but at no other time of day.

● **Flight call** Birds that have been frightened into taking flight typically give a short sharp variation of their usual alarm call. This is thought to serve as an alert to other members of its species that it has departed under threat. It typically triggers other members of the group to take flight.

DIALECTS AND REPERTOIRES

You may have noticed that the songs and calls of familiar species sometimes vary from place to place. Cape Sparrows in Cape Town, for instance, sound different from those in Johannesburg. This kind of regional variation is seen only among the songbirds.

As already mentioned, non-songbirds inherit all the genetic information they need to sing, and the chicks do not have to hear their parents singing in order to sing correctly themselves. This phenomenon is evident among cuckoos, for example, who lay their eggs in the nest of a host bird such as a sparrow. The chicks grow up hearing the sounds of their foster parents, yet cuckoos never give sparrows' calls. Members of a particular cuckoo species will also sound the same wherever they occur.

Thus, an apparent regional variation in the song of a non-songbird species may be good grounds for conducting further genetic research. In the United States, for example, call differences were noted in the eastern and western populations of the Western Flycatcher and subsequent genetic studies found that they were in fact two different species.

In the case of a true songbird, however, regional variation is seldom grounds for splitting species, since vocal development in these birds naturally leads to the evolution of broader repertoires and, ultimately, regional dialects. To split songbirds into multiple species requires very detailed examination of their calls (particularly the genetically inherited portion of a songbird's repertoire), physiological differences and even differences in nesting and other behaviour.

Although some songbirds, particularly those that mimic many other species, may have substantial repertoires, there is a limit to the number of songs a given bird can retain in its memory. A young songbird listens to and copies its parents and immediate neighbours, refining its subsong until it can imitate the adults' song repertoires almost exactly. Once its repertoire reaches maximum capacity the bird may well drop one of the songs it has already learned in order to accommodate a new phrase or song. This gradual replacement of songs means that birds of one species in a given area may slowly change their entire repertoire within just a decade. If you have not visited the area for a while, you may find on your return that the species now sounds quite different.

Male birds sing not only to advertise themselves as mates, but also to stake out females and territory and then to defend them from intruders. During the breeding season, when every male in a given area has paired up and established a territory, song repertoires tend to converge so that males recognise the calls of their paired-up neighbours. Singing is often the way in which neighbours guage that each male is keeping the required distance. In addition,

A male Rufous-naped Lark may have as many as 20 distinct phrases in his repertoire.

A. Froneman / Images of Africa

a lone foreign male attempting to usurp a female is quickly identified and repelled. If the intruding male is successful in usurping a mate and territory for himself, then neighbouring birds will adopt phrases from his repertoire just as he adopts some of theirs. Thus, a shared phrase serves as a kind of password, and dialects evolve.

This is helpful if a species is fairly sedentary, but is less useful to migrant and nomadic birds that move around frequently. Often they do not return to the same place each year and since it takes time to learn and refine local phrases, there's little point in continually acquiring new dialects. Thus nomadic and migratory species do not tend to exhibit many dialects.

Environmental disaster can result in the evolution of dialects that are unrelated to shared learning. For instance, if one or two youngsters were to colonise a patch of regrowth in an area of burnt fynbos, they would not have the chance to refine their subsong to match the adults' songs. As adults they would still sing incomplete calls. Once the regrowth merged back into the surrounding habitat, these now mature birds would retain their repertoire, even after meeting up with other members of their species. Over many generations, with successive fires, this would lead to an ever-increasing number of dialects.

N. Dennis/ Images of Africa

Cape Sparrows (above) sound quite different from place to place. In the Rattling Cisticolas (shown here) regional variation is so marked that individuals within just a few kilometres of each other may not share a single phrase.

A. Froneman / Images of Africa

MIMICRY

Mimicry can result in great frustration when you're trying to identify a bird by its songs and calls. Often, just as you're congratulating yourself on identifying a Crowned Eagle, say, you find that you're actually listening to a Red-capped Robin-Chat! Where species mimic other sounds this is denoted in blue type in the accounts that follow.

Birds mimic for various reasons. Some species use mimicry to steal food or to keep competing species away from food sources. This has been observed among Fork-tailed Drongos, which may mimic the alarm call of a species seen feeding, causing the birds to scatter. The drongos then drop down and quickly poach their food.

This does not, however, explain mimicry in species such as Red-capped Robin-Chats, which mimic a wide range of sounds and have even been known to copy the calls of Crowned Eagles. Since monkeys are an important component of the Crowned Eagle's diet, clearly the robin-chat is not mimicking in order to poach food. Furthermore, some species, like the robin-chats and even the Pied Crow, mimic sounds like those made by cars and telephones. In such cases it is likely that mate attraction is the force driving

Red-capped Robin-Chats are excellent mimics, copying anything from a Crowned Eagle to a telephone.

mimicry. In these species the female probably selects her mate on the basis of his vocal competence. A large repertoire that includes a great deal of mimicry may serve as a sign of male fitness. For the male, it's probably far easier to copy the sounds around him than it is to invent a new repertoire.

In support of this sexual selection theory one has only to look at migrating birds like Marsh Warblers. When they return to their European breeding grounds they often include in their songs various phrases learned in southern Africa. As they're far from the birds they've been mimicking, the purpose is evidently not related to territorial proclamation or mate defence or to appropriating or defending food. Rather, a male with a broad and complex song repertoire has a far greater chance of attracting a female.

Crows, like this Pied Crow, are known for their complex vocalisations. They are also good mimics.

Marsh Warblers breed in Europe, but often win mates with song phrases learned in southern Africa.

DUETS

Many birds sing duets, chiefly during the breeding season. In this guide those birds that **duet** are denoted in blue type in the species accounts.

Duetting males and females sing in one of the following co-ordinated patterns:

● **Call and response** This type of duet is seen in a number of species. The Spotted Eagle-Owl is a good example. The male gives a two-note hoot to attract a mate. Once he has paired up, however, you'll notice that his two-note hoot is followed within a few seconds by the lower pitched three-note hoot from the female. This evening duet can be heard for quite some time within the pair's territory.

● **Antiphonal duetting** This kind of duet is highly synchronised and the singing alternates rapidly between male and female. The Black-collared Barbet provides an excellent example. It is famous for its *too-puddley* call, in which the male gives a *too* note and the female quickly responds with a *puddley* note. This call and response is so fast that it sounds like a single bird giving a rapidly repeated phrase.

● **Simultaneous duetting** Birds sometimes duet by singing together. They may sound the same and give identical phrases, or each sex may give a different call simultaneously. African Rails, for example, sing together giving identical phrases, while in the Black Crake male and female sound different but sing together. In the latter case the song sounds strange when one member is not singing; a portion of the song is 'missing'.

> Note that sometimes a male and female sing together, but their song is not regarded as a true duet because it is not co-ordinated or patterned and is not a distinguishing feature of the species' song.

The male Black-collared Barbet gives a too *note, to which the female responds with* puddley.

Duetting serves various purposes, the most important of which is that it announces and strengthens a pair bond. So, a male Tropical Boubou will not respond aggressively to a recording of Tropical Boubous duetting. This is because the presence of a pair is not a threat. However, remove the female's song from the recording and he'll react aggressively, because a lone male singing is a potential rival, and poses a threat to his pair bond and his territory.

A duet may also serve to let other males know that a given female is paired and thus not available. In some cases the male stings from a perch and the female responds now and then with a call that she gives only when she is paired. This may well be her way of announcing that she has paired with the particular male who is proclaiming his territory.

Black Crakes duet together, although male and female give different phrases.

13

THE DAWN CHORUS

The dawn chorus refers to the singing of large numbers of birds just before dawn every day. The purpose of this spectacular cacophony of calls is something of a mystery. It is particularly outstanding during the breeding season when birds are most active and their voices sound best. Each species calls for a certain period before it tires and tapers off. Changes in light levels seem to determine when a particular species starts singing. In Johannesburg, for instance, the Karoo Thrush is the first bird to sing. It is quickly followed by the Dark-capped Bulbul, and other species subsequently join in, often following a predictable order.

Although this has not been documented, my own observation is that the most impressive dawn choruses are heard on clear, sunny, not overcast, mornings. Perhaps in overcast conditions the sky grows lighter more gradually and singing is therefore drawn out over a longer period, whereas on a sunny day the sky brightens rapidly, triggering a more rapid progression and a more spectacular chorus.

The dawn chorus probably serves several purposes, and the reasons may also differ depending on whether a species is resident or migrant.

One theory is that because birds more often succumb to the weather or predators during the night, they call as energetically as possible in the morning to announce that they are still alive and that their territory remains occupied.

Large numbers of birds sing just before dawn.

In Sedge Warblers the sexes migrate separately, so males call at dawn to attract females that have arrived in the night.

Thrushes are usually the first to call at dawn, shortly followed by bulbuls, like the Dark-capped Bulbul.

Robin-Chats are among those species in which males use the dawn chorus as their opportunity to try mating with females who have already paired up. This strategy can be surprisingly successful.

Another possibility is that they're making use of the cooler, denser morning air to project their calls as far as possible. An infrared scan of a singing bird shows that its head is several degrees warmer than the rest of its body, which illustrates the amount of effort and energy required for a small bird to produce such a loud sound. To conserve energy, birds may have evolved to take advantage of the time of day when their calls will travel furthest.

The dawn chorus is often also the time when a rogue male may try to lure a female away from the male she's paired with. (Rogue males may be rather successful. For example, a researcher working in central Africa reported taking genetic samples from four White-browed Robin-Chat chicks and the two adults attending them, only to discover that the chicks were the offspring of three different fathers, none of which was the male actually assisting the female at her nest!)

Finally, among many migrating birds the males and females do not travel together, or at the same time, and may well be separated by a few days. Among smaller birds migration flights occur in the cooler evening hours in order to conserve energy. As soon as the sun comes up, unpaired males call energetically to attract any new females that may have arrived overnight.

In combination these theories help to explain the striking phenomenon of the dawn chorus.

PENGUINS

Most penguins encountered in the region are rare vagrants and tend to be silent here. The only penguin that breeds in southern Africa is the African Penguin; its calls are easily recognised.

African Penguin *Spheniscus demersus*   *Brilpikkewyn*

1 Track detail 0:37 (total length) = 0:02–0:31 (song), 0:31–0:37 (pair interaction)

Song A *dah-dah-dah-dah-dah* that accelerates, ending on a highly distinctive donkey-like bray. Given by male when displaying at a nest site or proclaiming his territory in the vicinity of the nest. Also, a guttural rolling sound, given by members of a breeding pair in their courtship display.

Regional variation None.
Other sounds Alarm and contact calls have not been described.
Habitat Strictly coastal. Feeds at sea. Nests on small islands and suitable beaches along the shore.
Similar sounding None.

SEA BIRDS

Most sea birds are vocal only at their breeding colonies or when squabbling over food at sea. Given here are some of the species most likely to be encountered at a nesting colony or on a pelagic trip. Cape Gannets are the most vocal members of the group.

White-chinned Petrel *Procellaria aequinoctialis*   *Bassiaan*

2 Track detail 0:02–0:14 (nest site call*; context unknown)
    * Similar to calls heard at sea

Song Breeding and display song not heard in southern African region.
Other sounds Clucks and squeaks when fighting over food at sea; these sounds are similar to their calls at nest sites.

Regional variation None.
Habitat Only encountered on pelagic trips. Congregates with other sea bird species at fishing trawlers.
Similar sounding None.

Cape Gannet *Morus capensis*   *Witmalgas*

3 Track detail 0:02–0:52 (songs at breeding colony)

Song Male gives a grunting *haraah* in courtship displays at breeding colony.
Other sounds A two-note *hoo-ahh*, very similar to song, given in some pair interactions.

Regional variation None.
Habitat Breeds on rocky islands and at colonies on the coast. Feeds almost exclusively at sea.
Similar sounding None.

PELICANS

Pelicans give simple croaks and grunts – they are not known for their songs. Generally silent, they are more vocal at breeding colonies or when alarmed or taking flight.

Great White Pelican   *Pelecanus onocrolatus*

Witpelikaan

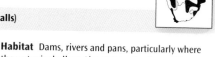

 Track detail 0:03–0:28 (alarm or aggression calls)

Song A series of low grunts, recalling those of a hippo, and some cow-like sounds.
Other sounds Generally silent outside the breeding season but gives guttural croaks in aggression, when alarmed or when taking flight.
Regional variation None.

Habitat Dams, rivers and pans, particularly where the water is shallow. Also some estuaries and lagoons.
Similar sounding Pink-backed Pelican (not included), Goliath (12) and Black-headed (15) herons and Little (17) and Great (16) egrets. Sounds similar to, but deeper and more guttural than, those species listed here.

FLAMINGOS

Flamingos are not known for their songs and calls. They're mainly heard in groups at their colonies and feeding grounds, or when paired birds sing together in ritual displays. Lesser and Greater flamingos sound similar and are not easily separated on sound.

Greater Flamingo   *Phoenicopterus roseus*

Grootflamink

Track detail 0:02–0:24 (calls at breeding colony)

Song Guttural goose-like honks and croaks given by the male or by both sexes during pairing displays. Male often sings when standing on or near to his nesting mound, to attract a female.
Other sounds Variations of song given by groups of birds when feeding and in flight.
Regional variation None.

Habitat Breeds at saltpans. Also found at shallow freshwater habitats such as dams, pans and river mouths.
Similar sounding Lesser Flamingo (not included). It is easy to identify flamingos to group level on sound, but separating the species is more difficult.

CORMORANTS AND DARTERS

These dark-plumaged freshwater diving birds give simple guttural songs and calls, but are more often silent. With the exception of the African Darter, which gives distinctive high-pitched quacks, most of these species are not easily separated on call alone.

White-breasted Cormorant   *Phalacrocorax lucidus*   Witborsduiker

 Track detail 0:02–0:38 (nest site calls; context uncertain)

Song Mainly silent, but gives a guttural croaking song in display at nesting colony.
Other sounds Gives a similar, repetitive, croaking *ghra-ghra-ghra* in confrontations and self-defence.
Regional variation None.

Habitat A wide range of waterbodies, both fresh and saline. Also rivers and coastal waters.
Similar sounding Cape Cormorant (7). A close acquaintance with both calls helps to separate these cormorants.

Cape Cormorant   *Phalacrocorax capensis*   Trekduiker

 Track detail 0:03–0:44 (nest site calls; context uncertain)

Song Male gives low-pitched clucks in display.
Other sounds Groups of birds at colonies give a guttural, high-pitched, whining *nah nah nah*, the context for which is uncertain.
Regional variation None.

Habitat Coastal, marine and estuarine habitats, including some saltpans.
Similar sounding White-breasted Cormorant (6). The guttural croaking sounds very similar to that of the White-breasted Cormorant.

African Darter   *Anhinga rufa*   Slanghalsvoël

8 **Track detail 0:02–0:28 (song)**

Song Short rasping *ghaak* notes, rather like the quacks of a duck, but higher pitched.
Other sounds Gives hisses and drawn-out variations of song at the nest; the context for these calls is uncertain.

Regional variation None.
Habitat Waterbodies including dams, lakes, pans and slow-flowing rivers.
Similar sounding None.

IBISES

The best-known member of this bird family is the Hadeda Ibis, which has a highly distinctive song. Hadedas give fairly basic songs and calls, with some unique high-pitched squawking and squeaking sounds.

African Sacred Ibis *Threskiornis aethiopicus*
Skoorsteenveër

 9 Track detail 0:02–0:41 (nest site calls; context unknown)

Song Generally silent, but gives a range of distinctive hoots and squeaks in courtship displays and at nest sites.
Other sounds Nest sounds include alarm and contact calls, as well as begging sounds given by the young. All are variations of notes from the song.

Regional variation None.
Habitat Found on the margins of wetlands and in flooded grasslands. Nests in reed beds.
Similar sounding None.

Hadeda Ibis *Bostrychia hagedash*
Hadeda

 10 Track detail 0:38 (total length) = 0:02–0:13 (song); 0:13–0:26 (flight call); 0:26–0:38 (begging call)

Song A very distinctive *ha-ha-ha-hadeeda* that has earned this bird its common name.
Other sounds Variations of the song, including a drawn-out *daaaaaaa* often given as initial alarm call when perched, and a rapid *hadeda-hadeda-hadeda*, when flushed, which is the sound most often heard. Young birds give a guttural hissing contact call.

Regional variation None.
Habitat Wide-ranging, including grasslands, cultivated fields, the margins of forests and wetlands, sports grounds and gardens.
Similar sounding None.

Glossy Ibis *Plegadis falcinellus*
Glansibis

 11 Track detail 0:02–0:06 (flight call)

Song Low-pitched guttural croaks, given in aerial breeding display and at the nest.
Other sounds Gives similar croaks in alarm and flight.
Regional variation None.

Habitat Margins of wetlands, dams and rivers. Also muddy habitats like freshly flooded grasslands.
Similar sounding Purple (13) and other herons. Similar to many herons, particularly the Purple Heron, but not as loud.

HERONS, EGRETS AND BITTERNS

Herons, egrets and bitterns are water birds that give basic guttural songs and calls. Although the sounds made by a Goliath Heron are distinctive, most other herons and egrets are difficult to separate. Experience may help you to distinguish some species. The deeper, far-carrying calls of bitterns are easier to tell apart.

Goliath Heron   *Ardea goliath*   Reusereier

12 Track detail 0:02–0:08 (song)

Song Easily identified by unique rhythm and tone. Croaks, as is typical of a heron, but sounds rhythmical and descends in pitch and volume. Probably the most vocal heron when away from the nest.
Other sounds Similar harsh croaks given when flushed.
Regional variation None.

Habitat Usually found at freshwater lakes, dams, pans and large rivers, but may also be seen in estuaries and at saltwater marshes.
Similar sounding Great White Pelican (4), Great (16) and Little (17) egrets. Rhythm and tone distinctive; resemblance to species listed is superficial.

Purple Heron   *Ardea purpurea*   Rooireier

13 Track detail 0:02–0:24 (flight call)

Song Like many other herons, male gives guttural croaks in breeding display.
Other sounds Typical croaks, given as alarm, flight and contact calls.
Regional variation None.
Habitat Dense vegetation at the margins of freshwater wetlands.

Similar sounding Glossy Ibis (11), Grey (14), Western Cattle (18) and Yellow-billed (not included) egrets. Sounds like Glossy Ibis and most large herons as well as the egrets listed. Take care when attempting to separate these species on call alone, paying special attention to tone and pitch.

Grey Heron   *Ardea cinerea*   Bloureier

14 Track detail 0:01–0:14 (flight call)

Song In display flight, male gives a range of guttural croaks, as is typical of most herons.
Other sounds Largely silent when not nesting, but gives characteristic guttural sounds in flight and alarm.
Regional variation None.
Habitat Wetlands, rivers, estuaries and some coastal habitats, provided there is shallow water in which to forage for food.

Similar sounding Purple (13) and Black-headed (15) herons, Little (17), Western Cattle (18), Great (16) and Yellow-billed (not included) egrets. Pay particular attention to tone and pitch when attempting to separate these very similar-sounding species.

Black-headed Heron *Ardea melanocephala* Swartkopreier

15 Track detail 0:02–0:21 (flight call)

Song As is typical for a heron, male displays on the ground, giving a harsh, raucous croak.
Other sounds A similar croak given when flushed.
Regional variation None.
Habitat Grasslands and freshly ploughed fields. Sometimes associated with wetlands, but usually found away from water.

Similar sounding Great White Pelican (4), Glossy Ibis (11), Grey Heron (14), and Great (16), Little (17) and Western Cattle (18) egrets. Pelican sounds deeper and more guttural. The Glossy Ibis has a higher pitched call. More nasal and screechy than the heron and egrets, and its croaks have a darter-like tone.

Great Egret *Ardea alba* Grootwitreier

16 Track detail 0:02–0:08 (flight call)

Song In courtship displays male clatters bill and thumps wings while giving a raucous croak.
Other sounds When flushed, gives raucous croaks like those in courtship display. Makes wheezing sounds at breeding colonies, as is typical of most egrets.
Regional variation None.
Habitat Large bodies of fresh water such as dams, lakes and pans. Sometimes also occurs at saltwater estuaries.

Similar sounding Great White Pelican (4), Glossy Ibis (11), Goliath (12), Grey (14) and Black-headed (15) herons and Little Egret (17). Great White Pelican sounds much deeper and more guttural. Glossy Ibis sounds significantly higher pitched. Except for the Goliath Heron, where the resemblance is superficial, most herons and egrets are tricky to separate without experience. Listen for the deeper and more guttural tone of the Great Egret.

Little Egret *Egretta garzetta* Kleinwitreier

17 Track detail 0:02–0:31 (flight call)

Song A low, harsh, guttural growl given in courtship display.
Other sounds Deep, short, whistled *poh* notes heard at colonies, but context not well understood. Alarm and flight calls similar to display song.
Regional variation None.
Habitat A wide range of aquatic habitats, including pans, dams, rivers, estuaries and the seashore.

Similar sounding Great White Pelican (4), Glossy Ibis (11), Goliath Heron (12), Grey Heron (14), Great Egret (16) and Black-headed Heron (15). Glossy Ibis is distinguished by the higher pitch of its calls. Great Egret sounds deeper. The herons sound similar in pitch and tone, so take care when attempting to separate their songs and calls from those of the Little Egret.

Western Cattle Egret *Bubulcus ibis* Veereier

 18 Track detail 0:02–0:33 (breeding colony calls; context uncertain)

Song In display, male gives guttural croaks similar to those of other herons and egrets.
Other sounds Silent, except at colony, where male gives typical guttural sounds and youngsters and females honk and hoot.
Regional variation None.

Habitat Colonies established in trees or in reed beds, either in or overlooking water. Feeds in grasslands and savanna, often in association with cattle and other hoofed mammals.
Similar sounding Glossy Ibis (11) and Purple (13), Grey (14), Black-headed (15) and other large herons. Very similar to Glossy Ibis, but not as high pitched. Take care when attempting to separate herons and egrets on call alone.

Squacco Heron *Ardeola ralloides* Ralreier

 19 Track detail 0:02–0:19 (flight or contact call)

Song A unique, rather narrow range of high-pitched, frog-like croaks, given rapidly in display flight.
Other sounds Flight and alarm calls very similar to main song.
Regional variation None.
Habitat Any freshwater wetland with reed beds or rank vegetation. Also found in freshly flooded grasslands.

Similar sounding Black-crowned Night Heron (not included), Malagasy Pond Heron (not included) and Black Heron (20). Song is a trilled croak, whereas Black-crowned Night Heron gives ghostly barks. So similar to Malagasy Pond Heron that call is not useful in separating these species. Croak is not drawn out like that of the Black Heron.

Black Heron *Egretta ardesiaca* Swartreier

20 Track detail 0:02–0:06 (flight call)

Song None.
Other sounds Typical heron's croak given when flushed. Also aggressive screams in defence of nest.
Regional variation None.
Habitat Found mainly in flooded grasslands, at pans and along the edges of dams and lakes.

Similar sounding Glossy Ibis (11) and Squacco Heron (19). Calls are higher pitched and thinner than those of either of these species, while croak is drawn out and monotone by comparison with rapid series of croaks given by Squacco Heron.

Eurasian Bittern *Botaurus stellaris* Grootrietreier

 21 Track detail 0:02–0:16 (song)

Song Visits but does not breed in region, so song, though very similar to other calls (see **Other sounds**), is not heard locally.
Other sounds Booming, far-carrying, guttural *gaaarr*, so deep that note is both heard and felt. Context for this call is not fully understood.

Regional variation None.
Habitat Mainly reed beds (but sometimes also tall vegetation) in freshwater wetlands.
Similar sounding Common Ostrich (58). Ostrich is quite distinctive, and bittern's calls are so deep that confusion is unlikely.

Little Bittern *Ixobrychus minutus*

Kleinrietreier

22 Track detail 0:02–0:32 (song)

Song A territorial booming *grah*, repeated at intervals of about a second.
Other sounds Similar, but harsher, sounds given in alarm or when flushed.
Regional variation None.
Habitat Associated with reed beds, but sometimes found among rank river or wetland vegetation.

Similar sounding Dwarf Bittern (not included). Little Bittern calls at one-second intervals for long periods, where Dwarf Bittern calls in short bursts of 3–4 notes.

Green-backed (Striated) Heron *Butorides striata*

Groenrugreier

23 Track detail 0:02–0:13 (flight call)

Song A range of harsh piercing *keoww* sounds given in display flight.
Other sounds Very distinctive, short, sharp variations of song given when flushed and in flight.
Regional variation None.

Habitat Prefers wooded rivers and margins of wetlands, but sometimes ventures into more open habitat.
Similar sounding None.

STORKS

Most storks are completely silent, except for some soft bill-clicking. The Woolly-necked Stork described here is one of the more vocal stork species.

Woolly-necked Stork *Ciconia episcopus*

Wolnekooievaar

24 Track detail 0:02–0:21 (nest calls; context uncertain)

Song Vaguely duck-like chuckling at nest site, usually in display.
Other sounds Generally silent, but may give some chuckling alarm calls in defence of nest. Young birds also make various begging sounds.

Regional variation None.
Habitat Wetlands and estuaries. Sometimes also occurs in man-made habitats.
Similar sounding None.

HAMERKOP

The Hamerkop generally gives comical piercing calls. Its distinctive shrill cries and chuckles make it easy to recongise by its call alone.

Hamerkop *Scopus umbretta*

Hamerkop

25 Track detail 0:02–0:40 (pair interactions)

Song Loud piercing *tuk* notes and distinctive rising and falling cackles, like raucous laughter.
Other sounds Short sections from song given in pair interactions, contact and other situations, but often without the rapid laughter-like cackling.
Regional variation None.

Habitat Found mostly on the margins of pans, dams and rivers.
Similar sounding Giant Kingfisher (188). Hamerkop's cackling far more raucous than chuckles typically given by Giant Kingfisher; also sounds deeper and more nasal than the kingfisher.

GREBES

Grebes are small water birds that prefer open water. Their calls vary widely, from guttural rasping phrases to very high-pitched chittering. Each species has a highly distinctive song that is easy to separate from those of other species in the family, as well as from the calls of other birds in the region.

Great Crested Grebe *Podiceps cristatus*

Kuifkopdobbertjie

26 Track detail 0:03–0:31 (song)

Song Mostly silent, except in breeding season when male gives distinctive guttural *hoo-raahh*.
Other sounds Gives drawn-out *raahh* when alarmed. Youngsters make high-pitched *peep* sounds as contact calls or when begging for food.

Regional variation None.
Habitat Large inland waterbodies such as lakes, dams and pans. Sometimes found at saltwater pans.
Similar sounding None.

Little Grebe (Dabchick) *Tachybaptus ruficollis*

Kleindobbertjie

27 Track detail 0:02–0:27 (duet)

Song In the breeding season gives distinctive, high-pitched, chittering giggle that quickly rises, then descends in pitch. Often given as a **duet** in which both sexes give the same song simultaneously.
Other sounds Alarm and contact calls comprise soft high-pitched *weet* and clucking sounds, similar in tone to main song.

Regional variation None.
Habitat Almost any body of still fresh water, including dams, pans and lakes. Sometimes also found in saltwater environments.
Similar sounding None.

DUCKS, GEESE AND THEIR ALLIES

These are familiar, easily recognised water birds. Their songs vary widely, and many species have an easily identifiable call, such as a piercing whistle or a goose's hiss. Quacks, however, are not always easy to separate.

White-faced Whistling Duck   *Dendrocygna viduata*   Nonnetjie-eend

 Track detail 0:03–0:32 (flight call by several individuals)

Song Not described.
Other sounds A clear whistled *swee-see-eeuu* given mainly in flight, but sometimes also from a perch just prior to takeoff. Also a single whistled *see* note given in alarm.
Regional variation None. Variations in pitch and tone of call probably individual rather than regional.

Habitat Waterbodies in savanna, woodland and open areas. Favours shallow water with partially submerged plants.
Similar sounding Fulvous Whistling Duck (29). White-faced's whistle is cleaner and higher pitched, with three (not two) notes.

Fulvous Whistling Duck   *Dendrocygna bicolor*   Fluiteend

 Track detail 0:03–0:23 (flight call)

Song A simple two-note *ka-seeu*; also given in flight.
Other sounds Single versions of the *seeu* note often given in alarm situations; also gives flight call (see **Song**).
Regional variation None.

Habitat Most inland waterbodies. Favours shallow water with edible aquatic vegetation.
Similar sounding White-faced Whistling Duck (28). Songs superficially similar, but that of Fulvous sounds harsher and comprises just two (not three) notes.

Egyptian Goose   *Alopochen aegyptiaca*   Kolgans

 Track detail 0:03–0:23 (pair interactions and duet)

Song Male's song incorporates wide range of hisses, honks and quacks, as is typical for a goose. Best-known song consists of repeated noisy honking and quacking, to which female often responds with hisses. Both honk when taking off and sing a rapid **duet** while flying close together, the male staying slightly ahead of the female.

Other sounds Many variations of main song. Contact call may consist of softly murmured quacks. Gives loud agitated honks in confrontations.
Regional variation None.
Habitat Wetlands and rivers, provided there is floating edible vegetation.
Similar sounding None.

South African Shelduck *Tadorna cana*　　　　　Kopereend

31 Track detail 0:03–0:24 (song)

Song In courtship, gives screeching version of territorial honk (see **Other sounds**).
Other sounds Goose- or duck-like honk, but with unique, somewhat comical tone, given as both contact and alarm call.

Regional variation None.
Habitat Shallow freshwater and saline habitats, often in muddy areas. Also small water holes in very arid regions.
Similar sounding None.

Yellow-billed Duck *Anas undulata*　　　　　Geelbekeend

32 Track detail 0:03–0:15 (flight call)

Song Male silent, except for soft grunts and whistles in head-bobbing courtship displays.
Other sounds Female gives a repetitive descending *qauuuaaa-qua-qua-qua-qua-quack*, like that of a domestic duck; context for this call is unknown. Flight call, given on takeoff, comprises slower quacks, at a rate of about two per second. Alarm and contact calls are also quacks.

Regional variation None.
Habitat Slow-flowing or still waterbodies such as dams and wetlands. Avoids rivers, unless quite static.
Similar sounding African Black Duck (33) and Mallard (not included). Comparison with song of African Black Duck may assist in separating their very similar quacks. Mallard also similar in tone and phrasing.

African Black Duck *Anas sparsa*　　　　　Swarteend

33 Track detail 0:03–0:21 (female's quack)

Song Male gives soft peeping. To attract a mate, lone male gives more persistent version of this song.
Other sounds Flight call, often given by members of a breeding pair, comprises both the loud quack and the softer peeping song.
Regional variation None.

Habitat Never strays far from rivers and favours shallow, wooded streams in particular. Sometimes found on dams.
Similar sounding Yellow-billed Duck (32) and Mallard (not included). Quacks sound very similar.

Cape Teal *Anas capensis*　　　　　Teeleend

34 Track detail 0:02–0:19 (song)

Song Male's song a soft, nasal, whistled *seeyoo* note that rises and falls in pitch.
Other sounds Generally silent, but female gives a soft nasal *querk* call, presumably in both contact and alarm situations.

Regional variation None.
Habitat Most abundant in saltwater wetlands and estuaries, but also at home in some freshwater wetlands.
Similar sounding None.

DIURNAL RAPTORS

Diurnal birds of prey are a varied group whose members range in size from large vultures to tiny falcons like the Taita Falcon, which is smaller than a Laughing Dove. Their sounds may vary as much as their appearance. Some sing frequently, while many others are silent for much of the year, singing only during mating displays prior to nesting. It is often easy to identify a call as belonging to a kestrel, vulture or falcon, for example, but more difficult to separate closely related species within these groups. However, a few species, like the African Fish Eagle, are highly distinctive.

Cape Vulture   *Gyps coprotheres*   Kransaasvoël

35   Track detail 0:03–0:16 (distress call)

Song Like all vultures, song (and calls) very primitive and scratchy, with little variation.
Other sounds Silent when flying and feeding, but hisses and cackles at the nest. Also gives harsh hissing screech in conflict, alarm and distress situations.
Regional variation None.
Habitat Varies. Always nests and roosts on a cliff, but may travel great distances from home range,

gliding in search of food. Closely associated with game reserves, stock farms and vulture restaurants, where there are plentiful carcasses available for the birds.
Similar sounding White-backed (not included) and other vultures. Most vultures give scratchy, hissing calls.

African Fish Eagle   *Haliaeetus vocifer*   Visarend

36   Track detail 0:03–0:20 (duet)

Song A beautiful far-carrying *heeeuuu-weya-weya-weya*. Sometimes given as part of a **duet** in which female sings same phrase, but at a lower pitch.
Other sounds None.
Regional variation None.

Habitat Large waterbodies including rivers, dams, lakes and wetlands with open water, provided there are suitable trees in which to nest.
Similar sounding None. This iconic song is sometimes known as the 'call of Africa'.

Bateleur   *Terathopius ecaudatus*   Berghaan

37   Track detail 0:02–1:01 (alarm call at nest)

Song Largely silent, like most raptors. The *kow-oww* courtship song is seldom heard. One of the few eagles that deliberately thumps its wings in aerial displays.
Other sounds A high-pitched, rasping, whistled sound near the nest; possibly also given as alarm call.
Habitat Predominantly woodlands, especially broad-leaved. May extend along river courses into more arid regions, provided there are large trees.

Regional variation None.
Similar sounding Yellow-billed Kite (42). Sneering whistle at nest very similar to that of Yellow-billed Kite, but sound does not drop as much in pitch and is harsher than that of the kite.

Martial Eagle *Polemaetus bellicosus* Breëkoparend

 Track detail 0:02–0:26 (*klu-wee-yoo* call)

Song Seldom heard, but comprises a rapid *kowe-ki-ki-ki-ki-ki-ki*, given by male in display flight.
Other sounds A double-note *klu-wee-yoo* given once; context unclear. Contact and alarm calls each only a single phrase.
Regional variation None.
Habitat Open woodlands and arid areas, provided there are large trees or power lines on which to roost.

Similar sounding African Harrier-Hawk (52) and Red-knobbed Coot (76). Display call unique, but single-phrase contact and alarm call resembles song of African Harrier-Hawk and call of fledgling Red-knobbed Coot. Martial Eagle's song and call significantly lower pitched than either the fledgling coot or the harrier-hawk.

Crowned Eagle *Stephanoaetus coronatus* Kroonarend

 Track detail 0:03–0:25 (song)

Song A plaintive *weeooooa*, immediately followed by a series of quick *keu-keu-keu-keu* notes. Male and female give territorial defence calls year-round.
Other sounds Some rapid variations of the song, without the plaintive lead-in note; context not well understood.
Regional variation None.

Habitat Large areas of forest, very dense woodlands and wooded ravines.
Similar sounding Dark Chanting Goshawk (not included). Almost identical to the goshawk, but introductory note more plaintive and varies in pitch, while the rapid whistled notes that follow descend more noticeably.

Long-crested Eagle *Lophaetus occipitalis* Langkuifarend

 Track detail 0:03–0:15 (male song with female reponse)

Song Plaintive *tiu* notes, given about two seconds apart; piercing whistled note may be preceded by a shorter, sharper introductory note. Female sometimes responds with a lower-pitched note, although this is not considered a duet.
Other sounds Contact whistles.
Regional variation None.

Habitat Forests and dense woodlands, always close to open grasslands or farms.
Similar sounding Shikra (51) and Gabar Goshawk (49). Shikra also gives plaintive, piercing whistles, but phrase comprises groups of 3–4 notes and is not as deep and full as song of Long-crested Eagle. Far slower and deeper than song of Gabar Goshawk.

Southern Banded Snake Eagle *Circaetus fasciolatus*
Dubbelbandslangarend

 Track detail 0:03–0:25 (song)

Song A distinctive *ker-kowa-kowa-kowa-kaaar*.
Other sounds A single *kwaak*, given as both alarm and contact calls.
Regional variation None.

Habitat Favours evergreen forests, but also known to frequent plantations.
Similar sounding Western Banded Snake Eagle (not included). A vague resemblance; should be distinctive.

Yellow-billed Kite   *Milvus parasitus*   Geelbekwou

42 Track detail 0:02–0:11 (flight or contact call)

Song Yellow-billed and Black kites, previously grouped together as a single species, have very similar songs, although the latter is usually silent in our region. Yellow-billed Kite gives a distinctive *kleeuuu-ti-tii* in breeding pair interactions.
Other sounds A fairly high-pitched piercing *kleeeu* that descends, and a trilling *keeeerrrrr*, both presumed to be contact and alarm calls.

Regional variation None. There is little variation in raptor calls.
Habitat Frequents a wide range of habitats, but avoids arid areas. Often associated with people.
Similar sounding Bateleur (37), Steppe Buzzard (44). Yellow-billed Kite's *kleeeuuuuu* note reminiscent of, but much longer than, Steppe Buzzard's *peuuu*.

Jackal Buzzard   *Buteo rufofuscus*   Rooiborsjakkalsvoël

43 Track detail 0:02–0:24 (song)

Song A *yeeeoww*, often given by the male and repeated several times. Species derives its common name from song's jackal-like tone.
Other sounds Contact and alarm calls are mewing variations of song, with short, sharp introductory note.
Regional variation None.

Habitat Common in mountainous regions, where it occupies woodlands, karoo scrub and grasslands.
Similar sounding Steppe (44) and Forest (45) buzzards and Indian Peafowl (61). Resemblance with species listed is superficial and confusion unlikely, as the jackal-like tone is easily recognised.

Steppe Buzzard   *Buteo vulpinus*   Bruinjakkalsvoël

44 Track detail 0:02–0:19 (call; context uncertain)

Song Considered silent in our region.
Other sounds A descending whistled *peuuu*, heard quite frequently at the beginning and end of summer.
Regional variation None.
Habitat Mainly grasslands and open woodlands. Sometimes ventures into small plantations.

Similar sounding Yellow-billed Kite (42), Jackal (43) and Forest (45) buzzards, Indian Peafowl (61) and Red-winged (423) and Pale-winged (424) starlings. Almost indistinguishable from Forest Buzzard. Steppe is usually silent in the region, but don't just assume you're hearing a Forest Buzzard. Superficially resembles Jackal Buzzard, Red-winged Starling and Indian Peafowl. Pale-winged Starling's whistle is more piercing

Forest Buzzard   *Buteo trizonatus*   Bosjakkalsvoël

45 Track detail 0:03–0:28 (song)

Song A sharp, descending *peeeooo*, given at random wide intervals. Sound is typical of a buzzard.
Other sounds Rasping *dzeeee* contact calls.
Regional variation None.
Habitat Forests and dense plantations along the escarpment. Also ventures southwards into forested habitat in Western Cape.

Similar sounding Jackal (43) and Steppe (44) buzzards, Indian Peafowl (61) and Red-winged Starling (423). Steppe and Forest buzzards almost indistinguishable by ear; take care in identification as Steppe Buzzard, while usually silent here, does sometimes call. Superficially resembles Jackal Buzzard, Red-winged Starling and Indian Peafowl.

Black-shouldered Kite *Elanus caeruleus* Blouvalk

46 Track detail 0:03–0:16 (song)

Song Male's *dzeep-dzeep-dzeeep* display call seldom heard.
Other sounds A rasping *tsuu-dzerrrr*, given in many contexts.
Regional variation None.

Habitat Grasslands and other open habitat where it can hover in search of prey; avoids dense vegetation.
Similar sounding Marsh Owl (165), Ground Woodpecker (228) and some rollers. Resemblance to these species only superficial.

Lizard Buzzard *Kaupifalco monogrammicus* Akkedisvalk

47 Track detail 0:03–0:48 (song)

Song Largely silent, but pre-breeding display song is a distinctive *weeuuuu-too-too-too-too-too*.
Other sounds None, apart from piercing calls given by chicks begging for food.
Regional variation None.

Habitat Woodlands, especially broad-leaved types.
Similar sounding Pale (48) and Dark (not included) chanting goshawks. Sounds similar to both chanting goshawks, but their calls are lower pitched, less piercing and much faster.

Pale Chanting Goshawk *Melierax canorus* Bleeksingvalk

48 Track detail 0:58 (total length) = 0:03–0:20 (song);
0:20–0:41 (*titititititi* call; context unknown); 0:41–0:58 (alarm call)

Song During the breeding season, both male and female sing with a stirring *kyow-wow-tu-du-du-du*, increasing in speed and descending in pitch.
Other sounds A *ti-ti-ti-ti-ti-ti*, the context for which is unknown, and a descending, piercing, whistled alarm call.
Regional variation None.

Habitat Arid and woodland areas, with tall trees in which to roost and perch, and open areas for hunting.
Similar sounding Lizard Buzzard (47) and Fiery-necked Nightjar (176). Lizard Buzzard is higher pitched and slower. Nightjar's song is far more bubbly and melodious, with trilled notes.

Gabar Goshawk *Micronisus gabar* Witkruissperwer/Kleinsingvalk

49 Track detail 0:02–0:23 (song)

Song Male gives piercing *ti-ti-ti-ti-ti-ti* whistle, vaguely reminiscent of a cuckoo's song.
Other sounds Nest interaction sounds include varied two-note whistles, similar in tone and pitch to male's song.
Regional variation None.
Habitat Open acacia and some broad-leaved woodlands; also along tree-lined rivers in arid areas.

Similar sounding Shikra (51), Long-crested Eagle (40) and Chirping Cisticola (351). The Goshawk's higher pitch and the spacing of its 4–6-note whistled song are distinctive. Long-crested Eagle gives fuller, more eagle-like whistled note, repeated at intervals of about two seconds. Separated from Chirping Cisticola by preferred habitat.

African Goshawk   *Accipiter tachiro*   Afrikaanse Sperwer

50   Track detail 0:02–0:27 (song)

Song The display song, often given in flight, is an almost quail-like *tlik-tlik-tlik*, repeated at intervals of about two seconds. Call is ventriloquial, frequently sounding as if it emanates from surrounding bushes. Look above you, rather than searching close to the ground.

Other sounds Rapid *wit-wit* sounds around the nest, probably given by both sexes. Female gives mewing sounds, but context for this unknown.
Regional variation None.
Habitat Forests, dense woodlands and plantations.
Similar sounding None.

Shikra   *Accipiter badius*   Gebande Sperwer

51   Track detail 0:02–0:25 (song)

Song Almost plaintive; comprises four *tiu-tiu-tiu-tiu* notes given mainly in breeding season.
Other sounds A *tli-wit* used as a soliciting call, a rapid *tu-tu-tu-tu* given by female around the nest and a *tu-wii* used in alarm situations.
Regional variation None.
Habitat Most woodland habitats, including arid, acacia and dense broad-leaved types.

Similar sounding Gabar Goshawk (49) and Long-crested Eagle (40). Shikra's song slower and lower pitched than that of the goshawk, with fewer notes. Long-crested Eagle's call more typical of an eagle; listen for fuller whistled note, repeated at approximately two-second intervals, where Shikra gives four notes.

African Harrier-Hawk (Gymnogene)   *Polyboroides typus*   Kaalwangvalk

52   Track detail 0:03–0:26 (song)

Song A seldom-heard *sweeeee-ooh* given by male in display flight.
Other sounds Other high-pitched whistles and *hweep* sounds. The context for these calls is unknown.
Regional variation None.

Habitat Acacia and broad-leaved woodlands; may also breed in well-wooded suburban habitats.
Similar sounding Martial Eagle (38) and Red-knobbed Coot (76). Display song *very* similar to whistled contact calls of Martial Eagle and young Red-knobbed Coot; separated on habitat and context.

Lanner Falcon   *Falco biarmicus*   Edelvalk

53   Track detail 0:02–0:11 (alarm call)

Song In courtship displays gives trilled *kerrrr-kerrr-kerrr*, as is typical for a raptor.
Other sounds In alarm, gives short sharp *kik* calls.

Regional variations None.
Habitat Desert, mountain and grassland habitats.
Similar sounding None.

Eurasian Hobby *Falco subbuteo* Europese Boomvalk

54 Track detail 0:03–0:18 (alarm call)

Song Not heard in our region.
Other sounds Falcon-like *keek* repeated rapidly when alarmed.
Regional variation None.
Habitat Sometimes ventures into very open habitat, but prefers woodlands, suburbs and parks.

Similar sounding Most kestrels and falcons such as Taita (not included) and Rock Kestrel (56). Falcons and kestrels generally give very similar nondescript sounds, making them difficult to differentiate by ear.

Red-necked Falcon *Falco chicquera* Rooinekvalk

55 Track detail 0:38 (total length) = 0:03–0:30 (alarm call); 0:30–0:38 (pair interactions)

Song Various high-pitched rasping *zree-zree-zree-zree* sounds are almost always given by both members of a breeding pair, although it is not a true duet.
Other sounds Variations of song, given in alarm.
Regional variation None.

Habitat Arid savanna and woodland habitats.
Similar sounding Magpie Shrike (397). Song vaguely reminiscent of this shrike's alarm call, but confusion highly unlikely.

Rock Kestrel *Falco rupicolus* Kransvalk

56 Track detail 0:03–0:50 (mixed alarm and soliciting calls)

Song A rapid and metallic *ti-ti-ti-ti-ti-ti* given in summer as part of courtship display.
Other sounds Alarm and contact calls similar to main song.
Regional variation None.

Habitat Mountainous areas in the breeding season. Otherwise ranges widely in grasslands, semi-arid and karoo scrub country.
Similar sounding Eurasian Hobby (54) and Blacksmith Lapwing (102). Difficult to separate from the hobby. Song and calls are faster and less metallic than those of the lapwing.

Pygmy Falcon *Polihierax semitorquatus* Dwergvalk

57 Track detail 0:02–0:26 (song)

Song A distinctive repetitive *ri-di-di* or *ri-di-di-da* given year-round.
Other sounds Varied *ti-ti-ti* and *ki-ki-ki* alarm and contact calls.

Regional variation None.
Habitat Open arid grasslands. Often closely associated with colonies of Sociable Weavers.
Similar sounding None.

OSTRICHES

A unique family comprising just one (or possibly two) species of large flightless birds. Generally silent, ostriches are more vocal during the mating season.

Common Ostrich *Struthio camelus*   Volstruis

58 Track detail 0:02–0:09 (song)

Song Male utters three-note booming song comprising two short notes and a longer, deeper, descending note. Most often heard during breeding season.
Other sounds Silent except when displaying. Female seldom vocalises.

Regional variation None.
Habitat Open woodlands, grasslands and some arid areas.
Similar sounding Eurasian Bittern (21). Confusion unlikely, as phrase distinctive enough to be easily recognised.

GUINEAFOWL

Like other members of the game-bird (wildfowl) family, guineafowl most often chatter in groups, giving a steady stream of clucking sounds, although males do sometimes give a few piercing whistled phrases. The two guineafowl species are difficult to separate on call alone.

Helmeted Guineafowl *Numida meleagris*   Gewone Tarentaal

59 Track detail 0:36 (total length) = 0:02–0:22 (male's song);
0:22–0:36 (group contact calls)

Song Main song, given by leading male in a group, is a piercing *chuk-wee* whistle, repeated many times.
Other sounds Contact and alarm calls comprise mainly guttural cackles and clucks, given by groups of birds.
Regional variation None.

Habitat Mainly grasslands, farms and woodlands; roosts in trees. Avoids dense vegetation.
Similar sounding Crested Guineafowl (60). Male's whistled song fairly distinctive. Clucking sounds similar to those of Crested Guineafowl, but not as full and deep.

Crested Guineafowl *Guttera pucherani*   Kuifkoptarentaal

60 Track detail 0:02–1:25 (mixed group contact calls and song)

Song Varies, but a piercing guttural *chuk* forms basis of main song.
Other sounds Contact calls like main song, but softer. May call well after dark or if disturbed.
Regional variation None.

Habitat Heavily wooded and forested areas; may venture into the open, but remains close to cover.
Similar sounding Helmeted Guineafowl (59). Gives fuller, deeper chuck than Helmeted Guineafowl and male's call lacks the piercing whistle.

PEAFOWL

An introduced ornamental species. Feral and pet birds are becoming increasingly widespread, so their unique eerie calls are heard quite often.

Indian Peafowl *Pavo cristatus* Makpou

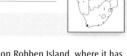

 61 Track detail 0:02–0:18 (song)

Song A distinctive far-carrying *pree-yeouw* wail, something like a toy trumpet.
Other sounds Contact and alarm calls include chicken-like clucks and hoots.
Regional variation None.

Habitat Dense cover on Robben Island, where it has established a viable breeding population. Also kept as ornamental pets on farms and smallholdings.
Similar sounding Jackal (43), Steppe (44) and Forest (45) buzzards. Similar to these buzzards, but only when heard at a distance.

FRANCOLINS, SPURFOWL AND QUAILS

The songs of these distinctive-looking game-birds comprise brief phrases, repeated frequently in short bursts. These birds often sing from secluded spots in grass or dense undergrowth, making identification of the particular species responsible for a call quite difficult. In addition, some smaller members of the group, particularly quails, sound very similar. Most francolins, spurfowl and quails give rapid clucking calls when flushed, as well as soft rasping contact calls to keep a group together in long grass. Domestic chickens, to which game-birds are related, give different alarm calls for various types of threat; the same is probably true of some francolins, spurfowl and quails. Among songbirds individuals within a species may vary their songs, but there is little such variation within the members of this group – only a few very subtle differences are noted in some species. These birds sing mainly in the early morning, although alarm calls may be heard at any time.

Grey-winged Francolin *Scleroptila africanus* Bergpatrys

 62 Track detail 0:03–0:14 (duet)

Song A **duet** in which male gives distinctive *tiu-tiu-tiu-tiu* advertisement call, repeated 4–6 times, followed by a *kachee-weeuu-wip*. Female chimes in with the *kachee-weeuu-wip*.
Other sounds When flushed, gives a flurry of mixed sounds that are similar to, but faster than, main song.

Regional variation None.
Habitat Montane grasslands; often prefers hill tops.
Similar sounding Red-winged Francolin (63). The *kachee-kleeu* in song of Red-winged Francolin is shorter and more rhythmical than the *kachee-weeuu-wip* of Grey-winged.

Red-winged Francolin *Scleroptila levaillantii* Rooivlerkpatrys

63 Track detail 0:02–0:49 (group song)

Song A lead-in *ti-ti-ti-ti*, repeated 3–5 times, followed by a *ka-chee-kleeu*, 2–3 times. Several members of a group sing this song together.
Other sounds None. In other similar species, alarm call is a jumble of phrases resembling excited version of song. Presumably Red-winged's alarm call fits this pattern.

Regional variation None.
Habitat Grassland areas, usually on flat ground.
Similar sounding Grey-winged Francolin (62). To separate, listen for the more complex notes following lead-in to Grey-winged Francolin's song. Red-winged's *ka-chee-kleeu* is faster and more rhythmical.

Shelley's Francolin *Scleroptila shelleyi* Laeveldpatrys

64 Track detail 0:03–0:47 (group song)

Song Male's main song a clear, four-note, rhythmical *ki-chi-ti-kleu*; sounds almost musical. Males often sing in groups, while prominently perched, providing best opportunity to view this species.
Other sounds When flushed, gives piercing and excited variations of song.

Regional variation None.
Habitat Common in a wide range of savanna and woodland habitats.
Similar sounding Orange River Francolin (65). Shelley's song more continuous and rhythmical, with evenly spaced notes.

Orange River Francolin *Scleroptila levaillantoides* Kalaharipatrys

65 Track detail 0:03–1:03 (song)

Song A clear piercing *kira-tiru*, repeated several times. Birds often call together, while prominently perched.
Other sounds Contact call when alarmed is a rasping croak. When flushed, gives excited high-pitched variation of song.
Regional variation None.

Habitat Semi-arid savanna, lush grasslands and woodlands.
Similar sounding Shelley's Francolin (64). Song is faster and less rhythmical, with two closely sounded, bisyllabic notes, whereas Shelley's gives four monosyllabic notes per phrase.

Crested Francolin *Dendroperdix sephaena* Bospatrys

66 Track detail 0:28 (total length) = 0:02–0:15 (duet);
0:15–0:28 (contact or alarm call)

Song A harsh *chee-churruk, chee-churruk* duet between male and female; unclear which part each sex sings.
Other sounds A soft *zee-hrrrrrr* contact call. Male uses same contact call to warn nearby females of intruders.
Regional variation None. Any variations recorded in song of Kirk's Francolin would suggest that this subspecies should be elevated to full species status.

Habitat Woodland thickets and long grass, as well as open areas adjoining patches of thicket and long grass.
Similar sounding Hartlaub's Spurfowl (72) and Black-collared Barbet (214). Song similar in structure to that of barbet, but piercing and harsh; confusion unlikely. Bears only a superficial resemblance to the song of the spurfowl.

Red-billed Spurfowl   *Pternistis adspersus*   Rooibekfisant

67 **Track detail** 1:38 (total length) = 0:02–0:26 (song); 0:26–0:38 (contact call); 0:38–1:01
(group song); 1:01–1:29 (unknown vocalisation); 1:29–1:38 (song variation)

Song A clucking *chuk-chuk-chuk-chrrrrrr*, given most often at dawn, presumably by male, although this is not confirmed.
Other sounds Like other spurfowl, excited and frantic clucking when flushed.
Regional variation None.

Habitat Dry woodlands and teak savanna, often near water.
Similar sounding Natal Spurfowl (69). Clucking song similar, but deeper and more rasping than that of Natal Spurfowl, with rapid rattled sound ending the phrase.

Cape Spurfowl   *Pternistis capensis*   Kaapse Fisant

68 **Track detail** 0:24 (total length) = 0:02–0:19 (song); 0:19–0:24 (contact call)

Song Shrill, clucking *do-it, do-it, do-it, do-it-it, do-it-it*, mainly in the early morning. Can be heard from a distance. Serves both as a territorial advertisement and to solicit mates.
Other sounds Like most other spurfowl, gives frantic burst of clucks when flushed.

Regional variation None.
Habitat Coastal scrub and fynbos.
Similar sounding None. No other spurfowl species occur in its range.

Natal Spurfowl   *Pternistis natalensis*   Natalse Fisant

69 **Track detail** 0:21 (total length) = 0:02–0:13 (group song); 0:13–0:21 (flight call)

Song Male announces himself with a series of piercing *chuk-kee chuk-kee-chuk-kee* clucks. Most vocal at dawn and dusk.
Other sounds Rapid clucking when flushed. Various alarm calls, including distinctive low-pitched nasal *meeeeuuuwwww*, reminiscent of a raptor's call.

Regional variation None. Calls do naturally include a wide variety of clucks.
Habitat Grassy areas and undergrowth in woodlands, particularly near rivers.
Similar sounding Red-billed Spurfowl (67). Sounds higher pitched and less rasping than Red-billed.

Red-necked Spurfowl   *Pternistis afer*   Rooikeelfisant

70 **Track detail** 0:50 (total length) = 0:02–0:43 (song); 0:43–0:50 (flight call)

Song Rasping song, given at dawn and dusk, includes clucks and *chucka* sounds.
Other sounds Like other spurfowl, gives excited clucks and rasping sounds when flushed.
Regional variation None.

Habitat Dense vegetation in forests and along watercourses. May be seen with Swainson's Spurfowl.
Similar sounding Swainson's Spurfowl (71). Song has a similar tone, but Red-necked Spurfowl's song lacks the two-syllable phrases of Swainson's.

Swainson's Spurfowl · *Pternistis swainsonii* · Bosveldfisant

71 Track detail 0:48 (total length) = 0:02–0:38 (male song); 0:38–0:48 (flight call)

Song Distinctive rasping *karrrrrrra*, repeated several times; often given from a prominent position.
Other sounds Like other spurfowl, gives excited clucks and trills when flushed.
Regional variation None.

Habitat Grasslands, open woodlands and cultivated fields. Unlike Red-billed, does not venture into forests, but both spurfowl may feed together on farm lands.
Similar sounding Red-necked Spurfowl (70). Song similar to, but slower, than that of Red-necked Spurfowl.

Hartlaub's Spurfowl · *Pternistis hartlaubi* · Klipfisant

72 Track detail 0:03–0:26 (duet)

Song A loud rasping **duet**, with some variations. Female typically sings a harsh *zreeya* to which male quickly responds with higher-pitched *reeya*. Together, they call *zreeya reeya*, in an obvious see-saw rhythm.
Other sounds Soft, guttural, rasping contact call like that of Crested Francolin, and harsh alarm calls typical of francolins generally. Twelve different calls and songs described.

Regional variation None. Distinct variations in combined duetted phrase regularly noted but probably not geographical.
Habitat Rocky outcrops in semidesert areas.
Similar sounding Crested Francolin (66). Resemblance very superficial; rhythm and tone of Hartlaub's sufficiently distinctive that it should be easy to recognise.

Coqui Francolin · *Peliperdix coqui* · Swempie

73 Track detail 0:03–0:51 (song)

Song A piercing and repeated *ko-kir-kir-kir-kir-kir* song, tapering off in pitch and volume. Often given from a low perch.
Other sounds Soft *took* contact call given in long grass. Alarm call comprises piercing trills and drawn-out whistles.

Regional variation None.
Habitat Dense grass in savanna and woodland areas.
Similar sounding None.

Common Quail · *Coturnix coturnix* · Afrikaanse Kwartel

74 Track detail 0:03–0:08 (song)

Song Male gives very rhythmical, high-pitched *whit-it-it*, 5–10 times, then pauses and repeats. Female sometimes responds with low whistles and trills, but this is not a duet. Song heard mainly in the mornings.
Other sounds Various grating contact sounds. When flushed, gives rapid series of piercing whistles.

Regional variation None.
Habitat Chiefly moist grasslands. Also ventures into semi-arid and lightly wooded areas.
Similar sounding Harlequin Quail (75). Both sing clear repetitive songs, but listen for the three-note pattern and faster phrases of Common Quail.

37

Harlequin Quail   *Coturnix delegorguei*   Bontkwartel

75 Track detail 0:03–0:30 (song with female response)

Song Male initiates **duet** with series of evenly spaced budgie-like *whit-whit-whit-whit* phrases, lacking any obvious rhythm. Female responds with softer *kweee-it* sounds.
Other sounds When flushed, gives rapid piercing *kreee* calls.

Regional variation None.
Habitat Found in various grassland habitats, but especially wooded and flooded rank grasslands.
Similar sounding Common Quail (74). Sounds more metallic and lacks precise rhythmical phrasing of Common Quail.

COOTS, MOORHENS AND GALLINULES

These waterfowl give varied clucking songs and calls. While moorhens and coots are readily visible, often feeding in the open, gallinules are rather shy.

Red-knobbed Coot   *Fulica cristata*   Bleshoender

76 Track detail 0:32 (total length) = 0:03–0:20 (*klu-hup* call);
0:20–0:32 (*doh* call given in aggressive interaction on water)

Song No specific song described. See **Other sounds**.
Other sounds Many different sounds documented, but contexts not well understood. Calls include wide range of muted clucks and quacks, the most recognisable of which are a slightly piercing two-note *klu-hup*, a dull *doh-doh-doh-doh* and a liquid trilling *trrrpp*. Fledglings give a wailing whistle.
Regional variation Unknown. Vocalisations still poorly understood.

Habitat Fresh water in wetlands, dams and lakes; sometimes found on slow-flowing rivers.
Similar sounding Martial Eagle (38), African Harrier-Hawk (52) and Common Moorhen (77). Wailing whistles given by fledgling coots resemble calls of African Harrier-Hawk and Martial Eagle, but the latter sound deeper than fledgling. Slight similarity to calls of Common Moorhen, but fuller and duller.

Common Moorhen   *Gallinula chloropus*   Grootwaterhoender

77 Track detail 0:23 (total length) = 0:03–0:21 (*turrk* call);
0:21–0:23 (aggressive interaction)

Song No specific song described. See **Other sounds**.
Other sounds Gives wide range of clucks and toots, including a short liquid *turrk* note. Alarm call is a brief sharp *tuk*. Exact context for most sounds still uncertain.
Regional variation None.

Habitat Fresh water in wetlands, rivers or dams, provided there is nearby cover.
Similar sounding A range of wetland birds including Red-knobbed Coot (76) and Allen's Gallinule (79). Allen's Gallinule's phrases higher pitched and simpler. Resemblance to coot is superficial.

African Swamphen   *Porphyrio madagascariensis*   Grootkoningriethaan

 Track detail 0:19 (total length) = 0:03–0:09 (song); 0:09–0:19 (call; context unknown)

Song A series of raucous, hooted, guttural sounds given to protect territory.
Other sounds A distinctive mewing, along with many other sounds. Contexts not well understood.

Regional variation None.
Habitat Reed beds along slow-flowing rivers and in wetlands. Will venture into the open to feed.
Similar sounding Allen's Gallinule (79). The gallinule is higher pitched and more repetitive than the swamphen.

Allen's Gallinule   *Porphyrio alleni*   Kleinkoningriethaan

79 **Track detail** 1:03 (total length) = 0:02–0:23 (song); 0:23–0:35 (call; context unknown); 0:35–1:03 (song)

Song Abrupt *kep, kerr* and *kepurr* notes.
Other sounds Clucking sounds given in alarm; also wader-like *ti-ti-ti-ti* flight calls.
Regional variation None.
Habitat Reed beds, flooded grasslands and dense growth along the margins of waterbodies.

Similar sounding African Swamphen (78) and Common (77) and Lesser (not included) moorhens. Gives far more abrupt, less varied notes than does swamphen. Single-note phrases similar to those of both Common and Lesser moorhens.

CRAKES, RAILS AND FLUFFTAILS

Secretive wetland birds that give various whistling, churring or clucking songs. These species are frequently located and told apart by their unique songs, as they are often heard, but seldom seen.

Black Crake   *Amaurornis flavirostra*   Swartriethaan

80 **Track detail** 0:03–0:39 (duet)

Song Jumbled chattering laugh, comprising different sounds by **duetting** pairs or small groups of birds; notes sound very different when given by a lone bird.
Other sounds A chicken-like cluck, presumably given as a begging or contact call, but context uncertain.
Regional variation None.

Habitat Reed beds and dense vegetation on wetland and river margins. Less secretive than other members of this group; may venture into the open, staying close to cover.
Similar sounding None.

African Rail   *Rallus caerulescens*   Grootriethaan

81 **Track detail** 0:02–0:12 (song)

Song A unique series of whistles. Initially high-pitched and rapid, song descends and slows down.
Other sounds High-pitched rattles and wheezes, given in confrontations. Also group chatter.

Regional variation None.
Habitat Wetlands. Restricted mainly to reed beds but sometimes ventures into other types of dense cover.
Similar sounding None.

African Crake   *Crecopsis egregia*   Afrikaanse Riethaan

 82   Track detail 0:02–0:10 (song)

Song Male's song a distinctive series of rapid churring *krrr* notes.
Other sounds Soft, almost chicken-like clucking.
Regional variation None.

Habitat Both dry and flooded grasslands as well as grass in open savanna habitat.
Similar sounding None.

Baillon's Crake   *Porzana pusilla*   Kleinriethaan

 83   Track detail 0:03–0:36 (song)

Song A range of frog-like croaks and trills, in particular a series of short, quick, purring sounds.
Other sounds Clucks, as is typical for a crake, although context not well understood. Also short, sharp, harsh alarm calls.

Regional variation None.
Habitat A typical wetland bird, found in reed beds and flooded grass. Takes cover in short vegetation, particularly when breeding.
Similar sounding None.

FLUFFTAILS

Members of this family of highly secretive birds are often heard but seldom seen. Their hooting songs emanate from reed beds and, in some cases, from dense forests and woodlands. Some species can be separated by ear.

Red-chested Flufftail   *Sarothrura rufa*   Rooiborsvleikuiken

 84   Track detail 0:03–1:22 (song)

Song A series of short *hoooo* or *hoooaaa* notes, given about once per second, repeatedly.
Other sounds Like most flufftails, over 100 different calls described, including rapid hoots, clucks and trills.
Regional variation Unknown. Reason for high variability in sounds not fully understood, but unlikely to be geographical.

Habitat Occupies flooded grasslands and various types of wetland, as well as reed beds or dense cover along rivers, dams and streams.
Similar sounding Most flufftails. The wide range of sounds made by Red-chested Flufftail often overlap with those made by other flufftails.

Buff-spotted Flufftail
Sarothrura elegans

Gevlekte Vleikuiken

85 Track detail 0:03–0:35 (song)

Song A deep hooting *ooooooooo*, lasting several seconds at a time.
Other sounds Like other flufftails, over 100 different calls described, among them rapid hoots, clucks and trills.

Regional variation Unknown. High variability in sounds unlikely to be related to geographical location.
Habitat Dense cover in woodlands and forests. Also found in bushy undergrowth in parks and gardens.
Similar sounding None.

CRANES

Like other birds of their size, including storks, herons and korhaans, cranes sing guttural grating songs. Each of the three cranes in this group sounds sufficiently distinctive to be easily identified by ear.

Grey Crowned Crane
Balearica regulorum

Mahem

86 Track detail 0:03–0:22 (group song)

Song A trumpeting *ooo-wah-ooo*, sometimes given by a group of birds.
Other sounds Flight calls sound similar to song.
Regional variation None.

Habitat Breeds around wetlands, but forages in open grasslands and savanna. May gather in large numbers on cultivated fields.
Similar sounding None.

Blue Crane
Anthropoides paradiseus

Bloukraanvoël

87 Track detail 0:02–0:18 (song)

Song A trilled *puuuuurrrr* and *pur-urrrrrrrr*.
Other sounds Similar sounds, given in alarm and in flight.
Regional variation None.

Habitat A range of natural habitats, including karoo scrub and grasslands, but will also venture into cultivated fields.
Similar sounding None.

SECRETARYBIRD

This unique bird of prey is recognised by its long legs, which are adapted for roaming through grasslands in search of snakes. Generally silent, the songs and calls it does give are simple, harsh and quite easy to recognise.

Secretarybird *Sagittarius serpentarius*　　　　　　　　　Sekretarisvoël

88　Track detail 0:03–0:17 (alarm or contact call at nest)

Song Croaks recalling sound of a wood-saw, given in breeding display at nest.
Other sounds A rapid and repeated *keu-keu-keu* also given at nest, presumably as contact or alarm call.

Regional variation None.
Habitat Open grasslands, provided there are scattered large bushes or trees in which to nest.
Similar sounding None.

KORHAANS

Harsh grating songs are typical of most members of this group, and of the bustards, to which korhaans are related, although some korhaans give piercing whistled songs that are easy to tell apart. Generally, each species' song has a unique rhythm, although the two black korhaans are an exception.

Red-crested Korhaan *Lophotis ruficrista*　　　　　　　Boskorhaan

89　Track detail 0:03–0:37 (song)

Song A series of shrill, gradually descending whistles, interspersed with some tongue clicks. Sometimes ends on a double note.
Other sounds Female gives repetitive croaks as is typical for a korhaan. Soft peep alarm calls also noted.

Regional variation None.
Habitat Confined to acacia and broad-leaved woodlands, where it favours sandy areas.
Similar sounding Neddicky (345). Korhaan calls from the ground, while Neddicky calls from the top of a tree or bush.

Southern Black Korhaan *Afrotis afra*　　　　　　　Swartvlerkkorhaan

90　Track detail 0:03–0:12 (song)

Song Male sings *kraak-kraak-kraak*, repeatedly, from a mound or other territorial perch.
Other sounds A similar *keraak-keraak-keraak*, given in flight. Alarm calls are much the same.
Regional variation None.

Habitat Fynbos, particularly renosterveld and strandveld. Ventures slightly into succulent karoo habitat.
Similar sounding Northern Black Korhaan (91). Southern and Northern black kornhaans not readily separated by ear.

Northern Black Korhaan   *Afrotis afraoides*

Witvlerkkorhaan

91 Track detail 0:51 (total length) = 0:03–0:35 (song); 0:35–0:51 (display song)

Song As with Southern Black Korhaan, male gives a repeated sequence of *kraak-kraak-kraak* sounds from a mound used as a territorial perch.
Other sounds A similar *keraak-keraak-keraak*, given in flight; alarm calls also comprise variations on song.
Regional variation None.

Habitat Grasslands, but avoids taller grass. Also sometimes occurs in acacia savanna and on farms with vegetation cover.
Similar sounding Southern Black Korhaan (90). Songs very similar. Northern and Southern black korhaans not easily separated by ear.

Rüppell's Korhaan   *Eupodotis rueppellii*

Woestynkorhaan

92 Track detail 0:03–0:25 (song)

Song A rhythmical grating *graar-zee-zee*, with one low and two higher-pitched notes.
Other sounds In flight gives a quack, as is typical for a korhaan.
Regional variation None.

Habitat Desert with scattered trees. Favours sandy areas.
Similar sounding Blue Korhaan (93). Song is more rhythmical and lacks the three distinct pitch changes heard in Blue Korhaan's song.

Blue Korhaan   *Eupodotis caerulescens*

Bloukorhaan

93 Track detail 0:03–0:31 (song)

Song A rhythmical grating *graar-zaa-zee*, with three distinct pitch changes. Sometimes also gives a bisyllabic phrase.
Other sounds When flushed, gives excited variation of main song.
Regional variation None.

Habitat Found towards the tops of gentle slopes in otherwise fairly flat grasslands.
Similar sounding Rüppell's Korhaan (92). Song less rhythmical than that of Rüppell's, with three (not two) distinct pitch changes.

STILTS AND AVOCETS

Black-and-white wading birds all with very similar flight and feeding behaviour. Their songs, too, are very much alike, generally comprising just a single, harsh, piercing note, given repeatedly.

Black-winged Stilt *Himantopus himantopus* Rooipootelsie

 94 Track detail 0:03–0:34 (flight call)

Song A *keek* similar to the songs and calls of some terns, but with a more metallic tone.
Other sounds A hoarse *kerr*, given on the ground as a contact call.
Regional variation None.

Habitat Wetlands, both fresh and salt water; also flooded grasslands.
Similar sounding Pied Avocet (95). Song monotone and more piercing than the *dooh* notes of the avocet.

Pied Avocet *Recurvirostra avosetta* Bontelsie

95 Track detail 0:02–0:22 (contact call)

Song None described.
Other sounds Contact and flight calls comprise a plaintive *diu diu diu*, reminiscent of a sandpiper, but with a distinctive tone.
Regional variation None.

Habitat Temporary and saline wetlands. Avoids rivers and dams.
Similar sounding Black-winged Stilt (94). Stilt sounds scratchy and harsh, while avocet is more plaintive.

African Jacana *Actophilornis africanus* Grootlangtoon

96 Track detail 0:02–0:18 (contact call)

Song Not fully described, but appears to comprise a wide range of *kerrr* and *kaarr* notes, like those given in other contexts.
Other sounds Gives range of *kerrr* and *kaarr* notes in disputes and to maintain group contact. In alarm gives some high-pitched sounds.

Regional variation None.
Habitat Open, still or slow-flowing fresh water, provided there is floating vegetation on which the jacana can forage for aquatic insects.
Similar sounding None.

African (Black) **Oystercatcher** *Haematopus moquini*   Swarttobie

97 Track detail 0:03–0:21 (flight calls)

Song A distinct piercing *ti-kleu*.
Other sounds In flight gives much faster variation of song.
Regional variation None.

Habitat Rocky and stony beaches, estuaries, lagoons and coastal salt marshes.
Similar sounding None.

THICK-KNEES

Being nocturnal, thick-knees are heard mainly at night. Their rapid whistled songs may sound quite eerie.

Spotted Thick-knee *Burhinus capensis*   Gewone Dikkop

98 Track detail 0:03–0:37 (song)

Song A high-pitched and ghostly *titititititit*, slowing to a *ti-ti-ti-ti* that gradually fades away. Also an eerie *kleu-kleu-kleu-kleu* that rises and falls in pitch.
Other sounds Soft hissing alarm calls.
Regional variation None.

Habitat Open savanna with stony ground. Often roosts on the ground under trees by day. Also sometimes occurs in large gardens.
Similar sounding None.

Water Thick-knee *Burhinus vermiculatus*   Waterdikkop

99 Track detail 0:03–0:26 (song)

Song A fast, very high-pitched *tititititititi-ti-ti-ti-ti-teee* that slows down and drops in pitch.
Other sounds Similar, high-pitched, whistled alarm calls.
Regional variation None.

Habitat Dams, freshwater rivers and estuaries. Occasionally seen on beaches.
Similar sounding African Grey Hornbill (205). Song is faster, higher pitched and lacks the plaintive wailing whistles of the hornbill.

PRATINCOLES

Pratincoles generally call in large flocks. They sing simple grating or rasping songs that sound most similar to those of terns and sandgrouse.

Collared (Red-winged) Pratincole *Glareola pratincola*
Rooivlerkspringkaanvoël

100 Track detail 0:03–0:25 (group chatter and interactions)

Song A series of tern-like sounds – often rapidly repeated monosyllabic notes, but may include bisyllabic sounds. May be given by a lone individual, but as this species flocks in large numbers, more often given by groups of birds.
Other sounds In alarm gives slightly more piercing 2–3-syllable phrases, reminiscent of a tern.

Regional variation None.
Habitat Muddy wetlands, flooded grasslands and flooded farm lands.
Similar sounding None.

COURSERS

Coursers resemble small lapwings. Their often eerie calls are distinctive at both the group and individual species levels.

Three-banded Courser *Rhinoptilus cinctus*
Driebanddrawwertjie

101 Track detail 0:02–0:28 (song)

Song A rising and falling nasal *peeu-peeu-peeu…*; may also be rendered as a rapidly repeated *kika*.
Other sounds A rising alarm-like *chirererererereer* along with other piercing whistled phrases reminiscent of parts of song.

Regional variation None.
Habitat Dry mopane and miombo woodlands, provided there are some areas of sand and short grass.
Similar sounding None.

LAPWINGS AND PLOVERS

These birds give many different sounds, ranging from the soft chirps and tweets of shore birds, like sandpipers, to the piercing notes of lapwings. Most of the species in this group have distinctive songs.

Blacksmith Lapwing (Plover) *Vanellus armatus*   Bontkiewiet

 102 Track detail 0:50 (total length) = 0:02–0:27 (alarm call); 0:27–0:32 (flight call); 0:32–0:50 (mobbing call)

Song The main song is a distinctive metallic *tink-tink-tink*. Derives English common name from song's resemblance to the sound of a blacksmith's hammer striking an anvil.
Other sounds In alarm, gives distressed variation of metallic song or, if alarmed in flight, a piercing repeated *pruueee*. Also gives rapid, repeated series of descending metallic trills, gradually fading away; context unknown but possibly a contact call.

Regional variation None.
Habitat Wide-ranging, but typically found on the margins of freshwater wetlands and mud flats, on sports fields and parks and in areas of short grass.
Similar sounding Rock Kestrel (56) and African Green Pigeon (140). Kestrel's call is shorter, faster and less metallic. African Green Pigeon also sounds less metallic than lapwing.

White-crowned Lapwing (Plover) *Vanellus albiceps*   Witkopkiewiet

103 Track detail 0:28 (total length) = 0:02–0:19 (alarm call); 0:19–0:28 (flight call)

Song A rapid high-pitched series of *tip* notes, given in short bursts and at variable speeds.
Other sounds An aggressive, tern-like *pee-reee*, repeated quite quickly.
Regional variation None.

Habitat A mud- or sandbank in the course of a river or other waterbody; avoids the shore.
Similar sounding Wood (116) and Marsh (not included) sandpipers. Difficult to separate from these sandpipers on sound alone, but tends to sing short bursts at random speeds, less repetitively. Confusion unlikely.

Crowned Lapwing (Plover) *Vanellus coronatus*   Kroonkiewiet

104 Track detail 0:24 (total length) = 0:02–0:14 (alarm call); 0:14–0:24 (flight call)

Song A rasping *prreeyip*; speed varies. Given by the male in defence of territory.
Other sounds Agitated version of song, given in alarm; also, a softer rolling trill heard on the ground, but context unclear. The same trill also given as a warning to intruders straying too close to nest.

Regional variation None.
Habitat Short grasslands, burnt and freshly grazed fields and sports fields.
Similar sounding African Green Pigeon (140). Bears superficial resemblance to calls of this pigeon, but confusion is unlikely.

Black-winged Lapwing (Plover) *Vanellus melanopterus* Grootswartvlerkkiewiet

 105 Track detail 0:03–0:35 (song by a group of individuals)

Song A rapidly repeated *tzee-tzee-tzee* with some birds responding with a trilled *zurrreee*. A few individuals may be heard at once, but not a true group call.
Other sounds Some high-pitched whistles, given in alarm.

Regional variation None.
Habitat Short grasslands in the upper Lowveld. Most common on freshly grazed or burnt land.
Similar sounding African Wattled Lapwing (106). Black-winged's song is softer, less shrill and not as full.

African Wattled Lapwing (Plover) *Vanellus senegallus* Lelkiewiet

106 Track detail 0:03–0:38 (alarm calls of breeding pair)

Song A piercing *yip-yip-yip-yip* that varies in pitch.
Other sounds Contact and alarm calls comprise the same *yip* given at different speeds and intensities.
Regional variation None.
Habitat Flooded grasslands and grassland habitats near water. Sometimes seen at human settlements.

Similar sounding Black-winged Lapwing (105) and Giant Kingfisher (188). Song is fuller and shriller than that of Black-winged, while kingfisher has a deeper song.

Grey Plover *Pluvialis squatarola* Grysstrandkiewiet

107 Track detail 0:02–0:15 (song)

Song Not heard in our region.
Other sounds Contact and alarm calls comprise unique whistled wail that falls, then rises slightly, but remains high pitched overall.
Regional variation None.
Habitat Coastal shores and saline estuaries. May visit freshwater wetlands, when migrating.

Similar sounding Eurasian Curlew (112) and Common Whimbrel (111). Resemblance to calls of curlew and whimbrel very slight; should be easy to distinguish.

Common Ringed Plover *Charadrius hiaticula* Ringnekstrandkiewiet

108 Track detail 0:02–0:16 (contact or flight call)

Song Not heard in our region.
Other sounds A high-pitched *tweeoo*, given as flight, contact and alarm calls.
Regional variation None.

Habitat Mud flats, sandbanks and other freshwater habitats. Also seen at estuaries, lagoons and on beaches.
Similar sounding None.

Three-banded Plover *Charadrius tricollaris* Driebandstrandkiewiet

109 Track detail 0:03–0:51 (territorial song)

Song A piercing three-note *dzeet-dzeet-dzeet*, with fairly distinctive tone.
Other sounds Alarm calls comprise *trrrrr* sounds. Also gives excited mixed chatter in confrontations.
Regional variation None.

Habitat Margins of freshwater wetlands, rivers and dams.
Similar sounding Wood Sandpiper (116) and other high-pitched sandpipers and parakeets. Superficial resemblance to high-pitched sandpipers and parakeets, but should be easy to distinguish.

SNIPES

Snipes give distinctive calls that include *chuk* sounds and short hoots. Some snipes are known for 'winnowing', a term used to describe the noise produced when the wind blows the tail feathers during a display flight. The African Snipe is the most often encountered member of this group.

African (Ethiopian) Snipe *Gallinago nigripennis* Afrikaanse Snip

110 Track detail 0:20 (total length) = 0:02–0:16 (territorial call); 0:16–0:20 (winnowing)

Song Main 'song' is winnowing (whirring of flight feathers), heard when a bird enters a dive as part of its breeding display. Usually takes place over wetlands in spring and early summer. Also, a repeated *wuk-wuk-wuk-wuk*, often given on the ground just before or after the display flight.

Other sounds A short grating *krek* when flushed.
Regional variation None.
Habitat Wetlands with reed beds for shelter; also flooded grasslands. Often feeds in the open on mud flats, but doesn't stray too far from cover.
Similar sounding None.

WHIMBRELS AND CURLEWS

The soft trills, wailing whistles and toots of whimbrels and curlews are heard in many wetland areas. It is easy to identify that a particular song belongs to a member of this group, but separating species by ear requires some effort.

Common Whimbrel *Numenius phaeopus* Kleinwulp

111 Track detail 0:02–0:32 (contact call)

Song A soft plaintive *ti-ti-ti-ti-ti-ti* and a *tu-tu-tu-tu-tu*, sung rapidly; often descending slightly in pitch.
Other sounds Gives song variations as contact call while feeding. Flight and alarm call is a sharp *ti* or *tiu*.
Regional variation None.

Habitat Estuaries, salt marshes and coastal shores.
Similar sounding Grey Plover (107), Eurasian Curlew (112) and Bar-tailed Godwit (113). Superficially like Grey Plover. Curlew's song includes more complex notes and trills. Godwit sounds harsher and more nasal.

Eurasian Curlew *Numenius arquata* Grootwulp

112 Track detail 0:02–0:19 (contact and flight calls)

Song Not heard in our region.
Other sounds Short whistled phrases and a distinctive trilled *kur-leeww* given both as contact and alarm call.
Regional variation None.
Habitat Coastal wetlands and tidal zones.

Similar sounding Grey Plover (107), Common Whimbrel (111) and Bar-tailed Godwit (113). Resemblance to plover superficial – confusion unlikely. Distinguished from whimbrel and godwit by the trilled notes.

GODWITS

Godwits are rare vagrants to southern Africa, except for the Bar-tailed Godwit, which is relatively common in suitable habitat. Like most water birds in the region, godwits are fairly quiet, except when breeding and displaying, but birds may call to establish and maintain group contact.

Bar-tailed Godwit *Limosa lapponica* Bandstertgriet

113 Track detail 0:02–0:12 (contact call)

Song Not heard in our region.
Other sounds Short *ti-ti-ti-ti* alarm and flight calls.
Regional variation None.
Habitat Estuaries and lagoons and, rarely, pans in the interior.

Similar sounding Common Whimbrel (111) and Eurasian Curlew (112). Some resemblance to Common Whimbrel, but harsher and with a more nasal quality. Eurasian Curlew gives more trilled call.

TYPICAL WADERS

Typical waders spend most of their time feeding on mud flats and in shallow water. Most species give similar piercing *ti* calls and are often only vocal in our region when flushed. Despite their apparent similarity, with a little experience calls can serve as an aid to identification, since species may be separated by pattern, pitch and note inflections.

Common Greenshank *Tringa nebularia* Groenpootruiter

114 Track detail 0:02–0:16 (flight call)

Song Not heard in our region.
Other sounds A piercing *tiu-tiu-tiu-tiu-tiu* given when flushed into flight.
Regional variation None.
Habitat Shallow water and mud flats along the margins of wetlands, rivers, dams and estuaries.

Similar sounding Marsh (115), Wood (116), Common (117) and Green (not included) sandpipers. Wood and Common sandpipers give a *ti* rather than a *teu* note and are higher pitched. Green and Marsh sandpipers do give a *teu* note, but at a much higher pitch than that of Common Greenshank.

Marsh Sandpiper *Tringa stagnatalis* Moerasruiter

115 Track detail 0:02–0:11 (flight call)

Song Not heard in our region.
Other sounds Gives rapid, high-pitched, slightly slurring *teu-teu-teu* in flight and when alarmed.
Regional variation None.
Habitat Largely a wetland bird; frequents freshwater pans and dams, estuaries and lagoons.

Similar sounding Green Sandpiper (not included), Common Greenshank (114) and Wood Sandpiper (116). Unslurred notes distinguish it from Green Sandpiper and Common Greenshank. The latter also sounds higher pitched. Most closely resembles Wood Sandpiper.

Wood Sandpiper *Tringa glareola* Bosruiter

116 Track detail 0:02–0:12 (flight call)

Song Not heard in our region.
Other sounds Most contact calls not given in southern Africa. Most commonly heard sounds in our region are short piercing *ti-ti-ti-ti-ti* flight whistle and slower version of this whistle given in alarm, often from the ground.
Regional variation None.
Habitat Most freshwater habitats, especially the muddy margins of pans and rivers.

Similar sounding White-crowned Lapwing (103), Three-banded Plover (109), Green Sandpiper (not included), Common Greenshank (114), Marsh Sandpiper (115) and Common Sandpipper (117). The lapwing and plover sound higher pitched and harsher. Less plaintive than Green Sandpiper, not as deep and slurred as Common Greenshank and not as high-pitched as Common Sandpiper. Most closely resembles flight call of Marsh Sandpiper.

Common Sandpiper *Actitis hypoleucos* Gewone Ruiter

117 Track detail 0:03–0:21 (song)

Song Not heard in our region; similar to other sounds.
Other sounds A high-pitched *tititititititi*, given rapidly in flight or more slowly and briefly as alarm call when perched.
Regional variation None.
Habitat A typical wetland bird; also occurs around streams and dams.

Similar sounding Common Greenshank (114), Wood Sandpiper (116), Meyer's Parrot (147) and Burnt-necked Eremomela (319). Told from greenshank, sandpiper and other waders by higher pitched and unique lack of note inflection. Some sounds made by the eremomela may resemble the sounds of a Common Sandpiper. Meyer's Parrot may have sandpiper-like tone; confusion unlikely.

Sanderling *Calidris alba* Drietoonstrandloper

118 Track detail 0:01–0:07 (contact call)

Song Not heard in our region.
Other sounds A sparrow-like chirp, given in flight. Also nondescript wader-like twitterings, when feeding in a group.
Regional variation None.

Habitat Largely a seashore and estuarine bird, but sometimes ventures inland.
Similar sounding House Sparrow (444). The sparrow-like flight chirp is unique for a wader. Superficial resemblance to chirp of female House Sparrow unlikely to cause confusion.

Little Stint *Calidris minuta*

Kleinstrandloper

119 Track detail 0:02–0:13 (contact call)

Song Not heard in our region.
Other sounds Soft, very high-pitched *peep* notes that are typical of small stints and their allies, and that have earned this group the nickname *peeps*.
Regional variation None.

Habitat Largely a wetland bird. Prefers pans and dams with muddy shores, as well as tidal mud flats.
Similar sounding Red-necked Stint (not included). The call of this rare vagrant is difficult to separate from that of the Red-necked Stint.

GULLS AND TERNS

Gulls and terns give simple grating and rasping songs. Although some species sound unique, many are very similar, so song is not always the best means of identifying these birds.

Kelp Gull *Larus dominicanus*

Kelpmeeu

120 Track detail 0:24 (total length) = 0:02–0:12 (flight calls); 0:12–0:24 (nest site calls; context uncertain)

Song Mostly gives typical gull's *kraaw* or *kraawu*.
Other sounds Complex and not well described, but around breeding sites often gives rapid descending *kraaw-wow-wow-wow-wow*. In group interactions, gives an agitated *kyow-kyow-kyow-kyow-kyow*.
Regional variation None.

Habitat On coast. Sometimes ventures inland to scavenge, but never strays too far from the sea.
Similar sounding Grey-headed (121) and Hartlaub's (122) gulls. Superficially like Hartlaub's and Grey-headed gulls, but confusion is unlikely.

Grey-headed Gull *Chroicocephalus cirrocephalus*

Gryskopmeeu

121 Track detail 0:02–1:13 (mixed flight and alarm calls)

Song A typical gull-like *kaaarr*; sometimes also a slight double-note *ka-kaaarr*.
Other sounds Variations of the song given in alarm.
Regional variation None.
Habitat Fresh water like pans and wetlands; also saltwater pans and estuaries. Forages at landfills.

Similar sounding Kelp (120) and Hartlaub's (122) gulls. Superficial resemblance to Kelp Gull, but confusion unlikely. Song is slightly fuller and lower pitched than that of Hartlaub's.

Hartlaub's Gull *Chroicocephalus hartlaubii*

Hartlaubmeeu

122 Track detail 0:02–0:27 (mixed flight, alarm and begging calls)

Song Like Grey-headed Gull, gives typical *kaaarr*, sometimes a double-note *ka-kaaarrr*.
Other sounds In alarm gives variation of the *kaaarr*.
Regional variation None.

Habitat Never strays very far from the coast.
Similar sounding Kelp (120) and Grey-headed (121) gulls. Superficially like Kelp Gull. Hartlaub's song is subtly higher pitched and thinner.

Caspian Tern   *Hydroprogne caspia*   Reusesterretjie

123 Track detail 0:03–0:25 (flight call)

Song Not heard in our region.
Other sounds Deep, guttural, rasping alarm calls such as a harsh *kraak*.
Regional variation None.
Habitat Estuaries, lagoons, and inland waterbodies.

Similar sounding White-backed Night Heron (not included) and Marsh Owl (165). Recalls songs of night heron and of Marsh Owl, but shorter; confusion unlikely.

Sandwich Tern   *Thalasseus sandvicensis*   Grootsterretjie

124 Track detail 0:02–0:10 (flight call)

Song Not heard in our region.
Other sounds Grating *kree* and *krek* sounds, given in alarm. Flight call comprises these same sounds, but with a more piercing, lapwing-like tone.
Regional variation None.

Habitat Beaches; sometimes estuaries and lagoons.
Similar sounding Common (125), Little (126), Arctic (not included) and Black (not included) terns. Listen for the slight lapwing-like tone in the flight call.

Common Tern   *Sterna hirundo*   Gewone Sterretjie

125 Track detail 0:02–0:22 (flight call)

Song Not heard in our region.
Other sounds Typical tern-like *kiep* and grating *kerrrr* calls.
Regional variation None.

Habitat Wide range of coastal habitats; also occurs offshore.
Similar sounding Other terns, including the Sandwich (124) and Little (126) terns. Terns can sound so alike that call may not aid identification.

Little Tern   *Sternula albifrons*   Kleinsterretjie

126 Track detail 0:02–0:15 (flight call)

Song Not heard in our region.
Other sounds A short, sharp, grating *kerr*.
Regional variation None.
Habitat Estuaries, lagoons and some saltpans; also occurs offshore.

Similar sounding Common (125), Sandwich (124), Damara (127), Arctic (not included) and Black (not included) terns. Pay special attention to tone and pitch. Sandwich Tern's call has lapwing-like tone. Damara's call resembles squeaky polystyrene.

Damara Tern *Sternula balaenarum* Damarasterretjie

127 Track detail 0:02–0:23 (group song)

Song A high-pitched rasping *tzee-wee*. Uniquely for a tern, song recalls squeaky polystyrene.
Other sounds Contact and alarm calls comprise soft and loud variations of main song.

Regional variation None.
Habitat Along the coast, at saltpans and at estuaries.
Similar sounding Little Tern (126). Squeaky polystyrene tone is not heard in calls of Little Tern.

Whiskered Tern *Chlidonias hybrida* Witbaardsterretjie

128 Track detail 0:02–0:26 (flight call)

Song A soft scratchy *kreek* sound.
Other sounds None.
Regional variation None.

Habitat Inland waterbodies such as dams, pans and seasonally flooded areas.
Similar sounding White-winged Tern (129). Whiskered Tern sounds scratchier and higher pitched.

White-winged Tern *Chlidonias leucopterus* Witvlerksterretjie

129 Track detail 0:02–0:16 (flight call)

Song Not heard in our region.
Other sounds A scratchy *kreek*, given both as alarm and contact call; sound is typical for a tern.
Regional variation None.

Habitat Wetlands, dams and temporary pans. Often also forages in habitats away from water.
Similar sounding Whiskered (128) and other terns. White-winged tends to sound scratchier and more distinctive than terns listed here.

SANDGROUSES

Sandgrouses utter a range of nasal and bubbly sounds that are unique to this family. Their calls are sufficiently distinctive that these species can be identified by ear alone.

Namaqua Sandgrouse *Pterocles namaqua* Kelkiewyn

130 Track detail 0:02–0:20 (group song by a large number of birds)

Song Gives short, nasal, almost wheezing *kel-kie-wyn* notes, from which it gets its Afrikaans name.
Other sounds Groups of birds give *kip* notes both on the ground and at takeoff.

Regional variation None.
Habitat Sandy ground in arid areas.
Similar sounding None.

Yellow-throated Sandgrouse   *Pterocles gutturalis*   Geelkeelsandpatrys

131 Track detail 0:36 (total length) = 0:03–0:29 (song); 0:29–0:36 (flight call)

Song A guttural *kuwaar-ar-ar*.
Other sounds A short repeated *yip*, given by groups of birds both on the ground and on takeoff.
Regional variation None.
Habitat Grassy habitats with some sandy areas.

Similar sounding Grey Go-away-bird (150). Sometimes bears slight resemblance to go-away-bird, but sandgrouse's rhythmical three-note song sufficiently distinctive; confusion unlikely.

Double-banded Sandgrouse   *Pterocles bicinctus*   Dubbelbandsandpatrys

132 Track detail 0:03–0:30 (contact call)

Song A metallic, bubbly *wheet-wheet-weuu*.
Other sounds Rasping *chuk* sounds sometimes given at takeoff. Groups of birds give excited song variations at water holes and as contact call.

Regional variation None.
Habitat Mostly seen in sandy areas in mopane woodlands, but also found in acacia woodlands.
Similar sounding None.

PIGEONS AND DOVES

The songs of pigeons and doves are already familiar to many birders. Species in this group have distinctive songs that are usually easy to recognise. Wood doves are an exception, however. Their calls are very similar, making it more of a challenge to separate these birds by their songs and calls.

Speckled Pigeon   *Columba guinea*   Kransduif

133 Track detail 0:03–0:26 (song of several males)

Song A series of the drawn-out *doo-doo-doo* notes typical of a pigeon, as well as a *doo-zoo-woooooo*.
Other sounds Contact call comprises soft dove-like sounds.
Regional variation None.

Habitat Cliffs, rocky and mountainous areas as well as urban areas with tall buildings. Ventures into gardens and crop lands to feed.
Similar sounding Purple-crested Turaco (149). Introductory notes are more rasping and dove-like.

Eastern Bronze-naped (Delegorgue's) Pigeon   *Columba delegorguei*   Withalsbosduif

134 Track detail 0:03–1:01 (song)

Song A distinct *doo-doooo-dududududududu* phrase, given 4–5 times; final phrase falls slightly in pitch.
Other sounds An almost duck-like *kaarrgg*, given as flight call.

Regional variation None.
Habitat Very restricted. Found only in mature evergreen coastal forests.
Similar sounding None.

Rock Dove (Feral Pigeon) *Columba livia*   Tuinduif

135 Track detail 0:01–0:15 (song)

Song Male's display song is a trilling *coo*, like that of a typical dove, but faster.
Other sounds Alarm and contact calls comprise range of low-pitched, muffled hoots and coos, as well as other guttural sounds.

Regional variation None.
Habitat Built-up urban areas. Will venture into suburbs and periurban areas when food is scarce.
Similar sounding None.

African Mourning Dove *Streptopelia decipiens*   Rooioogtortelduif

136 Track detail 0:34 (total length) = 0:03–0:17 (*dzu-wuuuuu coorrrrr* song); 0:17–0:25 (*doo-woooo* song); 0:25–0:34 (alarm or contact call)

Song A *dzu-wuuuuu coorrrrr*, easily recognised as a dove's song. Also gives *doo-woooo* similar to song of Red-eyed Dove.
Other sounds Sometimes gives a drawn-out, rolling *cooooorrrrrr*, presumably as alarm or contact call.
Regional variation None.
Habitat Lowveld savanna, acacia woodlands, riverine habitats, well-wooded gardens and cultivated lands.

Similar sounding Red-eyed Dove (137) and Southern White-faced Owl (166). Elements of song recall Red-eyed Dove, but African Mourning Dove gives just two notes per phrase, not 4–5. Rapid rattling tone of alarm call faster than rattle given by Southern White-faced Owl.

Red-eyed Dove *Streptopelia semitorquata*   Grootringduif

137 Track detail 0:03–0:30 (song)

Song A *doo-doo-doodoo-doo* phrase, easily recognised as that of a dove. May add an extra note at the end – *doo-doo-doodoo-doo-doo*. Also gives rasping sounds in breeding display.
Other sounds Rasping sounds, similar to breeding display song, given as both alarm and contact call.
Regional variation None.

Habitat Woodlands and acacia savanna, as well as gardens and parks. Also occurs in commercial plantations of exotic trees.
Similar sounding African Mourning Dove (136). Song similar to that of African Mourning Dove, but comprises 4–5 notes.

Cape Turtle Dove *Streptopelia capicola*   Gewone Tortelduif

138 Track detail 0:02–0:29 (song)

Song A distinctive *coo-cooora*, repeated for long periods of time. Probably the best-known dove song.
Other sounds A rasping and excited *caaarrrrra*, given most often when landing in a tree (but not on the ground).

Regional variation None.
Habitat Woodlands, farms, parks and gardens.
Similar sounding None.

Laughing Dove *Streptopelia senegalensis* Rooiborsduifie

139 Track detail 0:02–0:26 (song)

Song A soft *do-do-do-do-do* that rises and falls in pitch, given mainly to proclaim territory; sounds a little like laughter. Faster version given in display.
Other sounds Sometimes gives soft bleat in flight or alarm.

Regional variation None.
Habitat Wide ranging, but avoids broad-leaved woodlands. In arid areas, favours human settlements.
Similar sounding None.

African Green Pigeon *Treron calvus* Papegaaiduif

140 Track detail 0:02–0:12 (song)

Song A series of high-pitched whistles that vary in pitch, followed by throaty grating sounds.
Other sounds Alarm and contact calls not described.
Regional variation None.
Habitat A range of broad-leaved woodland habitats. Figs are a primary food source.

Similar sounding Crowned (104) and Blacksmith (102) lapwings. Song superficially resembles those of some lapwings, including those listed here, but confusion not likely.

Emerald-spotted Wood Dove *Turtur chalcospilos* Groenvlekduifie

141 Track detail 0:03–0:42 (song)

Song A soft hooted *doo-woo doo*, speeding up and ending with a descending series of *do-do-do-do-do* notes.
Other sounds Alarm and contact calls not yet described.
Regional variation None.

Habitat Acacia savanna, woodlands and gardens.
Similar sounding Blue-spotted Wood (not included) and Tambourine (142) doves. Song higher pitched than in either of these species. Phrase longer than that of Blue-spotted Dove. Tambourine Dove's pitch does not descend as song tapers off.

Tambourine Dove *Turtur tympanistria* Witborsduif

142 Track detail 0:03–0:40 (song)

Song A soft hooted *doo doo*, starting slowly and culminating in rapid, evenly pitched *doo* notes.
Other sounds Must have both alarm and contact calls, but none yet described.
Regional variation None.

Habitat Evergreen forests and riverine bush.
Similar sounding Blue-spotted (not included) and Emerald-spotted wood doves (141). Song is lower and more evenly pitched than that of Emerald-spotted and longer than that of Blue-spotted.

Namaqua Dove *Oena capensis* Namakwaduifie

143 Track detail 0:02–0:20 (song)

Song A mournful *koo-woooo*, rising on *woooo*.
Other sounds Similar, but slightly harsher, flight calls.
Regional variation None.

Habitat Dry woodlands, acacia savanna and fallow farm land.
Similar sounding None.

PARROTS, PARAKEETS AND LOVEBIRDS

The shrill song of a parrot or lovebird is easily recognised. This kind of song is typical of all birds within the group, so these species are often hard to tell apart by ear.

Rosy-faced Lovebird *Agapornis roseicollis* Rooiwangparkiet

144 Track detail 0:03–0:32 (contact call)

Song Mixed shrieks, recalling those of a parakeet.
Other sounds Alarm call is faster version of song. Groups of birds give trill sounds to stay in contact.
Regional variation None.
Habitat Woodlands and shrub lands.

Similar sounding Black-cheeked and Lilian's lovebirds (not included), Meyer's (147) and Rüppell's (148) parrots and Rose-ringed Parakeet (not included). Difficult to separate from the lovebirds; higher pitch helps to distinguish it from parrots and parakeets.

Cape Parrot *Poicephalus robustus* Woudpapegaai

145 Track detail 0:03–1:08 (song)

Song A range of the usual parrot sounds. Includes *dzeek*, *zu-eet* and *zu-zee* phrases.
Other sounds Alarm call is a typical parrot's screech.
Regional variation Some minor variations have been recorded.
Habitat Occurs mainly in forests with yellowwood trees. May venture into fruit plantations to feed.

Similar sounding Larger parrots, especially Grey-headed (not included); also the smaller Brown-headed (146) and Meyer's (147) parrots. Song is lower pitched than those of smaller parrots like Rüppell's (148). Could be mistaken for one of the larger species; especially difficult to distinguish from Grey-headed, as Cape and Grey-headed were once considered the same species. Meyer's Parrot is higher pitched.

Brown-headed Parrot *Poicephalus cryptoxanthus* Bruinkoppapegaai

146 Track detail 0:03–1:05 (contact call)

Song Not described. Probably a typical parrot's song.
Other sounds Harsh screeching given in alarm, as is usual for a parrot.
Regional variation Unknown; some variation likely.
Habitat Acacia and mopane woodlands.

Similar sounding Cape (145), Grey-headed (not included), Meyer's (147) and Rüppell's (148) parrots. Higher pitched than Cape or Grey-headed. Very difficult to separate from Meyer's. Rüppell's vocalisations include more monosyllabic phrases.

Meyer's Parrot *Poicephalus meyeri*   Bosveldpapegaai

147 Track detail 0:03–0:34 (song)

Song A series of high-pitched parrot's screeches and swizzles. Sometimes has sandpiper-like tone.
Other sounds Gives harsh screeches when alarmed.
Regional variation Some regional variation likely.
Habitat Acacia, savanna and broad-leaved woodlands; favours baobab trees.

Similar sounding Common Sandpiper (117), Rosy-faced Lovebird (144) and Cape (145), Grey-headed (not included), Brown-headed (146) and Rüppell's (148) parrots. Tone harsher and more parrot-like than in sandpiper and deeper than in lovebird. Higher pitched than Cape or Grey-headed parrots. Has more bisyllabic phrases than Rüppell's. Very similar to Brown-headed.

Rüppell's Parrot *Poicephalus rueppellii*   Bloupenspapegaai

148 Track detail 0:02–0:16 (song)

Song Largely monosyllabic, piercing screeches.
Other sounds Harsh screeches given when alarmed.
Regional variation Some variation likely.
Habitat Riparian and mixed woodlands; also lala palm forests.

Similar sounding Rosy-faced Lovebird (144), Cape (145), Grey-headed (not included), Brown-headed (146) and Meyer's (147) parrots. Song is slightly deeper than that of lovebird and higher pitched than that of Cape Parrot. Monosyllabic phrases distinguish it from songs of Brown-headed and Meyer's.

TURACOS AND GO-AWAY-BIRDS

Birds in this group are highly vocal, with distinctive noisy songs. Only the three Knysna turacos (formerly considered a single species) present any problems, as they sound very similar.

Purple-crested Turaco (Lourie) *Tauraco porphyreolopha*   Bloukuifloerie

149 Track detail 0:03–0:49 (song)

Song Soft rasping introductory notes, followed by a loud, far-carrying *ko-ko-ko-ko-ko*.
Other sounds Some grating *kaar-kaar-kaar* sounds, presumably given as alarm or contact call.
Regional variation None.

Habitat Forests and densely wooded gardens; sometimes ventures into woodlands. Avoids open habitats.
Similar sounding Speckled Pigeon (133). Turaco's tone is not as rasping and dove-like.

Grey Go-away-bird (Lourie) *Corythaixoides concolor*   Kwêvoël

150 Track detail 0:03–0:34 (mixed song and alarm call)

Song A *kwê* sound; sometimes a *go-away* phrase from which it gets its English common name.
Other sounds Nasal, gurgling contact and alarm calls.
Regional variation None.
Habitat Dry and acacia woodlands and suburban gardens. Avoids dense broad-leaved woodlands.

Similar sounding Yellow-throated Sandgrouse (131) and Broad-billed Roller (202). Sandgrouse distinguished by its three-note rhythm. Resemblance to Broad-billed Roller is superficial.

CUCKOOS

Cuckoos are easy to separate by ear, as each species has a unique song. Songs may comprise various whistled phrases, like those of the distinctive Red-chested Cuckoo, or shriller sounds, like those of the Great Spotted and Jacobin cuckoos.

African Cuckoo *Cuculus gularis*

Afrikaanse Koekoek

 Track detail 0:02–0:19 (song)

Song A two-note *coo-coo*, repeated at intervals of about two seconds.
Other sounds Like most other cuckoos, female gives a piercing *ki-ki-ki-ki-ki*; context uncertain.
Regional variation None.

Habitat Woodlands and acacia and semi-arid savanna. Absent from forests.
Similar sounding Black Coucal (163) and African Hoopoe (212). Song slower than that of the coucal and fuller, deeper and less muted than that of the hoopoe.

Red-chested Cuckoo *Cuculus solitarius*

Piet-my-vrou

152 **Track detail** 0:02–0:27 (song)

Song A loud whistled *wit-wee-woo* phrase, rendered as *piet-my-vrou* in Afrikaans. Each note descends in pitch.
Other sounds Female may give a loud and piercing *ki-ki-ki-ki-ki-ki*; context uncertain.

Regional variation None.
Habitat Lush forests, broad-leaved woodlands and very well-wooded gardens.
Similar sounding None. Among the best-known birdsongs in southern Africa.

Black Cuckoo *Cuculus clamosus*

Swartkoekoek

153 **Track detail** 0:47 (total length) = 0:02–0:36 (song); 0:36–0:47 (bubbling call; context uncertain)

Song A highly distinctive, almost eerie *doo-doo doooooooo*. Last note is longer and rises in pitch.
Other sounds Male gives rising, bubbling, excited chatter; ends on a short descending *dooo*. Female gives *ki-ki-ki-ki-ki* call. Context for both calls uncertain.

Regional variation None.
Habitat Thick bushveld, broad-leaved woodlands and large exotic trees in lush suburbs.
Similar sounding None.

Levaillant's Cuckoo   *Oxylophus levaillantii*   Gestreepte Nuwejaarsvoël

154 Track detail 0:24 (total length) = 0:02–0:09 (song); 0:09–0:24 (contact calls)

Song A short, whistled, bisyllabic *kla-weeuu*, repeated at intervals of about a second; often followed by a rapid *too-too-too-too-too-too-too*.
Other sounds Alarm and contact calls similar to song, but with variations in number of notes and including some chattering sounds. The *kleeuu* notes sometimes spread very far apart.
Regional variation None.

Habitat Acacia and broad-leaved woodlands. Favours dense vegetation and tall trees.
Similar sounding Jacobin Cuckoo (155) and Great Spotted Cuckoo (156). Levaillant's song comprises a single *kla-weeuu* note, repeated frequently; its chattering is less harsh than that of Jacobin. Levaillant's alarm and contact calls higher pitched than those of Great Spotted Cuckoo.

Jacobin Cuckoo   *Oxylophus jacobinus*   Bontnuwejaarsvoël

155 Track detail 0:36 (total length) = 0:02–0:28 (song); 0:28–0:36 (contact call)

Song A series of piercing *kleeu* notes. Phrases closely spaced and number of notes per phrase varies.
Other sounds Contact call a raucous cackle, given by pairs or groups of birds. Alarm call is a rattled *tuka-tuka-tuka*.
Regional variation None.
Habitat Acacia savanna, dense woodlands and some coastal forests.

Similar sounding Levaillant's (154) and Great Spotted (156) cuckoos. The number of whistled notes in Jacobin's song varies, while Levaillant's always gives a bisyllabic whistle. Jacobin's chattering also sounds harsher than that of Levaillant's and its call is thinner than that of Great Spotted.

Great Spotted Cuckoo   *Clamator glandarius*   Gevlekte Koekoek

156 Track detail 0:02–0:12 (song)

Song A raptor-like *keeuuww*, repeated at approximately one-second intervals.
Other sounds A distinctive chattering, often given in alarm.
Regional variation None.

Habitat Open savanna and woodlands.
Similar sounding Levaillant's (154) and Jacobin (155) cuckoos. Great Spotted sounds lower and fuller than either of these cuckoos.

Dideric Cuckoo   *Chrysococcyx caprius*   Diederikkie

157 Track detail 0:35 (total length) = 0:02–0:19 (song); 0:19–0:35 (aggressive interactions between males)

Song Distinctive *di-di-di-diderik*.
Other sounds A series of rapidly sounded piercing whistles, similar in tone and pitch to the *di-di-di* notes in the main song, but faster.
Regional variation None.

Habitat Has wide habitat tolerance for a cuckoo, being found in acacia woodlands, on forest margins and in arid and grassland areas. Never strays far from trees.
Similar sounding None.

Klaas's Cuckoo *Chrysococcyx klaas*   Meitjie

158 Track detail 0:02–0:40 (song)

Song A unique and piercing *tee-hee*, given about 4–6 times in quick succession; leaves lengthy gap before repeating the phrase.
Other sounds Rapid *tee* notes, given in alarm.

Regional variation None.
Habitat Mainly broad-leaved but also dense acacia woodlands, forest margins and well-wooded gardens.
Similar sounding None.

African Emerald Cuckoo *Chrysococcyx cupreus*   Mooimeisie

159 Track detail 0:03–0:37 (song)

Song Distinctive four-note *do-deuuu doo dweet*.
Other sounds A loud descending trill.
Regional variation None.

Habitat Evergreen and escarpment forests. May be found in densely wooded gardens and thick woodlands.
Similar sounding None.

COUCALS

Coucals quite often occur near water. Their songs are similar; most give a series of rising or falling *do* notes.

Coppery-tailed Coucal *Centropus cupreicaudus*   Grootvleiloerie

160 Track detail 0:03–1:00 (duet)

Song Bubbling *do-do-do-do* notes that descend and gradually slow down; members of a **duetting** pair sing at different pitches.
Other sounds Like most coucals, gives a series of *tuk* notes when alarmed.
Regional variation None.

Habitat Found mainly in Botswana's papyrus swamps. May venture into seasonally flooded areas.
Similar sounding All other coucals, except Black Coucal. Coppery-tailed has deepest song, but not easily separated in the field. Pitch descends at end of the phrase, but Burchell's falls, then rises. Senegal's song is slower.

Burchell's Coucal *Centropus burchelli*   Gewone Vleiloerie

161 Track detail 0:02–0:15 (male song with response from distant female)

Song Both sexes give a bubbly decelerating *do-do-do-do*. In some cases the pitch falls then rises, in others it just falls. Context for these variations is unknown; also not yet known whether one of the sexes gives each variation.
Other sounds Alarm call a series of *tuk* notes, as is typical of most coucals.

Regional variation None.
Habitat Well-wooded gardens, wetlands, forest margins and thicket vegetation.
Similar sounding All other coucals, except Black Coucal. Burchell's song faster and higher-pitched than those of other coucals.

Senegal Coucal *Centropus senegalensis*

Senegalvleiloerie

162 Track detail 0:03–0:41 (song)

Song A series of *do-do-do-do* notes that rise then fall in pitch; phrase slower and less bubbling than usual for a coucal.
Other sounds A series of *tuk* alarm calls, as is typical of most coucals.
Regional variation None.
Habitat Favours dense cover. May stray quite far from water.

Similar sounding All other coucals, except Black Coucal; also Southern Yellow-billed (206) and Southern Red-billed (208) hornbills. Song distinguished from that of other coucals by slower speed and brief rise then fall in pitch; also has less bubbling tone. May recall a hornbill, but resemblance fairly superficial.

Black Coucal *Centropus grillii*

Swartvleiloerie

163 Track detail 0:02–0:18 (song)

Song A staccato, almost whistled *do-doot*.
Other sounds Contact call a series of rapidly sounded *tok* notes. Alarm call comprises slow *tuk* notes. Contact and alarm calls similar to those given by most other coucals.
Regional variation None.
Habitat Seasonally flooded, rank grassland habitats.

Similar sounding African Cuckoo (151) and African Hoopoe (212). Song unique within its wetland environment, although alarm and contact calls of most coucals are very similar. Songs of both African Cuckoo and African Hoopoe sound similar, but slower and lower pitched.

OWLS

Owls are nocturnal birds with enigmatic, easily recognised songs. Sounds range from hoots to screeches and grunts. All species are easily identified by ear.

African Wood Owl *Strix woodfordii*

Bosuil

164 Track detail 0:03–1:18 (song and either contact call or female song response)

Song Phrases comprise a quizzical *woo-hooooo* repeated a few times, followed by a pause. Somewhat reminiscent of a hyaena's call. The short rapid series of hoots thought to be a contact call (see **Other sounds**) may actually be female's response to male's song, but this is uncertain.

Other sounds A short rapid series of hoots; may be contact call, or song response by female (see **Song**).
Regional variation None.
Habitat Densely wooded forests as well as broad-leaved woodlands.
Similar sounding None.

Marsh Owl   *Asio capensis*

Vlei-uil

165 Track detail 0:43 (total length) = 0:02–0:36 (song);
0:36–0:43 (rapid croaks; context unknown)

Song Croaking phrases, like sound of fabric tearing.
Other sounds Gives high-pitched squeals in
confrontations as well as a rapid series of croaks;
context for this call uncertain.
Regional variation None.

Habitat Wetlands and tall grasslands; often
near water.
Similar sounding Black-shouldered Kite (46),
Caspian Tern (123) and European Roller (200). Marsh
Owl gives far shorter, more croaking notes.

Southern White-faced Owl   *Ptilopsis granti*

Witwanguil

166 Track detail 0:03–0:24 (song)

Song A dove-like *dudududududuwooooo*.
Other sounds Growls and hisses when disturbed.
Regional variation None.

Habitat Varied. Includes tall broad-leaved
woodlands, acacia woodlands and savanna.
Similar sounding African Mourning Dove (136).
Resemblance is superficial.

African Barred Owlet   *Glaucidium capense*

Gebande Uil

167 Track detail 0:03–0:22 (song)

Song Whistled trilling *preeu* notes, repeated several
times; sometimes also a two-note *pruur-ruuurrr*.
Other sounds Chicks' begging call comprises some
wheezing sounds.
Regional variation Isolated Eastern Cape
population may be separate species, but no song
variation recorded.

Habitat Mainly broad-leaved woodlands, where it
favours dense vegetation.
Similar sounding Pearl-spotted Owlet (169).
Gives trilled song notes, not plain whistles like
Pearl-spotted.

African Scops Owl   *Otus senegalensis*

Skopsuil

168 Track detail 0:03–0:45 (song)

Song A loud liquid *purrp*, given about every
10 seconds.
Other sounds Gives low croaks around the nest;
context uncertain.
Regional variation None.

Habitat Varies from arid savanna to dense acacia
and mopane woodlands.
Similar sounding None.

Pearl-spotted Owlet *Glaucidium perlatum*   Witkoluil

 Track detail 1:24 (total length) = 0:03–1:11 (song);
1:11–1:24 (nest site calls; context unknown)

Song Repeated *woo-woo-woo-woo-woo* whistles, building to a crescendo, followed by some descending *weeuu* whistles. The latter whistles sometimes given without the introductory *woo-woo-woo-woo-woo*.
Other sounds Some nest interaction whistles noted; context for these sounds not described.
Regional variation None.

Habitat Wide range of acacia and mopane woodlands. Avoids grasslands and very dense habitats.
Similar sounding African Barred Owlet (167). Pearl-spotted lacks the trill characteristic of the song of its barred cousin.

Verreaux's (Giant) Eagle-Owl *Bubo lacteus*   Reuse-ooruil

170 **Track detail 0:04–0:56 (song)**

Song A distinctive very low-pitched grunt of short duration. Usually pauses between grunting notes, but may string a few notes together in a brief phrase.
Other sounds When alarmed gives deep dog-like bark and nervous chittering.
Regional variation None.

Habitat Savanna and woodlands as well as arid savanna, always close to tall roosts and nesting sites such as large trees or pylons.
Similar sounding Pel's Fishing-Owl (171). Song and calls harsher and louder than those of Pel's.

Pel's Fishing Owl *Scotopelia peli*   Visuil

171 **Track detail 0:55 (total length) = 0:03–0:35 (song); 0:35–0:55 (contact calls)**

Song Gives 2–3 short, deep, booming hoots and sometimes also includes a long hoot. May give some soft grunts before song.
Other sounds Begging chicks give eerie loud wail.
Regional variation None.

Habitat Dense woodlands along large streams, where trees provide perches overhanging the water. Also occurs in densely wooded swamps.
Similar sounding Verreaux's Eagle-Owl (170). Song less grunting and more booming than that of Verreaux's.

Cape Eagle-Owl *Bubo capensis*   Kaapse Ooruil

172 **Track detail 0:02–0:30 (song)**

Song A far-carrying double or, sometimes, triple-note hoot.
Other sounds Dog-like yaps, but context unknown. Also hissing and bill snapping when alarmed, as is typical of many eagle-owls.
Regional variation None.

Habitat Woodlands, grasslands and higher-altitude karoo vegetation, always in association with cliffs, mountains and rocky outcrops.
Similar sounding Spotted Eagle-Owl (173). Notes are shorter and more piercing than softer hoots of Spotted.

Spotted Eagle-Owl *Bubo africanus*

Gevlekte Ooruil

 173 Track detail 0:03–0:35 (female song; recorded in captivity)

Song Male gives soft two-note *hoo-hoooo*; second note is longer and lower pitched. In **duet**, female responds from nearby with a three-note *hoo-hoo-hooooo*.
Other sounds Gives dog-like yaps, but context uncertain. Like many other eagle-owls, hisses and snaps its bill when alarmed.
Regional variation None.

Habitat Wide ranging, but includes arid areas, grasslands, woodlands, suburban and even built-up urban environments. Requires large trees or rocky areas to provide suitable nesting sites.
Similar sounding Cape Eagle-Owl (172). Song is a soft hoot with a long final note that is quite distinct from song of Cape Eagle-Owl.

Western Barn Owl *Tyto alba*

Nonnetjie-uil

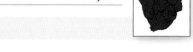

174 Track detail 0:03–0:24 (song)

Song A loud, shrill, human-like screech.
Other sounds Hisses and many variations on the screech from song, given as alarm, contact and begging calls.
Regional variation None.

Habitat Broad-leaved woodlands, acacia savanna and open grasslands; requires roosting sites. Moves to take advantage of available food sources.
Similar sounding Scaly-throated Honeyguide (not included). Honeyguide's screech rises more in pitch and is not usually given at night.

NIGHTJARS

Song is of great help in identifying nightjars, since these birds have highly cryptic plumage. Each species' song is distinctive and easily recognised, usually comprising a beautiful, liquid, whistled phrase or some purring notes.

Freckled Nightjar *Caprimulgus tristigma*

Donkernaguil

175 Track detail 0:02–0:24 (song)

Song A dog-like yapping *kow-wow*, repeated several times; sometimes gives third *wow* note.
Other sounds Some hooting sounds, in confrontations.
Regional variation None.

Habitat Broad-leaved woodlands in rocky areas or near rocky outcrops; requires rock-face roosts.
Similar sounding Green Barbet (213). The two- or three-note phrase separates this song from the repetitive single-note yaps of the barbet.

Fiery-necked Nightjar   *Caprimulgus pectoralis*   Afrikaanse Naguil

176   Track detail 0:02–0:25 (song)

Song Sings *good-lord-deliver-us*, sometimes repeating the *deliver-us* notes; an archetypal sound of the veld, often used to establish an African setting in films.
Other sounds Many other calls, including some soft *wow* sounds, given both as alarm and contact calls.
Regional variation None. Birds more vocal in warm weather; may falsely suggest regional differences.

Habitat Established acacia and broad-leaved woodlands, where thick layers of dead leaves provide cover on the ground.
Similar sounding Pale Chanting Goshawk (48). Goshawk's song is faster and less liquid than that of the nightjar.

Rufous-cheeked Nightjar   *Caprimulgus rufigena*   Rooiwangnaguil

177   Track detail 0:03–0:47 (song)

Song A lead-in series of *koo-ip* notes, followed by a drawn-out monotone churring.
Other sounds Gives same *koo-ip* call in flight and in confrontations.
Regional variation None.

Habitat Open areas in savanna and woodlands. Avoids grasslands.
Similar sounding Square-tailed Nightjar (179). Rufous-cheeked's *chur* is monotone, whereas Square-tailed's *chur* changes pitch.

Swamp (Natal) Nightjar   *Caprimulgus natalensis*   Natalse Naguil

178   Track detail 0:02–0:13 (song)

Song A unique repetitive *chop-chop-chop-chop*.
Other sounds Rapidly repeated *wuwuwuwuwuw*, given in flight.

Regional variation None.
Habitat Favours tall grasslands close to water.
Similar sounding None.

Square-tailed (Mozambique) Nightjar   *Caprimulgus fossii*   Laeveldnaguil

179   Track detail 0:03–0:30 (song)

Song A drawn-out churring; switches between two pitches at regular intervals.
Other sounds Some *ip* sounds given in alarm.
Regional variation None.
Habitat Favours sandy patches in both acacia and mopane woodlands.

Similar sounding Rufous-cheeked Nightjar (177). Continual switches in pitch distinguish song from Rufous-cheeked's monotone *chur*.

SWIFTS AND SPINETAILS

Swifts and spinetails have a rudimentary syrinx and their songs are therefore simple, often comprising just short scratchy notes. Most swifts sound similar and may be difficult to separate by ear. However, there are exceptions such as the diagnostic shrill chatter of the Little Swift and the rhythmical scratchy calls of the Horus Swift.

Alpine Swift *Tachymarptis melba*   Witpenswindswael

 180 Track detail 0:03–0:41 (nest site calls; context uncertain)

Song A drawn-out trill, typical of a swift.
Other sounds A series of agitated *titititititititi* phrases, given near nest site, presumably as alarm or contact call.
Regional variation None.

Habitat Forms breeding colonies in rocky areas, but disperses over a wider area to feed.
Similar sounding Little (181) and other swifts. Drawn-out shrill notes typical of swifts generally and difficult to distinguish, but the agitated twittering is distinctive, like that of Little Swift but without trills.

Little Swift *Apus affinis*   Kleinwindswael

 181 Track detail 0:03–0:50 (mixed song and contact calls)

Song Very shrill chattering that often descends in pitch.
Other sounds Typical swift-like scratchy noises sometimes heard. Also gives a *tri-tri-tri* similar in tone to the chattering in song, both as contact and alarm call.
Regional variation None.

Habitat Usually seen at nest sites on cliffs, bridges or tall buildings. Disperses to feed, often near water.
Similar sounding Alpine Swift (180), Burnt-necked Eremomela (319) and Namaqua Warbler (359). Distinguished from these species by its shrill chattering.

Horus Swift *Apus horus*   Horuswindswael

182 Track detail 0:02–0:23 (song)

Song A distinctive *zree-zee-zoo* or a four-note *za-zree-zee-zoo* phrase.
Other sounds Harsh, scratchy alarm calls, as is typical for a swift.
Regional variation None.
Habitat Like most swifts, forages widely over many types of habitat. Requires sites at which to build a hole nest, such as a quarry or sand bank. May excavate nest hole alongside other hole-nesting species like Pied Starlings.
Similar sounding White-rumped Swift (183). Like most swifts, song phrase fairly easy to distinguish. Listen for scratchy quality. Superficially resembles White-rumped Swift, but slower and less jumbled.

White-rumped Swift   *Apus caffer*

Witkruiswindswael

183 Track detail 0:03–0:27 (song)

Song Usually silent, except near nest sites, where it gives scratchy *zweeu* and *pree-ree-ti-ti* songs, presumably to attract a mate.
Other sounds Not known; must have distress calls.
Regional variation None.

Habitat Open karoo, savanna and shrub lands.
Similar sounding Horus (182) and many other swifts, and Grey Waxbill (479). Its *pree-ree-ti-ti* song superficially like that of Horus, but faster and less clearly patterned. Calls very similar to those of many other swifts. Resemblance to waxbill is superficial.

MOUSEBIRDS

Mousebirds tend to be shy, quiet birds and often their songs don't stand out. They may give swizzles and chirps similar to some weavers. It takes patience to learn their songs.

Speckled Mousebird   *Colius striatus*

Gevlekte Muisvoël

184 Track detail 0:03–0:55 (contact calls)

Song A weaver-like *dzeet*, repeated in groups of about 2–5 notes.
Other sounds An occasional soft, metallic rattle given as contact call. Alarm call is a grating *zit*.
Regional variation None.

Habitat Acacia (but not broad-leaved) woodlands, gardens and stands of exotic trees in grasslands.
Similar sounding Some weavers. Song has weaver-like tone, but repetitive *dzeet* and absence of weaver-like swizzling notes make it easy to distinguish.

White-backed Mousebird   *Colius colius*

Witrugmuisvoël

185 Track detail 0:02–0:19 (group contact and alarm calls)

Song No specific display or territorial song described.
Other sounds Metallic *zrik* notes, like a handful of coins shaken. Also a short, sharp *zwee* whistle, presumably given both as contact and alarm call.
Regional variation None.

Habitat Coastal fynbos and scrub, gardens and parks. Also riverine thicket in arid areas.
Similar sounding River Warbler (329) and White-winged Widowbird (465). Rapid *zrik* notes like songs of River Warbler or White-winged Widowbird, but given by groups of mousebirds, not lone individuals.

Red-faced Mousebird   *Urocolius indicus*

Rooiwangmuisvoël

186 Track detail 0:03–0:30 (song)

Song Unique; a soft three-note *tsee-wee-wi* whistle.
Other sounds An almost sparrow-like *chew-rip*.
Regional variation None.
Habitat Savanna, gardens and parks, often near water.

Similar sounding Cape (443) and House (444) sparrows. Mousebird gives some sparrow-like notes, but they are low and whispered, not as piercing; confusion unlikely.

TROGONS

A trogon's grating and ghostly hoots are easily recognised in its forest habitat.

Narina Trogon *Apaloderma narina* — Bosloerie

 Track detail 0:02–0:36 (song*) * Note Dark-backed Weaver and Red-capped Robin-Chat in recording

Song A soft, hoarse, grating *hroo-hroo-hroo-hroo*.
Other sounds Variations of the rasping hoot given as both alarm and contact call.
Regional variation None.

Habitat Various forest types as well as dense broad-leaved woodlands.
Similar sounding None.

KINGFISHERS

Kingfisher songs are typically piercing whistles, which may range from the very high-pitched whistle of an African Pygmy Kingfisher (not included here) to the whistled laugh of a Woodland Kingfisher – the iconic sound of summer in the bushveld. The songs of kingfishers are generally quite distinctive. Only the three small blue kingfishers, the Malachite, Half-collared and African Pygmy, sound at all similar. However, their songs differ in tone.

Giant Kingfisher *Megaceryle maximus* — Reusevisvanger

 Track detail 0:02–0:35 (song and female response)

Song A loud cackling *keh*, repeated at a rate of about two notes per second. Female sometimes gives a raucous cackle similar in tone, but both sexes seldom call simultaneously.
Other sounds Alarm and contact calls variations of the harsh chatter; all calls fairly similar.
Regional variation None.

Habitat Waterbodies with overhanging perches. Favours wooded river margins.
Similar sounding Hamerkop (25) and African Wattled Lapwing (106). Song not as deep and nasal as that of Hamerkop and lacks drawn-out screechy notes. African Wattled Lapwing's song not as full and cackling.

Pied Kingfisher *Ceryle rudis* — Bontvisvanger

 Track detail 0:02–0:15 (song with female response)

Song Both sexes give a sharp *kik* and a rolling *kika-ti-yip*. They may give these high-pitched metallic songs simultaneously, but it's unclear whether or not this is a duet.
Other sounds Soft trills to keep mates in contact. Gives highly agitated variation of song when alarmed.

Regional variation None.
Habitat Always near water, including streams, dams, pans and wetlands.
Similar sounding Little Bee-eater (198). Confusion unlikely as song sounds far more metallic and piercing than that of bee-eater.

Malachite Kingfisher *Alcedo cristata*   Kuifkopvisvanger

190 Track detail 0:02–0:17 (song)

Song Male gives a piercing whistled *tseek-tseek-tseek*. In **duet** gives less piercing *cha* notes, to which female responds with chattering very similar to male's song. **Other sounds** A single *tseek*, much like song, generally given as contact call. Faster variations of song when excited or alarmed.

Regional variation None.
Habitat Always at water (dams, pans and streams).
Similar sounding White-fronted Bee-eater (196) and Half-collared Kingfisher (not included). Bee-eater sounds softer and higher pitched, while Half-collared Kingfisher sounds lower pitched and less piercing.

Woodland Kingfisher *Halcyon senegalensis*   Bosveldvisvanger

191 Track detail 0:02–0:37 (song)

Song A clearly recognisable *tchip-trrrrrrrrrrrrrrrrrrr*. **Other sounds** Contact call a series of about four trilled *trrrrrrrrrrrrrrrrrrr* phrases, joined together without the introductory *tchip* note given in song. Alarm call an agitated *ke-ke-ke-ke*. **Regional variation** None. Individual variations noted in pitch and length of introductory *tchip* and in length of trilling *rrrrrrrrrrrrrrrrrrr* note, but such differences seem to be hereditary.

Habitat Mainly acacia and mopane woodlands. Sometime occurs in broad-leaved woodlands.
Similar sounding Mangrove Kingfisher (192). Song consists of a single introductory note, followed by a trill, whereas Mangrove's song is more stuttering.

Mangrove Kingfisher *Halcyon senegaloides*   Manglietvisvanger

192 Track detail 0:03–0:30 (song)

Song An accelerating series of introductory *tchip* notes, decreasing in pitch and ending on a trilled *trrrrrrrr*. **Other sounds** None recorded, but presumably gives both contact and alarm calls. **Regional variation** None.

Habitat Mainly mangrove swamps and estuaries in southern Africa. May be found in woodland habitats when migrating.
Similar sounding Woodland Kingfisher (191). Song speeds up and is more stuttering than the *tchip-trrrrrrrrrrr* of Woodland Kingfisher, which comprises just a single single introductory note (not a series) and a slower, more stuttering trill.

Brown-hooded Kingfisher *Halcyon albiventris*   Bruinkopvisvanger

193 Track detail 0:24 (total length) = 0:03–0:19 (song); 0:19–0:24 (alarm call)

Song A series of about four *ti* notes, each lower than the last, repeated every one or two seconds. **Other sounds** Some trilling in contact situations, and a rapidly repeated *cheee-it* alarm call.

Regional variation None.
Habitat Wetlands, woodlands, parks and gardens.
Similar sounding None.

Striped Kingfisher *Halcyon chelicuti*   Gestreepte Visvanger

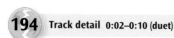

194 Track detail 0:02–0:10 (duet)

Song Both sexes give soft rolling *preuuuurrrrr*, repeated several times without intervals. Male may sing alone or in **duet** with a female.
Other sounds Rasping alarm calls.
Regional variation Some variations recorded, but basic song structure still recognisable.

Habitat Restricted to broad-leaved woodlands in some parts of its range; elsewhere may occur in acacia woodlands perhaps because competing species are absent there.
Similar sounding None.

BEE-EATERS

Bee-eaters are quite vocal, but their simple purping, chirping and sneering sounds generally don't carry well. Though unique, the songs are not crucial to identification, since these birds are often seen and heard at the same time.

European Bee-eater *Merops apiaster*   Europese Byvreter

195 Track detail 0:02–0:20 (song)

Song A distinctive liquid *purp* and a similar-sounding *pip* note.
Other sounds At the roost, groups of birds give rolling liquid calls.
Regional variation None.

Habitat Gardens, parks and acacia woodlands. Avoids both very dry and very wet areas.
Similar sounding Sclater's Lark (252), Black-eared Sparrow-Lark (254).

White-fronted Bee-eater *Merops bullockoides*   Rooikeelbyvreter

196 Track detail 0:03–0:49 (song*) * Listen for Woodland Kingfisher in recording

Song A rasping, almost comical *churra*, as well as other sounds including a nasal *kark* and louder ringing *kerrr*.
Other sounds Softer sounds, like a metallic, rattling *chip* and tern-like rasping *kee-keeyerrrr*. Context unknown.
Regional variation None.

Habitat Sandy river banks and eroded gullies in woodlands and scrub.
Similar sounding Malachite Kingfisher (190) and Gull-billed Tern (not included). Contact call similar to, but higher pitched than that of Malachite Kingfisher. Song recalls Gull-billed Tern, but can be separated by habitat preference.

Southern Carmine Bee-eater *Merops nubicoides*   Rooiborsbyvreter

 197 Track detail 0:29 (total length) = 0:02–0:25 (song); 0:25–0:29 (flight call)

Song A rasping *kirr*, repeated regularly.
Other sounds Flight call a full-sounding *ki-ki-ki-ki*, given on takeoff.
Regional variation None.

Habitat Flood plains, rivers and the shores of lakes in savanna habitat.
Similar sounding None.

Little Bee-eater *Merops pusillus*   Kleinbyvreter

198 Track detail 0:02–0:22 (song)

Song High-pitched, agitated, jumbled notes and a few trills.
Other sounds Contact and alarm calls comprise single *tjip* notes and trills.
Regional variation None.

Habitat Open areas in dry savanna; not bound to water, but may be found near dams.
Similar sounding Pied Kingfisher (189) and Black-eared Sparrow-Lark (254). Higher pitched, softer and less metallic than the kingfisher or the sparrow-lark.

ROLLERS

Rollers sing grating, scratchy songs. Some species sound unique and can be identified by call, but they are so conspicuous that one generally identifies them by sight long before they sing.

Lilac-breasted Roller *Coracias caudatus*   Gewone Troupant

199 Track detail 0:30 (total length) = 0:03–0:17 (contact or alarm call); 0:17–0:30 (song with crescendo)

Song Often silent, but display song comprises harsh *gaaarrr* sounds, speeding up to a crescendo.
Other sounds Slower variations of the *gaaarrr* sound, given in alarm; otherwise typically silent.
Regional variation None.
Habitat Acacia and broad-leaved woodlands. Avoids rocky and hilly areas.

Similar sounding European Roller (200). Alarm call most closely resembles alarm call of European Roller. Other common rollers have more distinctive phrases than does Lilac-breasted.

European Roller *Coracias garrulus*   Europese Troupant

 Track detail 0:03–1:00 (alarm call)

Song Breeding and display song not heard in our region.
Other sounds Harsh, grating, scratchy notes given in alarm and disputes. More vocal as it prepares to migrate.
Regional variation None.

Habitat Savanna and woodlands; may range into open grasslands, provided there are occasional trees.
Similar sounding Marsh Owl (165) and Lilac-breasted Roller (199). Song and calls are higher-pitched than those of Lilac-breasted Roller, with longer notes that sound like fabric tearing. Notes also longer than those of Marsh Owl.

Purple Roller *Coracias naevius*   Groottroupant

 Track detail 0:31 (total length) = 0:02–0:26 (song); 0:26–0:31 (aggressive defence of nest)

Song Grating *gaaarrr* and *chi-gaaaarrrr* notes, often culminating in excited cackles.
Other sounds A *hu-kaaarrrr* announces its presence to territorial intruders.
Regional variation None.
Habitat Acacia and broad-leaved woodlands, provided there are large trees in which to breed. Avoids savanna and the margins of wooded areas.

Similar sounding Broad-billed Roller (202) and Black-collared Barbet (214). Unlike Broad-billed Roller, doesn't sound like Grey Go-away-bird.Black-collared Barbet soon settles into its distinctive *too-puddley* sound.

Broad-billed Roller *Eurystomus glaucurus*   Geelbektroupant

 Track detail 0:02–0:33 (song)

Song Soft grating *kerrrrr* sounds, followed by a louder piercing *kweeerrrrrr*, almost like a baby's cry.
Other sounds Frantic repetition of the baby-like *kwerrrrr*, given in alarm.
Regional variation None.
Habitat Various types of savanna forest. Often found near water.

Similar sounding Grey-Go-away-bird (150), Purple Roller (201) and Black-collared Barbet (214). Resemblance to Grey Go-away-bird is superficial. Like Black-collared Barbet, song starts with slow nasal sneers, but the excited baby-like cry that follows helps to separate them. Song more nasal and wailing than that of Purple Roller and also lacks that roller's two-note *chi-gaaaarrrrr*.

HORNBILLS

Hornbills give strong, far-carrying whistles, wails and *chuck* sounds. Some species, like the Trumpeter Hornbill, have readily identifiable songs, but members of the yellow- and red-billed hornbill groups are not as easily distinguished and require more care. To separate these species on song alone, listen for subtle differences in the structure of the song phrases.

Southern Ground-Hornbill *Bucorvus leadbeateri*   Bromvoël

 Track detail 0:03–1:00 (song)

Song A series of short, deep, booming *doo-doo-doo-dadoo-da* notes, repeated with only brief intervals, usually given by a family of birds.
Other sounds Nasal *neh-neh-neh* sounds, something like a donkey's bray.

Regional variation None.
Habitat Wide variety of savanna and broad-leaved woodland habitats. Avoids wide open grasslands and stays within range of the ravines where it roosts.
Similar sounding None.

Trumpeter Hornbill *Bycanistes bucinator*   Gewone Boskraai

 Track detail 0:29 (total length) = 0:02–0:25 (song); 0:25–0:29 (flight call)

Song Plaintive wailing, like a baby's cry.
Other sounds Loud croaks when alarmed. Also gives soft churring contact calls.
Regional variation None.

Habitat Predominantly forests, dense woodlands and the margins of heavily wooded river courses.
Similar sounding None.

African Grey Hornbill *Tockus nasutus*   Grysneushoringvoël

Track detail 0:03–0:36 (song)

Song A loud, very piercing, whistled *ti-ti-ti-ti-ti-titeeuu-titeeuu-titeeuu* that varies in pitch and is accompanied by a wing-flicking display.
Other sounds Harsh, screechy whistles when mobbing predators such as raptors.
Regional variation None.

Habitat Most often found in riverine thickets and dense wooded areas, but may also occur in acacia and broad-leaved woodlands.
Similar sounding Water Thick-knee (99). Thick-knee's song is higher pitched, faster and lacks the plaintive whistles of African Grey Hornbill.

Southern Yellow-billed Hornbill *Tockus leucomelas* Geelbekneushoringvoël

206 Track detail 1:11 (total length) = 0:03–0:57 (song); 0:57–1:11 (alarm call)

Song Rapid monosyllabic *wuk-wuk-wuk-wuk* notes.
Other sounds A single *wuk* sound given in alarm.
Regional variation None.
Habitat A wide range of woodland habitats, usually with a low understorey.

Similar sounding Senegal Coucal (162), Southern Red-billed (208) and Damara (not included) hornbills. Superficially resembles the coucal but confusion unlikely. Notes are monosyllabic throughout the song, but Southern Red-billed and Damara hornbills switch to bisyllabic notes.

Crowned Hornbill *Tockus alboterminatus* Gekroonde Neushoringvoël

207 Track detail 0:28 (total length) = 0:02–0:21 (contact call); 0:21–0:28 (song)

Song A piercing *teeu-teeu-teeu* whistle, repeated many times.
Other sounds When alarmed, gives rapid series of agitated whistling notes, ending in a screech.
Regional variation None.

Habitat Dense woodlands and forests. Favours tall trees.
Similar sounding Somewhat evocative of a small raptor.

Southern Red-billed Hornbill *Tockus erythrorhynchus* Rooibekneushoringvoël

208 Track detail 0:03–0:33 (song)

Song Monosyllabic *wuk-wuk-wuk-wuk* notes; switches to bisyllabic *wuka-wuka-wuka* notes halfway through.
Other sounds In alarm gives faster version of the monosyllabic *wuk-wuk-wuk-wuk* song, along with some hissing sounds.
Regional variation None.
Habitat Arid and broad-leaved woodlands. Prefers an open understorey and thin ground cover.

Similar sounding Senegal Coucal (162), Southern Yellow-billed (206) and Damara (not included) hornbills. Superficially recalls the coucal. Song becomes bisyllabic halfway through, while Southern Yellow-billed maintains monosyllabic notes throughout. Damara Hornbill does switch to a series of bisyllabic notes, but both syllables are equal in volume, whereas the first is more dominant in song of Southern Red-billed.

HOOPOES, WOOD-HOOPOES AND SCIMITARBILLS

Members of this group are tricky to separate on song. While African Hoopoes are unmistakable in appearance, their song may be mistaken for that of the African Cuckoo with which they share their habitat. The two wood-hoopoe species are almost impossible to separate on call alone, although their cackles are quite distinct from the songs of other birds.

Green (Red-billed) Wood-Hoopoe   *Phoeniculus purpureus*   Rooibekkakelaar

209 Track detail 0:02–0:25 (group song)

Song An excited series of cackles, often given by groups of birds. Singing bird perches, rocking back and forth and bobbing its tail. Birds co-operatively raise young of a single breeding pair, so entire group calls to proclaim territory.
Other sounds Variations of song. Includes short, soft cackling phrase on takeoff and highly agitated cackles when in danger.
Regional variation None.

Habitat Acacia and broad-leaved woodlands, gardens and forest margins.
Similar sounding Violet Wood-Hoopoe (210), Spike-heeled Lark (232) and Arrow-marked Babbler (275). Wood-hoopoes are almost inseparable on song. Green Wood-Hoopoe defends both nesting and feeding territories, so will respond to playback throughout its range. Song vaguely like that of Spike-heeled Lark and Arrow-marked Babbler, but confusion unlikely.

Violet Wood-Hoopoe   *Phoeniculus damarensis*   Perskakelaar

210 Track detail 0:03–0:13 (group song)

Song Excited cackles, often given by groups of birds. Singing bird may perch and rocks its tail back and forth.
Other sounds Variations of cackling song given both as alarm and contact calls.
Regional variation None.
Habitat Broad-leaved and acacia woodlands, gardens and forest margins.

Similar sounding Green Wood-Hoopoe (209) and Arrow-marked Babbler (275). Wood-hoopoes almost inseparable on song. Responds to playback near nest, but does not defend feeding range, which is larger than that of Green Wood-Hoopoe. Song superficially resembles cackling of Arrow-marked Babbler, but not similar enough to cause confusion.

Common (Greater) Scimitarbill   *Rhinopomastus cyanomelas*   Swartbekkakelaar

211 Track detail 0:02–0:11 (song)

Song A plaintive piercing *tuuee-tuuee-tuuee-tuuee* whistle, rising at the end of each note; repeated in phrases of about four short notes, with brief pauses between phrases.
Other sounds Chattering sounds when alarmed and a raptor-like *ki-ki-ki-ki*, given as a contact call.
Regional variation None.

Habitat Acacia and open broad-leaved woodlands. Avoids habitat with a closed canopy.
Similar sounding Red-fronted (218), Yellow-fronted (219) and Yellow-rumped (220) tinkerbirds. Resemblance to tinkerbirds very superficial. Scimitarbill's plaintive whistle sufficiently distinctive; confusion highly unlikely.

African Hoopoe *Upupa africana*

Hoephoep

 Track detail 0:02–0:29 (song)

Song A distinct *hoep-hoep-hoep* phrase. Most often gives two *hoep* notes, but may give up to four.
Other sounds A scratchy *kgaaarr* on takeoff. Swizzling and churring sounds in pair interactions.
Regional variation None.

Habitat Woodlands and gardens. Favours patches of short ground cover within reach of trees.
Similar sounding African Cuckoo (151) and Black Coucal (163). Phrases vary from 2–4 notes and are more muffled than cuckoo's double-note phrase. Black Coucal sings faster and sounds higher pitched.

BARBETS AND ALLIES

The loud tooted whistles of barbets are easily identified by ear. However, some tinkerbirds sound very similar and it requires some care to tell them apart.

Green Barbet *Stactolaema olivacea*

Groenhoutkapper

213 Track detail 0:02–0:24 (song)

Song A loud, high-pitched *kow*, like a dog yapping. May be repeated for a minute or more at a time.
Other sounds Gives a rasping insect-like *bzzzzzt*, when alarmed.
Regional variation None.
Habitat Restricted to the Ongoye Forest in KwaZulu-Natal.

Similar sounding Red-fronted (218), Yellow-fronted (219) and Yellow-rumped (220) tinkerbirds; possibly also Freckled Nightjar (175) and Acacia Pied Barbet (217). Green Barbet's yapping *kow* more like the call of a Freckled Nightjar than the *tink* of these three tinkerbirds. Gives single, evenly spaced, notes, whereas Freckled Nightjar gives unevenly spaced double-note *kow-yow*. The barbet sounds more nasal.

Black-collared Barbet *Lybius torquatus*

Rooikophoutkapper

214 Track detail 0:03–0:42 (duet)

Song A highly synchronised, distinctive *too-puddley* duet, given several times: male sings *too*; female sings *puddley*. Scratchy nasal sounds often precede duet.
Other sounds A long *aaaarrrrr* in alarm or conflict, like drawn-out version of scratchy lead-in to duet. Rarely, lone males give the *too* from song that sounds a bit like a tinkerbird, but context uncertain. If it is used to attract a mate it would then constitute a song.

Regional variation None.
Habitat Most wooded habitats, but not evergreen forests and arid woodlands. Common in gardens.
Similar sounding Crested Francolin (66), Purple (201) and Broad-billed (202) rollers. Francolin's song is similar in structure to that of barbet, but harsher and more piercing. Barbet's scratchy introductory sounds are shorter and harsher than introductory notes given by the rollers.

White-eared Barbet   *Stactolaema leucotis*   Witoorhoutkapper

215 Track detail 0:02–0:32 (group chatter)

Song A harsh *shree*, repeated quite regularly. May sound a bit like an insect or frog.
Other sounds Alarm call is slightly harsher version of song. Also gives some general group chatter.

Regional variation None.
Habitat Coastal and low-altitude evergreen forests and woodlands.
Similar sounding None.

Crested Barbet   *Trachyphonus vaillantii*   Kuifkophoutkapper

216 Track detail 0:02–0:32 (song)

Song A duet in which male gives drawn-out rattling *trrrrrrrrrrrrrr* that is quite piercing, to which female responds with a slower *tika-tika-tika-tika*.
Other sounds A piercing *kek* note given in alarm.
Regional variation None.

Habitat Moist and arid acacia woodlands, as well as a range of broad-leaved woodland habitats. Also common in gardens.
Similar sounding None.

Acacia Pied Barbet   *Tricholaema leucomelas*   Bonthoutkapper

217 Track detail 0:03–0:26 (duet)

Song Male gives both a repeated sneering *neeah* and a *neh-neh-neh-neh* similar to the song of a tinkerbird, but more nasal. May form part of a duet to which female responds with a *duh-duh-duh-duh-duh* phrase.
Other sounds Weaver-like swizzling and buzzing given as both contact and alarm calls.
Regional variation None.
Habitat Varied. Includes open savanna, broad-leaved woodlands and gardens.

Similar sounding Green Barbet (213), Red-fronted (218), Yellow-fronted (219) and Yellow-rumped (220) tinkerbirds, Red-throated Wryneck (229), Terrestrial Brownbul (279), Yellow-bellied Greenbul (284) and Southern White-crowned Shrike (398). More nasal than the tinkerbirds. Some resemblance to Red-throated Wryneck, but less harsh. Vaguely like Terrestrial Brownbul, but confusion is unlikely. Yellow-bellied Greenbul more nasal and sneering. Fuller and carries further than call of Southern White-crowned Shrike.

Red-fronted Tinkerbird (Tinker Barbet)   *Pogoniulus pusillus*   Rooiblestinker

218 Track detail 0:03–0:21 (song)

Song A high-pitched series of *too-too-too* notes, repeated for several minutes.
Other sounds Trills, possibly given as contact or alarm calls. Also gives grating sounds when alarmed.
Regional variation None.
Habitat Forests, riverine bush and acacia woodlands.
Similar sounding Common Scimitarbill (211), Green (213) and Acacia Pied (217) barbets, Yellow-fronted (219) and Yellow-rumped Tinkerbird (220).

Song is slower with longer phrases than those of the scimitarbill and Yellow-fronted Tinkerbird. The continous *too-too-too notes* distinguish the song from the yapping song of the Green Barbet, while Acacia Pied Barbet sounds more nasal. Song is faster, more continuous and lower pitched than that of Yellow-rumped Tinkerbird – distribution is a useful aid in separating these species, but in areas where they co-exist they can be distinguished by ear with practice.

Yellow-fronted Tinkerbird (Tinker Barbet) *Pogoniulus chrysoconus*
Geelblestinker

 219 Track detail 0:02–0:17 (song)

Song A series of high-pitched *too-too-too* notes, repeated for several minutes.
Other sounds Various trill sounds.
Regional variation None.
Habitat Broad-leaved woodlands, as well as dense riverine bush.
Similar sounding Common Scimitarbill (211), Green Barbet (213), Red-fronted Tinkerbird (218), Acacia

Pied Barbet (217) and Yellow-rumped Tinkerbird (220). Vaguely like scimitarbill, but that species gives fairly distinctive whistle. The *too-too-too* notes separate it from yapping song of Green Barbet. Song is more continuous than that of Yellow-rumped Tinkerbird and slower and higher pitched than that of Red-fronted Tinkerbird. Acacia Pied Barbet's call is more nasal.

Yellow-rumped Tinkerbird (Golden-rumped Tinker Barbet)
Pogoniulus bilineatus
Swartblestinker

220 Track detail 0:02–0:27 (song)

Song A repetitive phrase of 4–6 *too-too-too-too* notes, with a brief pause between phrases. While singing, male displays by bobbing.
Other sounds Grating hisses given in alarm.
Regional variation None.
Habitat Coastal and lowland forests and densely wooded gardens.

Similar sounding Common Scimitarbill (211), Green Barbet (213), Red- (218) and Yellow-fronted (219) tinkerbirds and Acacia Pied Barbet (217). Vaguely like scimitarbill, but that species gives fairly distinctive whistle. Yellow-rumped Tinkerbird gives short phrases rather than a long series of notes, as do the species listed here. Acacia Pied Barbet sounds more nasal.

HONEYGUIDES

These secretive, parasitic birds sing from call sites and are often heard before being seen. Even when singing they can be difficult to find.

Greater Honeyguide *Indicator indicator*
Grootheuningwyser

221 Track detail 0:54 (total length) = 0:03–0:51 (song); 0:51-0:54 (guiding or alarm call)

Song Male's song is a distinctive *wit-pur wit-pur wit-pur* given repeatedly from any of several regular call sites, though singing bird is hard to spot. Song probably given to proclaim territory and attract mates.
Other sounds A repetitive agitated *tik-tik-tik-tik*, given to guide people or animals to beehives. Hissing alarm calls also documented.

Regional variation Unknown. Minor variations in number of repetitions and duration of call may be regional or seasonal.
Habitat Woodlands, forest margins, parks, gardens and exotic plantations.
Similar sounding None.

Lesser Honeyguide *Indicator minor*

Kleinheuningwyser

222 Track detail 0:03–0:44 (song*) * Listen for African Fish Eagle call at 0:09

Song A clear and repetitive *teeu-cheeu-cheeu-cheeu-cheeu* …, with about 19 but as many as 40 *cheeu* notes. Male sings from regular secluded perch.
Other sounds None.
Regional variation Unknown. Variation in number of notes in song may be seasonal rather than regional.

Habitat Well-wooded woodland or savanna habitat, parks and gardens. Avoids smaller clumps of trees in very open areas.
Similar sounding Pallid Honeyguide (not included). Confusion only likely in central Mozambique, where their ranges overlap.

WOODPECKERS AND WRYNECKS

A family known for distinctive loud drumming. This is an intentional territorial display, not a means of excavating nests or finding food. The songs of members of this group are easily told apart.

Golden-tailed Woodpecker *Campethera abingoni*

Goudstertspeg

223 Track detail 0:18 (total length) = 0:02–0:09 (foraging taps); 0:09–0:18 (contact call)

Song The main 'song' is a machine gun-like *trrrrr* … tapping that lasts for 1–2 seconds at a time.
Other sounds Most often identified by its commonly heard, nasal *neeeaaa* contact call. Also soft foraging taps.
Regional variation None.

Habitat Varied. Includes forests, woodlands and savanna.
Similar sounding Red-throated Wryneck (229) and other wrynecks and woodpeckers. Nasal sneer a little like song of Red-throated Wryneck, but is a single drawn-out note, given at wide intervals.

Knysna Woodpecker *Campethera notata*

Knysnaspeg

224 Track detail 0:03–0:24 (song; pauses between phrases have been shortened)

Song A two-note territorial *ti-wee*, with many minutes elapsing between phrases. One of the few woodpeckers not known to drum.
Other sounds Gives *ti-wee* phrase as a contact call. Also an excited *tri-tri-tri-tri*, but context unknown.

Regional variation None.
Habitat Restricted to coastal forests and thornveld across a small range.
Similar sounding None.

Bennett's Woodpecker *Campethera bennettii*

Bennettspeg

225 Track detail 0:03–0:43 (duet)

Song A distinctive harsh *grrrr-di-di-di-di-deeya-deeya-deeya-deeya-deeya* duet, by both male and female.
Other sounds None.
Regional variation None.

Habitat Woodlands with tall, broad-leaved trees; also acacia woodlands, if the trees are tall enough.
Similar sounding Southern Pied Babbler (277). The babbler's song lacks the bisyllabic *deeya* sound.

Bearded Woodpecker *Dendropicos namaquus*

Baardspeg

226 Track detail 0:46 (total length) = 0:02–0:25 (drumming display); 0:25–0:46 (male song)

Song Sings *wit-wit-wit-wit-wit-wit-ti-ti*, usually giving a series of about six *wit* notes and ending with a two-note *ti-ti*. Both sexes may give this song and both drum in bursts of about 10 taps.
Other sounds Softer *chuk* and *ti* sounds given as contact calls.

Regional variation None.
Habitat Broad-leaved woodlands and savanna. Avoids evergreen forests.
Similar sounding None.

Cardinal Woodpecker *Dendropicos fuscescens*

Kardinaalspeg

227 Track detail 0:02–0:29 (female song)

Song Both sexes may give a distinctive *chri-chri-chri-chri*, repeated rapidly, and a sequence of 30 drumming notes.
Other sounds In confrontations gives lower and more piercing versions of main song.

Regional variation None.
Habitat Woodlands and patches of large trees in more open grasslands. Avoids forests.
Similar sounding None.

Ground Woodpecker *Geocolaptes olivaceus*

Grondspeg

228 Track detail 0:03–0:30 (song)

Song A rasping and hoarse *kee-argg*, repeated several times in quick succession. Ground-based, so does not proclaim territory by drumming.
Other sounds Piercing two-note contact and alarm calls.
Regional variation None.

Habitat Rocky slopes, river banks and drainage ditches where nests can be excavated.
Similar sounding Black-shouldered Kite (46). Ground Woodpecker's *kee-argg* similar to the *kleeerrrrrr* note of the kite, but not as harsh.

Red-throated Wryneck *Jynx ruficollis*

Draaihals

229 Track detail 0:02–0:46 (song)

Song A loud nasal *kwee-kwee-kwee-kwee* varying from 4–6 notes. Always sing from a prominent perch.
Other sounds Paired birds give similar but more rasping *greeehh* contact calls and soft clicks when threatened near nest site. May tap weakly on a woody surface when foraging or excavating a nest, but taps softer than a woodpecker's territorial sounds.
Regional variation None.
Habitat Areas with widely spaced trees and short grass, including suburban parks and gardens.

Similar sounding Acacia Pied Barbet (217), Golden-tailed Woodpecker (223), Terrestrial Brownbul (279), Yellow-bellied Greenbul (284) and Southern White-crowned Shrike (398). The four-note nasal sneer is very distinctive. Far harsher and louder than the nasal sneer of barbet, and the woodpecker gives just one note at wide intervals. Sounds higher pitched than song of Terrestrial Brownbul. Fuller and carries further than song of shrike. Yellow-bellied Greenbul's song far more nasal and sneered.

LARKS AND SPARROW-LARKS

A group of nondescript 'little brown jobs (LBJs)', which can often be separated on song. For example, Red, Karoo, Barlow's and Dune larks (the red-billed lark complex) can be told apart with experience. Some species, however, are extremely difficult to separate on call alone, such as members of the long-billed lark complex. (Refer to *Southern African LBJs Made Simple* (Struik Nature), for guidance on how to separate these larks.) Songs are given either from a prominent perch or as part of an aerial display. Their phrases vary from a single piercing whistle to more elaborate jumbled twitterings and trills.

Red-capped Lark   *Calandrella cinerea*   Rooikoplewerik

230   **Track detail** 0:02–0:20 (song*)
* Listen for closely spaced two-note phrase repeated in latter half of track

Song A jumble of phrases, often incorporating two closely spaced descending *ti-ree* whistles, with a trill on the second note. Mimicry included in display song; mimics over 100 species.
Other sounds Contact and flight calls may comprise either the two-note whistle from its song, or a *ti-chick* like that of a pipit.
Regional variation Mimics those species present in the area.

Habitat A range of grassland habitats. Particularly favours ploughed farm lands and burnt fields.
Similar sounding Melodious (240), Pink-billed (250) and Botha's (251) larks. Botha's also has two-note whistle, but notes are more widely spaced and both are trilled. Pink-billed leaves noticeable gap between the two notes of its whistle and neither note is trilled. In breeding display mimics occasionally, whereas Melodious Lark mimics frequently.

Large-billed (Thick-billed) Lark   *Galerida magnirostris*   Dikbeklewerik

231   **Track detail** 0:03–0:43 (song)

Song A single lead-in note, followed by a full, fluty, jumbled whistle. Often includes phrases that mimic other birds' calls.
Other sounds Flight call is a soft single-note whistle.
Regional variation Mimics those birds present in its vicinity.

Habitat Dry fynbos, grasslands and cultivated land.
Similar sounding Karoo (235), Dune (236), Barlow's (237) and Red (238) larks. Superficial resemblance to these members of the red lark complex, but distinguished by comical tone of jumbled whistle.

Spike-heeled Lark   *Chersomanes albofasciata*   Vlaktelewerik

232   **Track detail** 0:02–0:21 (song)

Song May give a single soft chuckle or a rapid series of soft chuckling sounds.
Other sounds Versions of the main song given in alarm and contact situations. Also a soft *titititititit*, context for which uncertain.
Regional variation None.

Habitat Patchy grasslands and sparse karoo scrub.
Similar sounding Green Wood-Hoopoe (209) and Lazy Cisticola (346). Vaguely resembles Green Wood-Hoopoe, but its soft churring so distinctive that confusion is highly unlikely. Song resembles the contact call of the Lazy Cisticola, but lacks chip notes.

83

Sabota Lark *Calendulauda sabota*   Sabotalewerik

233 Track detail 0:03–0:51 (song)

Song Easily recognised. Gives a shrill introductory *tseeee*, followed by short phrases, often mimicking songs of other birds in the area. Frequently incorporates the introductory whistle into song phrases.
Other sounds In alarm, gives rapid chattering and mimics alarm calls of other birds.
Regional variation Mimics those species present in the area.

Habitat Open acacia woodlands and karoo scrub. In the latter instance, usually stays close to large bushes.
Similar sounding Melodious Lark (240). Separated by shriller tone, especially of introductory notes, shorter bursts of song and absence of the clear pattern distinguishable in Melodious Lark's song.

Fawn-coloured Lark *Calendulauda africanoides*   Vaalbruinlewerik

234 Track detail 0:02–0:35 (song)

Song Jumbled twittering phrases that accelerate. Song includes mimicry of other birds, both in display flight and when perching.
Other sounds A soft *tseek*, given in alarm.
Regional variation Mimics those birds present in the area.

Habitat A range of woodland habitats, particulary those with sandy soils. May extend into dune habitats in the Northern Cape.
Similar sounding African Stonechat (302) and Cape Grassbird (315). Vaguely reminiscent of the stonechat. Call is flutier, but not as liquid as that of grassbird.

Karoo Lark *Calendulauda albescens*   Karoolewerik

235 Track detail 0:02–0:17 (song)

Song Varied *chip* notes, followed by a complex swallow-like gurgle.
Other sounds Alarm call comprises low-pitched chittering.
Regional variation Subtle regional differences in notes and phrase structure.

Habitat Flat coastal and arid scrub habitat, on soft or stony ground.
Similar sounding Large-billed (231), Dune (236), Barlow's (237) and Red (238) larks. Song superficially like that of Large-billed Lark. Gives more varied range of chip notes than Dune or Barlow's larks and a longer and more complex swallow-like gurgle than Red Lark.

Dune Lark *Calendulauda erythrochlamys*   Duinlewerik

236 Track detail 0:02–0:37 (song)

Song Eight or more sparrow-like chirps, followed by a soft gurgle.
Other sounds Buzzing *zeet* sounds given as contact and alarm calls.
Regional variation None. The only red lark not to show any regional variation.

Habitat Grass-covered Namib dunes.
Similar sounding Large-billed (231), Karoo (235), Barlow's (237) and Red (238) larks. Faster and higher pitched than Large-billed Lark. Song less complex than that of the larks listed here. Song longer than that of any other red lark.

84

Barlow's Lark *Calendulauda barlowi* Barlowlewerik

 237 Track detail 0:02–0:37 (song)

Song A series of 6–9 *chip* notes, followed by a short swallow-like trill or rattle.
Other sounds Low-pitched chittering alarm call.
Regional variation Rattle in song may vary.
Habitat Sparse shrub lands and grassy dunes. Often associated with euphorbias.

Similar sounding Large-billed (231), Karoo (235), Dune (236) and Red (238) larks. Song superficially like that of Large-billed Lark and shorter than that of Dune Lark. Includes more lead-in notes than either Karoo or Red larks. Rattle is shorter than that of any of these larks.

Red Lark *Calendulauda burra* Rooilewerik

238 Track detail 0:02–0:24 (song)

Song A series of soft rattles, followed by fast jumbled phrase. Ends with a warble.
Other sounds Piercing whistles and scratchy notes given in alarm.
Regional variation Phrase variation, even between neighbouring males.

Habitat Grass-covered red dunes.
Similar sounding Large-billed (231), Karoo (235), Dune (236) and Barlow's (237) larks. Song closest to that of Karoo Lark, but slower and lower pitched. Has longest and most complex song of any red lark.

Monotonous Lark *Mirafra passerina* Bosveldlewerik

239 Track detail 0:03–0:35 (song)

Song Liquid, bubbly and rhythmical *zip-zirup-zur-rit*. Repeats phrase monotonously.
Other sounds A short *chip* alarm call.
Regional variation Unknown. Naturally includes many variations in its song and birds are nomadic. Variations may be geographical.

Habitat A range of woodland types. Avoids arid areas.
Similar sounding Cinnamon-breasted Bunting (498). Resemblance very superficial; song easily distinguished by liquid tone and monotonous repetition.

Melodious Lark *Mirafra cheniana* Spotlewerik

240 Track detail 0:02–0:34 (display song*) * Mimics Cape Longclaw and Common Myna

Song Accompanies long display flight with stream of trills, warbles and phrases mimicking many different birds. Like a reed-warbler, repeats a group of phrases at a time, before moving to the next group of phrases.
Other sounds Short, sharp alarm calls.
Regional variation Mimics locally present species.

Habitat True grasslands. Favours long grass and avoids open areas.
Similar sounding Red-capped (230), Sabota (233) and Pink-billed (250) larks. Told from these larks by its constant stream of mimicry.

Rufous-naped Lark   *Mirafra africana*   Rooineklewerik

241   Track detail 0:02–2:11 (song variations)

Song Distinctive, highly variable 3–4-note *tri-lee-tri-loo* or *tri-ree-loo* given from a fence post, bush or rock. Up to five variations may be heard in a small area. The maximum size of an average male's repertoire is unknown, but up to 20 phrases have been recorded. Singing bird may hop and rattle wings, but easily told from rattling display of a clapper lark. Twitters in flight display.

Other sounds In alarm gives soft plaintive whistle or clicks.
Regional variation None. Highly variable phrases unlikely to be geographical.
Habitat Seen frequently in savanna and grassland habitat, provided there are some perches from which to call.
Similar sounding None.

Flappet Lark   *Mirafra rufocinnamomea*   Laeveldklappertjie

242   Track detail 0:02–0:19 (wing-rattling display 'song')

Song One or two short wing rattles, followed by a longer rattle and a soft jumbled phrase audible only in ideal conditions.
Other sounds Soft twittering given on the ground; context uncertain, but presumably serves as both contact and alarm call.

Regional variation Wing rattle main component of song and shows no variation, but dialects and regional variations in the soft jumbled phrase have been noted and are annually consistent.
Habitat Clearings and gravel roads in broad-leaved woodlands. May venture into acacia woodlands.
Similar sounding None.

Eastern Clapper Lark   *Mirafra fasciolata*   Hoëveldklappertjie

243   Track detail 0:03–0:21 (song)

Song In display flight, rattles wings at constant tempo from takeoff, then drops back to the ground with ascending whistle.
Other sounds From a low perch, softly mimics calls of other birds, but context for this is unknown. Also gives grating alarm call.
Regional variation None.

Habitat Tall grasslands, either open or with some scattered bushes. Favours gentle slopes or flat ground.
Similar sounding Cape Clapper Lark (244) and Cinnamon-breasted Warbler (365). Cape Clapper Lark has a wing rattle that accelerates and there is more variation in the pitched of its whistled note. Cinnamon-breasted Warbler also lacks the wing rattle.

Cape Clapper Lark   *Mirafra apiata*   Kaapse Klappertjie

   Track detail 0:02–0:24 (display song)

Song Male gives accelerating wing rattle when taking off into display flight, then a whistle that varies in pitch as he drops back to ground.
Other sounds Occasionally mimics; context uncertain.
Regional variation Variations in wing rattle and whistle pitch noted in Agulhas race.

Habitat Dense scrub and fynbos. Sometimes strays into nearby crop lands.
Similar sounding Eastern Clapper Lark (243). The accelerating rattle and pitch variations in the whistle should be easy to distinguish from simple ascending whistle and steady wing rattling of Eastern Clapper Lark.

Short-clawed Lark   *Certhilauda chuana*   Kortkloulewerik

245   Track detail 0:03–0:48 (song*) * Listen for dual use of syrinx at 0:38

Song A piercing, floating whistle, similar in tone to a human's whistling, given when perched or in display flight. Also a series of whistles and liquid trills similar to those of a rock-thrush. Dual use of the syrinx is observed when a second note starts before the previous note ends.
Other sounds Variations on the piercing whistle given as alarm and contact call.

Regional variation Some regional differences in the complexity of the phrases.
Habitat Grasslands with scattered small bushes.
Similar sounding Long-billed (246–249) larks and rock-thrushes (291–293). Song tricky to separate from the long-billed larks, except by complex liquid trills. Separated from rock-thrushes by slow, plaintive whistle

Eastern Long-billed Lark   *Certhilauda semitorquata*   Grasveldlangbeklewerik

246   Track detail 0:03–0:49 (song)

Song A sharp descending whistle given when perched or in display flight.
Other sounds Alarm and contact calls comprise soft twittering given at lower pitch than the song.
Regional variation None.

Habitat Short grass in hilly areas with stony ground.
Similar sounding Short-clawed (245) and long-billed larks (247–249). Whistled phrase far less complex than that of Short-clawed Lark. Hard to separate from other long-billed larks.

Karoo Long-billed Lark   *Certhilauda subcoronata*   Karoolangbeklewerik

247   Track detail 0:03–0:29 (song)

Song A sharp descending whistle given when perched or in display flight, sometimes preceded by a softer introductory note.
Other sounds Alarm and contact calls comprise soft twittering, at lower pitch than in song.
Regional variation Introductory note not given in some parts of range.

Habitat Karoo scrub on stony ground, particularly where soils are reddish.
Similar sounding Short-clawed (245) and long-billed larks (246, 247 and 249). Members of the long-billed lark complex are extremely difficult to tell apart by ear. Floating whistled phrase not nearly as complex as that of Short-clawed Lark.

Cape Long-billed Lark   *Certhilauda curvirostris*   Weskuslangbeklewerik

248   Track detail 0:03–0:29 (song)

Song A shrill, generally descending whistle (occasionally ascending), given when perched or in display flight. Pitch sometimes wavers, rather than dropping smoothly.
Other sounds Lower-pitched soft twittering given as both alarm and contact calls.
Regional variation In some regions whistle descends smoothly; has wavering pitch elsewhere.

Habitat Coastal scrub and old farm lands, provided there is grass for cover.
Similar sounding Short-clawed (245) and long-billed larks (246, 247 and 249). Members of the long-billed lark complex extremely difficult to tell apart by ear. Floating whistled phrase not nearly as complex as that of Short-clawed Lark.

87

Agulhas Long-billed Lark · *Certhilauda brevirostris* · Overberglangbeklewerik

 Track detail 0:03–0:15 (song)

Song A shrill two-part whistle given when perched or in display flight. May also comprise a single descending whistle.
Other sounds Lower-pitched soft twittering given both as alarm and contact call.
Regional variation Variations in pitch. In some regions introductory note is absent.

Habitat Coastal scrub and unused farms, provided there is patchy vegetation cover.
Similar sounding Short-clawed (245) and long-billed larks (246–248). Members of the long-billed lark complex extremely difficult to tell apart by their songs and calls.

Pink-billed Lark · *Spizocorys conirostris* · Pienkbeklewerik

250 **Track detail** 0:02–0:14 (song)

Song A double-note trill, in which both notes are of equal length, separated by a short but noticeable gap. Sometimes accompanied by twittering, trills and jumbled musical phrases. Does not mimic other birds.
Other sounds Alarm and flight calls like the two-note whistle, but louder and more pronounced.
Regional variation None.

Habitat Grasslands, particularly when burnt or recently ploughed. Also unused sports fields in rural areas.
Similar sounding Red-capped (230), Melodious (240) and Botha's (251) larks. Two-note whistle includes fewer trills than that of either Red-capped or Botha's. Unlike Red-capped and Melodious larks, does not mimic other birds when twittering.

Botha's Lark · *Spizocorys fringillaris* · Vaalrivierlewerik

251 **Track detail** 0:02–0:20 (song)

Song A buzzing double-note *chi-ree*. First part of whistle is shorter, and gap between notes barely noticeable.
Other sounds Similar sounds given in alarm and flight.
Regional variation None.
Habitat Favours flatter areas within heavily grazed hilly grasslands.

Similar sounding Red-capped Lark (230) and Pink-billed Lark (250). Song resembles flight or contact call of Red-capped Lark, but that species gives two trilling notes of equal length. Pink-billed Lark trills on both notes of its whistle and leaves a more obvious gap between notes.

Sclater's Lark · *Spizocorys sclateri* · Namakwalewerik

 Track detail 0:02–0:20 (mixed song and contact calls)

Song Soft, almost bee-eater-like, *purp* notes.
Other sounds A mix of quiet sparrow-like chirps.
Regional variation None.
Habitat Arid areas with small bushes, usually on quartzitic soils.

Similar sounding European Bee-eater (195), Black-eared Sparrow-Lark (254) and Tractrac Chat (297). The *purp* notes superficially resemble the *purp* of the bee-eater, but are much higher pitched. Sclater's has more sparrow-like tone and lacks sparrow-lark's rasping notes. Song is less varied than that of Tractrac Chat.

Rudd's Lark *Heteromirafra ruddi* Drakensberglewerik

 Track detail 0:02–0:28 (song)

Song A very soft, nasal, buzzing *tzi-ri-ri-oo*, with highly distinctive tone and rhythm.
Other sounds Gives a soft pipit-like *chik* in flight and an agitated *peep* when intruders approach the nest.

Regional variation None. Male's song includes many phrases and variations, but they are not thought to be regional.
Habitat Upland grasslands; favours short grass regularly subject to burning.
Similar sounding None.

Black-eared Sparrow-Lark *Eremopterix australis* Swartoorlewerik

254 Track detail 0:03–0:26 (mixed song and contact calls)

Song A mixture of high-pitched sparrow-like *cheep* notes and buzzy *dzeep* notes, with a slight metallic tone.
Other sounds Components of song given in both alarm and contact situations.
Regional variation None.
Habitat Arid karoo shrub lands; favours red soils and stony ground.

Similar sounding Little (198) and European (195) bee-eaters, Sclater's Lark (252) and House Sparrow (444). Chirps vaguely resemble those of House Sparrow and Little Bee-eater, but higher pitched. Buzzing notes resemble those of European Bee-eater or Sclater's Lark, but thicker and higher-pitched. Most likely to be mistaken for a high-pitched House Sparrow, but all resemblances superficial.

Grey-backed Sparrow-Lark *Eremopterix verticalis* Grysruglewerik

255 Track detail 0:03–0:23 (contact call)

Song A series of *cheep* notes, each phrase ending in a distinctive *pree-ree-oo*.
Similar sounding Agitated versions of the main song given as alarm and contact calls. Also gives a soft metallic alarm note.

Regional variation None.
Habitat Arid grasslands and karoo scrub. Favours flat areas.
Similar sounding White-eyes (384–386). Resemblance very superficial.

SWALLOWS AND MARTINS

It is fairly easy to identify a call as being that of a swallow or martin: these birds sing mostly in groups, giving high-pitched metallic twittering and liquid trills. Only in a handful of species do individual birds sing alone, but as they nest so close together, their calls are often obscured by the sounds of other individuals nearby.

Barn (European) Swallow *Hirundo rustica*
Europese Swael

256 Track detail 0:02–0:26 (contact calls)

Song Not heard in our region; breeds in the northern hemisphere.
Other sounds In flight, gives a short, sharp *tsitt*. Contact call, generally given by male, is a fast metallic twittering, with many scratchy notes and some whistles.

Regional variation None.
Habitat Very widespread, but less common in arid areas.
Similar sounding White-throated Swallow (257). White-throated Swallow sounds musical and bubbly, not abrupt and scratchy.

White-throated Swallow *Hirundo albigularis*
Witkeelswael

257 Track detail 0:03–1:04 (song)

Song A typical swallow's song, containing House Sparrow-like chirps, nasal *wheeuu* notes and rising and falling *zeeeeooooweeee* whistles, as well as fast, gurgled twittering.
Other sounds Contact calls much like song. Often gives the same nasal *zeeeeooooooooweeeee* whistle in flight.

Regional variation None.
Habitat Wide ranging, but usually near water. Prefers open habitats and avoids forests and dense woodlands. Absent from very dry areas.
Similar sounding Barn Swallow (256) and House Sparrow (444). Less scratchy than Barn Swallow. Some notes like those of the sparrow, but phrase is distinctive.

Lesser Striped Swallow *Cecropis abyssinica*
Kleinstreepswael

258 Track detail 0:03–0:24 (song)

Song A distinctive nasal *tzee-tzee-tzoo-tzoo-tzoo*, each note lower pitched than the last. Number of notes per phrase varies.
Other sounds Swallow-like twittering, given to maintain contact with other Lesser Striped Swallows; also given in mixed species groups.

Regional variation None.
Habitat Often found near water in the wetter eastern half of the region. May be seen over grasslands, woodlands and, sometimes, suburban areas.
Similar sounding Greater Striped Swallow (259) has a similar gurgling call, but includes a trill.

Greater Striped Swallow   *Cecropis cucullata*   Grootstreepswael

259 Track detail 0:03–0:30 (song*)
* Listen for distinctive *turra* note at start of track

Song A gurgling and squeaky song characterised by a rapid *turrra* trill.
Other sounds A drawn-out high-pitched whistle that descends slowly, presumed to be a contact call.
Regional variation None.

Habitat Wide-ranging; occurs in grasslands, savanna, woodlands, farms and suburbs.
Similar sounding Lesser Striped Swallow (258). The rapid trill separates these swallows.

Red-breasted Swallow   *Cecropis semirufa*   Rooiborsswael

260 Track detail 0:03–0:26 (song)

Song Two short gurgled notes, followed by a long, bubbly, slightly descending *peeeuuuurrrr*.
Other sounds Some typical swallow-like twittering, given in flight and as contact call.

Regional variation None.
Habitat Occurs almost exclusively in savanna and grassland habitats.
Similar sounding None.

South African Cliff Swallow   *Petrochelidon spilodera*   Familieswael

261 Track detail 0:02–0:39 (mixed song and contact calls)

Song Almost always sings in groups, generally giving a short, sharp, nasal *neeerrr*.
Other sounds Repeats song excitedly in flight. In alarm gives short, sharp *tchik* sounds.

Regional variation None.
Habitat Scrub and grassland.
Similar sounding None.

Rock Martin   *Ptyonoprogne fuligula*   Kransswael

262 Track detail 0:02–0:34 (song)

Song Usually silent but sometimes gives chirping note like that of a House Sparrow, especially in breeding season.
Other sounds Variations of the sparrow-like chirp given as contact calls.
Regional variation None.

Habitat Steep rock faces and man-made 'cliffs', such as buildings of two stories or more.
Similar sounding House Sparrow (444). Chirp is higher pitched, without the clear *chirup* sound typical of the sparrow.

DRONGOS

Drongos sing very musical songs, although their repertoires do include scratchy and squeaky notes. It is easy to recognise that you're hearing a drongo, but separating species within the group often requires painstaking study of individual songs and phrases.

Fork-tailed Drongo *Dicrurus adsimilis*   Mikstertbyvanger

 Track detail 0:03–0:55 (song*) * Several other species can be heard in the background

Song A wide range of scratchy and squeaky sounds, as is typical of most drongos; mimics many species.
Other sounds A wide range of sounds; mimics other birds' alarm calls and even some mammals' sounds. Sometimes uses mimicry to poach food from other species, like babblers.
Regional variation Has wide call repertoire, but no dialects recorded. Mimics local species.

Habitat Wide ranging. Includes various types of savanna and woodland habitats, as well as forest margins, gardens and even grasslands, provided it can find suitable perches.
Similar sounding Square-tailed Drongo (264). Take care when trying to separate these drongos on call, since both give very similar squeaks and scratchy notes and both mimic other species.

Square-tailed Drongo *Dicrurus ludwigii*   Kleinbyvanger

264 **Track detail 0:03–0:37 (song)**

Song A wide range of scratchy and squeaky sounds, as is typical of most drongos; mimics many species, but the reasons for this aren't fully understood.
Other sounds A wide range of sounds; mimics alarm calls of other birds in competition for food.
Regional variation Has wide call repertoire, but no dialects known. Mimics local species.

Habitat Evergreen forests, forest margins and very well-wooded gardens.
Similar sounding Fork-tailed Drongo (263). Take care when separating drongos by ear, since both species mimic other birds and give same kinds of squeaky and scratchy notes, although the Square-tailed sounds slightly more thrush-like than Fork-tailed.

CUCKOOSHRIKES

Cuckooshrikes inhabit densely vegetated habitat, especially forests, where they feed on insects high in the canopy. Their songs and calls are typically high pitched, with an insect-like tone.

Black Cuckooshrike *Campephaga flava*   Swartkatakoeroe

265 **Track detail 0:03–0:33 (song)**

Song A cricket-like metallic *trrrrrrrrrrrr* that is unique in the region.
Other sounds When alarmed, gives a *kreeeuu* sound and hisses.
Regional variation None.

Habitat Broad-leaved woodlands; also mixed woodlands, particularly if they include some broad-leaved trees.
Similar sounding None.

Grey Cuckooshrike *Coracina caesia*

Bloukatakoeroe

 Track detail 0:02–0:26 (song)

Song A soft, high-pitched *tssseeeeeooooo*.
Other sounds Alarm and contact calls comprise high-pitched trilling sounds similar in tone to song.
Regional variation None.
Habitat Coastal forests. Sometimes ventures into more open wooded areas.

Similar sounding Cape Robin-Chat (310), African Dusky (371) and Spotted (372) flycatchers, and many others. While the song is distinctive, many young birds share the soft, piercing, high-pitched note, which also resembles the alarm calls of many adult birds.

ORIOLES

Orioles give beautiful, full, musical songs. It is relatively easy to identify the liquid phrases of an oriole, but more difficult to separate individual oriole species.

African Golden Oriole *Oriolus auratus*

Afrikaanse Wielewaal

 Track detail 0:03–0:52 (song)

Song A beautiful liquid song, something like that of a thrush.
Other sounds Nasal *neeeerrr* sounds, typical of an oriole, but context for this call uncertain.
Regional variation None.
Habitat Mainly miombo woodlands, rocky wooded areas and riverine forests.

Similar sounding Black-headed (268) and Green-headed (not included) orioles and Rockrunner (314). The orioles in the region all sound fairly similar, so care should be taken in separating them on call. African Golden Oriole lacks the single, short, sharp *tiuu* and *ti-liu* notes given by Black-headed and Green-headed orioles. Rockrunner's phrase is longer and a bit harsher.

Black-headed Oriole *Oriolus larvatus*

Swartkopwielewaal

 Track detail 0:02–0:33 (*ti-liu* song)

Song Two main song phrases are known: the liquid bubbly call typical of an oriole, and a short *tiuu* or bisyllablic *ti-liu*. **Mimics** various species, including buzzards, kingfishers and woodpeckers. Context for mimicry uncertain, but presumably aids mate attraction.
Other sounds A drawn-out, descending, nasal *neeerrr*; context uncertain.
Regional variation None.

Habitat Dense woodlands, gardens, parks and forests.
Similar sounding Green-headed (not included), African Golden (267) and all other orioles (not included) and Rockrunner (314). Very similar to other orioles but mimicry seems to be unique to Black-headed Oriole. The short notes are shared with Green-headed, but not African Golden orioles. Rockrunner gives longer phrase with harsher tone.

CROWS AND RAVENS

These birds are known for their guttural rasping and grating calls. Their vocalisations are fairly complex, particularly when groups or pairs of birds interact.

White-necked Raven *Corvus albicollis* Withalskraai

269 Track detail 0:03–0:32 (song)

Song A high-pitched, vibrating *kaaarrrhh*, vaguely resembling a car's hooter.
Other sounds Many other crow-like sounds, but gives unique gurgling noises not heard in crows; context uncertain. **Mimics** poultry and has even been known to mimic a telephone ringing; again context is not fully understood.

Regional variation Uncertain. Calls naturally diverse. Variation may not relate to geographical location.
Habitat Always associated with mountains, but often forages in nearby grasslands.
Similar sounding Pied (270) and Cape (271) crows. Much higher pitched than either of these crows; confusion unlikely.

Pied Crow *Corvus albus* Witborskraai

270 Track detail 0:02–0:22 (song)

Song A typical crow's *kraaah*, but harsh and more nasal. **Mimics** other birds and animals.
Other sounds Gives wide range of sounds in pair and group interactions.
Regional variation Unknown. Calls are naturally diverse. Variation may not relate to geographical location.

Habitat Savanna, mixed woodlands, crop lands and suburbia. Sometimes also seen in the open habitats frequented by Cape Crow.
Similar sounding White-necked Raven (269) and Cape Crow (271). Resemblances superficial. Cape Crow more guttural and less obviously crow-like. Raven has unique gurgles and gives higher-pitched sounds.

Cape Crow *Corvus capensis* Swartkraai

271 Track detail 0:02–0:18 (song)

Song Phrases comprise an abrupt, monotonous *kraaa*, repeated several times. Also gives short, liquid *kolop* notes.
Other sounds Like most crows, gives wide range of gurgling, grating and bubbling sounds in group interactions.
Regional variation Unknown. Calls naturally diverse, but this may not relate to geographical location.

Habitat Open country with scattered shrubs and trees, including grasslands, savanna, fynbos and desert areas.
Similar sounding White-necked Raven (269) and Pied Crow (270). Tone and gurgles of White-necked Raven help to distinguish it from Cape Crow. Phrases comprise a repeated monotone grating note, whereas Pied Crow sounds more typically crow-like.

TITS

Tits are small woodland birds that give loud buzzing alarm calls and beautiful, bubbly, warbled phrases, reminiscent of the high-pitched calls of a bushshrike, but incorporating a much greater variety of phrases.

Ashy Tit   *Parus cinerascens*   Akasiagrysmees

272 Track detail 0:02–1:06 (song)

Song A random mix of piercing warbles, whistles and a unique *dlu-dlu-dlu-dlu* phrase.
Other sounds In territorial conflicts, gives a distinctive *dzee-dzee-trrrrrrrrrr*.
Regional variation None.
Habitat Restricted to arid woodlands. Avoids all broad-leaved habitats.

Similar sounding Grey Tit (273), Chestnut-vented (321), Layard's (322) and other tit-babblers and some thrushes. More piercing and shrill than any thrush. Main song phrase reminiscent of a tit-babbler. Chestnut-vented Tit-babbler may cause confusion as it mimics many other birds (including Ashy Tit). Confrontational phrase sounds similar to that of Grey Tit, but these species are easily separated on range.

Grey Tit   *Parus afer*   Piet-tjou-tjougrysmees

273 Track detail 0:02–1:13 (song)

Song A range of beautiful phrases like those of a thrush, but less complex, as well as bubbling trills. Phrases include *tiu-tiu-tiu-tiu-tiu, tse-kswee-kswee-kswee* and a canary-like bubbling *tutututututututututu*.
Other sounds Contact and alarm calls are rasping trills and warbles, as is typical of most tits.
Regional variation None.

Habitat Dry woodlands, coastal scrub and scrub vegetation on the margins of cultivated lands.
Similar sounding Ashy Tit (272), Chestnut-vented (321) and Layard's (322) tit-babblers. Song phrases vary; difficult to separate from those of other tits. Alarm rattle very like that of Ashy Tit. Note that Chestnut-vented Tit-babbler mimics calls of many birds, including Grey Tit.

Southern Black Tit   *Parus niger*   Gewone Swartmees

 Track detail 0:03–0:42 (song)

Song A range of full, buzzing phrases. Most distinctive phrase is a short, high-pitched whistle, followed by 4–5 vibrating *dee-tiu-tiu-tiu-tiu* notes.
Other sounds Similar piercing whistles and buzzing calls given as alarm and contact calls.

Regional variation None.
Habitat Broad-leaved woodlands, but may venture into adjacent acacia woodlands.
Similar sounding None.

BABBLERS

Gregarious birds with raucous or scratchy songs and calls. As they spend much of their time in groups and even breed co-operatively, individual bird song is very seldom heard.

Arrow-marked Babbler *Turdoides jardineii*   Pylvlekkatlagter

 Track detail 0:38 (total length) = 0:03–0:25 (group song); 0:25–0:38 (contact call)

Song Groups of birds give a harsh cacophony of *garrrrr* sounds, with an obvious nasal sneer.
Other sounds Contact call a softer, cackling version of main song.
Regional variation None.
Habitat Varied. Includes both dry and moist acacia woodlands. Also gardens and, sometimes, reed beds.

Similar sounding Green (209) and Violet (210) wood-hoopoes. Nasal sneering cackle vaguely reminiscent of a wood-hoopoe's cackling, but confusion most unlikely.

Hartlaub's Babbler *Turdoides hartlaubii*   Witkruiskatlagter

 Track detail 0:02–0:35 (song)

Song A series of harsh, nasal *zee-zee-zee-zeeee zee-zee-zee-zeezeezee-zeeeee* notes, usually given by groups of birds, but sometimes also by a lone individual; recalls Morse code or a squeaky toy.
Other sounds Variations of the main song given in various contexts, particularly alarm and contact situations.

Regional variation None.
Habitat Dense riverine woodlands, reed beds and thickets.
Similar sounding Southern Pied (277) and Black-faced (not included) babblers. Hartlaub's song faster and more rhythmical than that of Southern Pied or Black-faced babblers.

Southern Pied Babbler *Turdoides bicolor*   Witkatlagter

Track detail 0:03–0:39 (group song)

Song A raucous cacophony of harsh chattering, comprising single-note *cherr* and double-note *cherra* sounds. Almost always given by groups of birds.
Other sounds Unknown.
Regional variation None.

Habitat Dry acacia savanna and thornveld.
Similar sounding Bennett's Woodpecker (225) and Hartlaub's Babbler (276). Harsher than Bennett's Woodpecker. Hartlaub's Babbler gives squeakier double-note phrase; resemblance is slight.

BUSH BLACKCAP

This forest-dwelling bird is known for its beautiful musical song. Its calls seem to fall midway between those of a bulbul and those of a warbler.

Bush Blackcap *Lioptilus nigricapillus* Rooibektiptol

 Track detail 0:03–0:39 (song)

Song A bubbly mix of notes given by male, and sometimes by female, although not considered a duet. **Other sounds** Rasping, guttural alarm calls. **Regional variation** Not described. Some regional differences have been observed but not yet recorded. **Habitat** Largely confined to escarpment forests and forest margins. Sometimes also seen in gardens.

Similar sounding Some robins, Dark-capped Bulbul (282), Thrush Nightingale (313) and Chestnut-vented (321) and Layard's (322) tit-babblers. Mixed bubbling notes in song vaguely like those of robins. Song like that of Dark-capped Bulbul but staccato and piercing. Knowledge of tone and phrasing helps to separate from Thrush Nightingale and tit-babblers.

BROWNBULS, BULBULS, GREENBULS AND NICATOR

Species within this group generally give repeated, brief, clear phrases, comprising full chips, chirps, warbles and other notes. Song phrases are separated by short gaps. In the breeding season, lone males sing to attract mates or proclaim their territory, but otherwise birds call in groups to maintain contact or when alarmed or mobbing intruders. Frantic mobbing calls from bulbuls often indicate the presence of predators such as owls, snakes or cats. A characteristic of bulbuls, but not other members of this group, is that they show marked song dialects. Often birds relatively near to one another share no phrases in their repertoires. Bulbuls, greenbuls and brownbuls are closely related. There are similarities in their songs and calls, but their behaviour tends to diverge more.

Terrestrial Brownbul *Phyllastrephus terrestris* Boskrapper

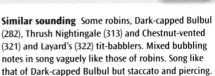

 Track detail 0:03–0:25 (song)

Song Distinctive resonant chattering. Song notes vary somewhat, but retain a similar feel and fairly constant tone. Members of a mating pair sometimes **duet**, in which case the song rises to a shrill crescendo, but retains its churring tone. **Other sounds** Groups give lower-pitched churring trills, presumably to establish and maintain contact. **Regional variation** None. **Habitat** Forests and dense bush, especially where protective undergrowth allows for ground-based foraging.

Similar sounding Acacia Pied Barbet (217), Red-throated Wryneck (229), Yellow-bellied Greenbul (284) and Southern White-crowned Shrike (398). Resemblance to song of Yellow-bellied Greenbul quite marked, but confusion with the barbet, wryneck or shrike far less likely, since Terrestrial Brownbul's calls are generally easy to identify as belonging within the bulbul group.

Cape Bulbul *Pycnonotus capensis*

Kaapse Tiptol

280 Track detail 0:27 (total length) = 0:02–0:17 (song); 0:17—0:27 (contact call)

Song A series of bright, slightly scratchy notes like *tjreep, preep* and *hoodley*. Dominant sound is *eep*. Also includes shorter, slurred *chip* notes. Phrases usually comprise about six notes.
Other sounds Main call an agitated and slurred *tjirup*, given in alarm and when mobbing intruders. Variation of this call also used to maintain group contact and as settling call, when birds congregate at a roost.
Regional variation Definite local dialects even over relatively short distances; birds within a few kilometres of one another may share no phrases.

Habitat Restricted to the winter-rainfall region. Prefers fynbos, coastal scrub and coastal forests; also occurs in gardens.
Similar sounding African Red-eyed (281) and Dark-capped (282) bulbuls. Cape Bulbul sounds thinner and scratchier than African Red-eyed and Dark-capped bulbuls, with fewer musical phrases.

African Red-eyed Bulbul *Pycnonotus nigricans*

Rooioogtiptol

281 Track detail 0:52 (total length) = 0:02–0:26 (song); 0:26–0:52 (contact call)

Song Phrases comprise about five *treep-tlop-preep-pirup-tleep* notes. Tone scratchier than in other bulbuls, but still bubbly. Each bird has a range of phrases in its repertoire.
Other sounds An agitated *trip-trip-trip* alarm call, given when mobbing predators. Similar call given to maintain group contact and as settling call when small groups congregate at a roost.
Regional variation Distinct local dialects. Birds within just a few kilometres of each other may have no phrases in common.

Habitat Replaces Dark-capped Bulbul in woodlands, gardens and arid savanna in the western parts of the region. There is a transition zone just southwest of Johannesburg, where they co-exist.
Similar sounding Cape (280) and Dark-capped (282) bulbuls, Eastern Nicator (285) and Red-billed Buffalo Weaver (449). Cape Bulbul's song scratchier and less musical, while Dark-capped sounds fuller and more melodic. Eastern Nicator's song is trilled, bubbly and piercing and includes mimicry. Group chatter does resemble the song of Red-billed Buffalo Weaver, but is less piercing.

Dark-capped (Black-eyed) Bulbul *Pycnonotus tricolor*

Swartoogtiptol

282 Track detail 0:55 (total length) = 0:03–0:46 (song); 0:46–0:55 (contact calls)

Song Among the first birds to sing in the morning. Phrases of about six short, lively notes, such as *de-droo-dzee-dee-droo-dziiip* are repeated at brief intervals. Each bird has a repertoire of several phrases.
Other sounds An agitated *trip-trip-trip* often given when mobbing predators. A variation of this is also given to maintain group contact and as a settling call when small groups congregate at a roost.
Regional variation Distinct local dialects. Birds within just a short distance may share no common phrases.
Habitat Woodlands. Attracted to fruit trees.

Similar sounding Bush Blackcap (278), Cape (280) and African Red-eyed (281) bulbuls, Eastern Nicator (285), White-throated Robin-Chat (311) and Red-billed Buffalo Weaver (449). Bush Blackcap sounds less repetitive and more energetic. African Red-eyed Bulbul's call is thicker and scratchier; Cape Bulbul sounds even scratchier and less musical. Eastern Nicator's call is trilled, bubbly and piercing, with mimicry. White-throated Robin-Chat more musical, with slightly longer phrases. Dark-capped Bulbul's group chatter sounds like song of Red-billed Buffalo Weaver, but less piercing.

Sombre Greenbul   *Andropadus importunus*   Gewone Willie

283 Track detail 0:26 (total length) = 0:02–0:20 (song); 0:20–0:26 (alarm call)

Song Highly distinctive and easily identified. A bubbly, musical phrase, followed by a drawn-out descending whistle. Often rendered as *Willie-come-out-and-have-a-fight, scaaaaaarrrreeeeedddd!*
Other sounds Contact call comprises soft murmurings. In alarm gives a *plee-plee-plee* call, a short, piercing variation of the descending whistle.

Regional variation Very slight variations in phrasing from region to region.
Habitat Forests, woodlands, gardens, karoo and fynbos country, provided the vegetation is dense.
Similar sounding None.

Yellow-bellied Greenbul   *Chlorocichla flaviventris*   Geelborswillie

284 Track detail 0:02–0:34 (song)

Song A nasal *neh-neh-neh-neh-neh-neh*, rising in pitch and intensity. Phrases usually comprise six or more notes.
Other sounds Gives two notes from song as contact call.
Regional variation None.

Habitat Forests, mangroves, thickets and gardens.
Similar sounding Acacia Pied Barbet (217), Red-throated Wryneck (229), Terrestrial Brownbul (279) and Southern White-crowned Shrike (398). Confusion unlikely, as Yellow-bellied Greenbul's song sounds far more nasal and sneering.

Eastern Nicator   *Nicator gularis*   Geelvleknikator

285 Track detail 0:03–0:33 (song)

Song Phrasing resembles that of a bulbul, but song is livelier, with more trills and greater variation in pitch. Short phrases are separated by brief pauses. May mimic other birds.
Other sounds Gives short, single-note *chuck* and *churr* sounds when alarmed.
Regional variation Mimics those species that occur locally.
Habitat Dense forest and scrub vegetation.

Similar sounding African Red-eyed (281) and Dark-capped (282) bulbuls, Thrush Nightingale (313) and Rockrunner (314). Phrasing similar to that of African Red-eyed and Dark-capped bulbuls, but their calls are less sharp and energetic, with fewer trills. Nicator also mimics, unlike true bulbuls. Similar tone to that of Thrush Nightingale, but nicator's phrases short, not long sequences. Song bears superficial resemblance to that of a Rockrunner, but the latter gives longer, more musical phrases.

THRUSHES AND ROCK-THRUSHES

Both thrushes and rock-thrushes are known for their beautiful songs, given by the male both to proclaim territory and to attract mates. The Cape Rock-Thrush is unique in the group in that both male and female may sing to proclaim territory. Thrushes sing the most tuneful phrases, with sweet whistles, yodels, trills and squeaks. Rock-thrushes sing similarly pretty songs, but with faster, shriller phrasing and some scratchier sounds. Both groups mimic other bird species.

Olive Thrush *Turdus olivaceus*   Olyflyster

286 Track detail 0:03–0:33 (song)

Song A series of sweet musical trills and whistles with a typical thrush-like quality. Highly varied, but almost always includes characteristic trilled whistle (heard in the recording).
Other sounds Alarm call a liquid *tchink*. Mimics other birds, although context for this not yet known.
Regional variation Like all thrushes, exhibits notable phrase variation. Mimics species that occur locally.

Habitat Evergreen forests and forest margins; common in suburban gardens. Avoids open habitats.
Similar sounding Karoo (287), Kurrichane (288) and Orange Ground (289) thrushes. Very similar to Karoo Thrush, but Olive Thrush mimics other species and its slightly longer, clearer, whistled notes are more musical. More trills and rattles than Kurrichane and Orange Ground thrushes.

Karoo Thrush *Turdus smithi*   Geelbeklyster

287 Track detail 0:50 (total length) = 0:02–0:32 (song); 0:32–0:50 (begging call)

Song Typical thrush-like song, with energetic, chirpy tone to phrases. Phrases highly varied, even within each individual's repertoire.
Other sounds A liquid *tchink* alarm call. Does not mimic other species. Begging call is a softer version of adult's alarm call.
Regional variation Phrases vary widely, even over short distances.

Habitat Riverine woodlands and bush; very common in suburban gardens.
Similar sounding Olive (286), Kurrichane (288) and Orange Ground (289) thrushes. Very similar to Olive Thrush, but has shorter, clearer, more energetic whistled notes and does not mimic. More trills and rattles than Kurrichane or Orange Ground thrushes.

Kurrichane Thrush *Turdus libonyanus*   Rooibeklyster

288 Track detail 0:03–0:35 (song)

Song A series of short piercing whistles and some trills with a clear *wiuu-wiuu-wiuu* repeated throughout the phrase.
Other sounds A very distinctive *whit-whiuu* flight call. Mimics various other birds, but context not well understood.
Regional variation Like all thrushes, exhibits marked variations in phrasing. Presumably mimics those species present in its environment.

Habitat Broad-leaved woodlands; also acacia habitats, if there is open ground on which to feed.
Similar sounding Olive (286), Karoo (287) and Orange Ground (289) thrushes and White-throated Robin-Chat (311). Closest to Karoo and Olive thrushes – pay careful attention to tone and phrasing. Told from Orange Ground Thrush by more plaintive and musical tone. Like the robin-chat, Kurrichane gives few shrill trills and no *chuck*.

Orange Ground Thrush   *Zoothera gurneyi*   Oranjelyster

 Track detail   0:03–0:30 (song)

Song The sweetest, clearest, most tuneful song of any thrush, with few or no trills. Each phrase comprises a few whistled *weet* notes varying in pitch, a brief pause, and then bulbul-like phrases. Pauses, then repeats this composite phrase, with variations. **Other sounds** No contact or alarm calls described, but presumably they do form part of its repertoire. Mimics other species; context not fully understood.

Regional variation Like most thrushes, exhibits enormous regional variation. Mimics local species. **Habitat** Montane and some escarpment forests. **Similar sounding** Olive (286), Karoo (287) and Kurrichane (288) thrushes and Miombo Rock-Thrush (292). Superfical resemblance to Olive, Karoo and Kurrichane thrushes, but confusion unlikely. Gives clearer, less trilled whistles than Miombo Rock-Thrush.

Groundscraper Thrush   *Psophocichla litsitsirupa*   Gevlekte Lyster

 Track detail   0:03–0:30 (song)

Song Piercing song comprising loud trilled notes. Phrases usually short and simple, interspersed with some clicks. **Other sounds** Clicking notes given in alarm. Mimics some bird species.

Regional variation Mimics those birds present in the area. **Habitat** A wide range of open woodland and garden habitats. **Similar sounding** None.

Cape Rock-Thrush   *Monticola rupestris*   Kaapse Kliplyster

 Track detail   0:03–0:41 (female song)

Song A see-sawing *zeeooo-zweee-yooo-krrr*, comprising piercing whistles and shrill trills. Phrases are longer, more varied, with less obvious repetition than in true thrushes. Sometimes mimics other birds; context not understood. Either sex may give the song. **Other sounds** Hissing and rattling when alarmed. **Regional variation** Mimics those species present in the area.

Habitat Rocky slopes and cliffs; also villages adjacent to such habitats. **Similar sounding** Miombo Rock-Thrush (292), Sentinel Rock-Thrush (293), Ant-eating (299) and Tractrac (297) chats and Mountain Wheatear (not included). More scratchy notes than Miombo and less wheatear-like than Sentinel rock-thrushes. Song fuller and more thrush-like than those of chats or wheatears.

Miombo Rock-Thrush   *Monticola angolensis*   Angolakliplyster

 Track detail   0:03–0:52 (song)

Song Short, tuneful, rising and falling notes, with slightly plaintive tone. Thrush-like, but without trills. **Other sounds** A two-note alarm call and general contact chatter. Mimics some birds, but context for this mimicry is uncertain. **Regional variation** None.

Habitat Open woodlands, with little ground cover. Not bound to rocky habitat like other rock-thrushes. **Similar sounding** Orange Ground Thrush (289) and Cape Rock-Thrush (291). Sounds less trilled than Orange Ground Thrush. Lack of scratchy notes makes Miombo's song atypical for a rock-thrush.

Sentinel Rock-Thrush *Monticola explorator* Langtoonkliplyster

293 Track detail 0:03–0:21 (song)

Song Sweet but shrill jumbled whistles, with many *shreee* sounds. A rather ineffective **mimic**.
Other sounds Alarm call similar to song, but generally harsher.
Regional variation Unknown. Not yet certain whether variations relate to geographical location.
Habitat Various types of grassland; needs scattered rocks on which to perch. Favours montane areas.

Similar sounding Short-clawed Lark (245), Cape Rock-thrush (291), some chats, like Buff-streaked Chat (298) and African Stonechat (302) and some wheatears. Resemblance to Short-clawed Lark and African Stonechat is superficial. Cape Rock-thrush gives more musical see-saw song. Sentinel sounds fuller and more tuneful than a chat or wheatear.

ROCKJUMPERS

A group of iconic birds endemic to mountainous regions in southern Africa. Distinctive, piercing, thrush-like alarm trills and sparrow-like tweets make it easy to identify members of the group by their calls. The ranges of the rockjumper species do not overlap and these birds are therefore easily separated on distribution.

Drakensberg Rockjumper *Chaetops aurantius* Oranjeborsberglyster

294 Track detail 0:40 (total length) = 0:02–0:14 (alarm call); 0:14–0:22 (song); 0:22–0:40 (aggressive interactions)

Song Gives two main song phrases: a piercing, almost sparrow-like *chee-chee-chee* and a *tree-tree-tree* like the distress call of a thrush.
Other sounds Agitated combinations of phrases from main song given in alarm. Excited variations of song used to establish and maintain group contact.
Regional variation Unknown. Variation unlikely owing to limited distribution.
Habitat Tall, rocky peaks in the Drakensberg and Malutis. Sometimes ventures down rocky slopes.

Similar sounding Cape Rockjumper (not included) and Rufous-eared Warbler (360). Although similar-sounding, rockjumpers are very range-bound and so are easily separated on distribution. Bears some similarity to a sparrow's chirps and a thrush's alarm calls, but the rockjumper's combination of these two types of sound is quite distinctive. Its whistles resemble those of a Rufous-eared Warbler, but that species gives a fast series that includes no other notes.

CHATS, STONECHATS AND WHEATEARS

A diverse group of birds whose songs may be simple and scratchy, with no mimicry of other species, or quite complex, with extensive mimicry. Small species like the African Stonechat and the wheaters mimic, while more typical chats (other than the Buff-streaked Chat) never mimic. The males of all these species sing from prominent perches.

Familiar Chat   *Cercomela familiaris*   Gewone Spekvreter

295 Track detail 0:02–0:18 (song)

Song A series of soft, scratchy *tzk* notes, with some short, piercing whistles. Sometimes also gives a rasping swizzling phrase.
Other sounds A distinctive *chirp-chit-chit* given both as an alarm and contact call.
Regional variation None.

Habitat Rocky and hilly areas in open woodlands, extending into the Karoo from the central interior. Also occurs in gardens.
Similar sounding Chat (370) and Spotted (372) flycatchers. Soft but scratchy song is unique, while alarm call sounds similar to, but a bit fuller than, that of Spotted and not as deep as that of Chat Flycatcher.

Sickle-winged Chat   *Cercomela sinuata*   Vlaktespekvreter

296 Track detail 0:02–0:15 (song)

Song Repeatedly gives a short, sharp *brrr*, some higher-pitched *dzeep* notes and a rattle. Context for song is poorly defined, but it probably serves for territorial defence and mate attraction.
Other sounds Not yet described.
Regional variation None.
Habitat Karoo scrub and bushy mountain slopes.
Similar sounding Budgerigars (not included), Rattling Cisticola (348), Cape Weaver (452) and

Chat Flycatcher (370). Short, sharp notes bear close resemblance to those of budgerigars, but feral budgies are uncommon in the region. Gives clicks and rattling sounds like those of Rattling Cisticola, but these aren't part of a structured phrase. Scratchier calls reminiscent of those of Cape Weaver, but distinguished by the mixture of whistles and other non-weaver-like sounds in chat's call. Sounds less harsh and scratchy than the Chat Flycatcher.

Tractrac Chat   *Cercomela tractrac*   Woestynspekvreter

297 Track detail 0:02–0:33 (song)

Song A nearly continuous jumble of trills, scratchy notes and whistles, with very brief intervals. Given so fast that no specific notes or phrases stand out.
Other sounds Short, sharp alarm calls, somewhat like the ticking of a clock.
Regional variation None.
Habitat Open plains with grass and small bushes, in arid regions. Also dune scrub.

Similar sounding Sclater's Lark (252), Cape Rock-Thrush (291) and Mountain and other vagrant wheaters (not included). Chirp notes similar to those of Sclater's Lark. Cape Rock-Thrush sounds slightly more musical and thrush-like than this chat. Those wheaters with long song phrases are not easily told from the Tractrac Chat by call alone.

Buff-streaked Chat *Campicoloides bifasciata* Bergklipwagter

 Track detail 0:03–0:55 (song*) * Listen for mimicry of African Stonechat at 0:28–0:38

Song A beautiful haphazard mix of sweet whistles and trills, with a few scratchy notes. Brief pauses separate jumbled phrases of 10 or more notes. Occasionally **mimics** other birds.
Other sounds A single harsh click, given as both an alarm and contact call.
Regional variation None.

Habitat Rocky parts of montane grasslands; also seen around buildings in rural settlements.
Similar sounding African Stonechat (302) and Sentinel Rock-Thrush (293). Song phrases faster, including fewer scratchy notes than stonechat's song. Bears superficial resemblance to rock-thrushes, but sounds thinner and more piercing.

Ant-eating Chat *Myrmecocichla formicivora* Swartpiek

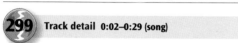

 Track detail 0:02–0:29 (song)

Song Like other chats, gives jumbled series of scratchy and tuneful notes. A two-note *too-ip* whistled phrase distinguishes this species. Sometimes **mimics** other birds.
Other sounds A plaintive drawn-out whistle, given in alarm and to establish and maintain group contact.
Regional variation Mimics those birds present locally.

Habitat A wide range of grassland habitats, as well as open savanna and semi-arid areas.
Similar sounding Cape Rock-Thrush (291), most wheatears, Arnot's (300) and other chats and Cape Longclaw (389). Cape Rock-Thrush sounds slightly more musical and thrush-like. Sounds similar to most wheatears and chats, but the plaintive two-note whistle (heard in this track) separates them. The whistle on its own can resemble that of Cape Longclaw, so take care when attempting to separate these species.

Arnot's Chat *Myrmecocichla arnoti* Bontpiek

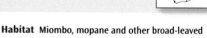

Track detail 0:02–0:31 (song)

Song Like other chats, gives jumbled series of scratchy and tuneful notes and a distinctive piercing whistle, but phrasing is slower. **Mimics** other birds more than is usual for a chat.
Other sounds Short, sharp, harsh contact calls and a plaintive alarm whistle.
Regional variation Mimics those birds present locally.

Habitat Miombo, mopane and other broad-leaved woodland habitats.
Similar sounding Most wheatears, Ant-eating (299) and other chats and Cape Longclaw (389). Song similar to those of most wheatears and chats, but slower and more piercing. Plaintive alarm whistle resembles the same note heard in Cape Longclaw and Ant-eating Chat's alarm and contact calls. Told from other chats by greater tendency to mimic.

Capped Wheatear *Oenanthe pileata* Hoëveldskaapwagter

 Track detail 0:03–0:50 (song*) * Listen for mimicry of Blacksmith Lapwing

Song Mixes short, piercing phrases with occasional longer ones. Blends notes typical of a wheatear, with a few warbler-like notes and mimics other birds extensively. Song incorporates more mimicked than unique sounds.
Other sounds Harsh, chat-like, clicking alarm calls. Contact call includes a whistle similar to that of African Stonechat.

Regional variation Mimics extensively; sounds heard depend on species found in the region.
Habitat Short dry or recently burnt grasslands, semi-arid scrub and crop lands.
Similar sounding African Stonechat (302). Contact and alarm calls similar to those of African Stonechat, but song, with its extensive mimicry and wheatear-like tone, should be sufficiently distinctive.

African Stonechat *Saxicola torquatus* Gewone Bontrokkie

Track detail 0:29 (total length) = 0:03–0:11 (song); 0:11–0:29 (alarm call)

Song Lovely jumbled phrases of 6–10 beautiful whistles and some scratchy notes, delivered rapidly and separated by brief pauses. Seldom mimics other birds.
Other sounds Contact and alarm calls comprise a short, sharp *tsee* whistle followed by one or two brief rasping *tik-tik* notes. May rearrange this *tsee-tik-tik* phrase in various ways.
Regional variation None.

Habitat Grassy slopes, grasslands with scattered bushes, forests and wetland margins.
Similar sounding Buff-streaked Chat (298), rock-thrushes (291–293), Capped (301) and Mountain (not included) wheatears, canaries and larks, like Fawn-coloured Lark (234). Phrases are shorter and more musical than those of Buff-streaked Chat and thinner than those of a rock-thrush. Calls recall Mountain Wheatear, but separated on habitat. Capped Wheatear mimics more. Song vaguely like that of a lark or canary.

SCRUB ROBINS AND ROBIN-CHATS

Scrub robins typically sing scratchy but distinctive phrases and are easily separated by ear. Robin-chats are known for their lovely songs, and many of these species give full, beautiful, whistled calls. They often also mimic other birds. In fact, one of the region's best mimics, the Red-capped Robin-Chat, falls into this group. In both scrub robins and robin-chats, it is always lone males who sing, generally just within dense cover.

Brown Scrub Robin *Cercotrichas signata* Bruinwipstert

 Track detail 0:03–1:03 (song)

Song A mournful whistle, typical of a robin, along with some *chuks* and trills. The only scrub robin that does not mimic other species.
Other sounds Very nasal, scratchy alarm calls.

Regional variation Phrase varies regionally, but length and tone are consistent.
Habitat Forests. Favours damp understorey.
Similar sounding None.

Bearded Scrub Robin   *Cercotrichas quadrivirgata*   Baardwipstert

304 Track detail 0:03–0:29 (song)

Song Like most scrub robins, gives complex phrases comprising beautiful shrill whistles and trills. Phrases may be brief, or last several minutes. Some, but not all, individuals **mimic** other birds. Incorporates bulbul-like *chirrup* notes within the phrase.
Other sounds Gives soft, nasal, rasping alarm call.
Regional variation Phrases highly varied, even among neighbours.

Habitat Sand forests, both moist and dry, as well as riverine forests and broad-leaved woodlands.
Similar sounding Kalahari (306) and White-browed (305) scrub robins and White-throated Robin-Chat (311). Very similar to Kalahari and White-browed scrub robins; take care in areas where their ranges overlap. White-throated Robin-Chat has more bulbul-like tone.

White-browed Scrub Robin   *Cercotrichas leucophrys*   Gestreepte Wipstert

305 Track detail 0:03–1:47 (song)

Song Bubbly and musical, with bulbul- or thrush-like characteristics, as well as whistles and trills typical of a robin. Also **mimics** other birds. Phrases usually start with one or two rapidly sounded whistled notes, followed by a complex phrase.
Other sounds Ratchety *krrr krrr krrr* alarm calls.
Regional variation Phrases of songs and calls vary tremendously from region to region, even among neighbours. Mimics species present locally.

Habitat Varied, but includes acacia savanna as well as acacia and miombo woodlands.
Similar sounding Bearded (304) and Kalahari (306) scrub robins and White-throated Robin-Chat (311). Difficult to separate from Bearded Scrub Robin on call. Does not give the *see-seeoooo see-seeooo* phrase of the Kalahari Scrub Robin. White-throated Robin-Chat also sounds similar, but its song has a bulbul-like character not heard in the scrub robin's song.

Kalahari Scrub Robin   *Cercotrichas paena*   Kalahariwipstert

306 Track detail 0:03–0:58 (song*) * Listen for distinctive *see-seeooo* at 0:46

Song A series of varied whistles, chirps and other typically robin-like sounds, but usually includes distinctive *see-seeoooo see-seeooo*. **Mimics** many other birds.
Other sounds In alarm gives insect-like buzzing.
Regional variation While trademark *see-seeoooo see-seeoooo* not highly varied, mimicry varies according to species present locally.

Habitat Dry thornveld with open patches of bare ground.
Similar sounding Bearded (304), White-browed (305) and Karoo (307) scrub robins. Although similar to other scrub robins confusion is highly unlikely, since the *see-seeoooo see-seeooo* phrase in the song is easily recognised.

Karoo Scrub Robin *Cercotrichas coryphoeus* Slangverklikker

307 Track detail 0:03–0:27 (contact and alarm calls)

Song A series of harsh *chit* and *tseet* notes, sometimes given quite rapidly. Mimics other birds.
Other sounds Gives nasal rasping notes in alarm.
Regional variation Complexity of call means general variations from region to region highly likely. Mimicry varies according to species present locally.

Habitat Karoo scrub, where it frequents open ground between bushes.
Similar sounding Kalahari Scrub Robin (306) and a range of sunbirds. Lacks *see-seeooo* notes of Kalahari Scrub Robin, and its sparrow-like chirps are unique. Calls slightly resemble a sunbird's alarm call.

Chorister Robin-Chat *Cossypha dichroa* Lawaaimakerjanfrederik

308 Track detail 0:03–1:18 (song*) * Listen for mimicry of Bokmakierie, Common Myna, African Fish Eagle and Olive Thrush

Song Whistled song chiefly comprised of a wide range of **mimicked** sounds, not just bird calls. Gives the most human-like whistle of any robin-chat.
Other sounds Contact call is a plaintive two-note whistle. Alarm call comprises some scratchy notes.
Regional variation Extensive mimicry means that local species and noises determine how song sounds.

Habitat Almost exclusively forests; sometimes ventures into gardens adjacent to forested habitat.
Similar sounding Red-capped Robin-Chat (309). Red-capped Robin-Chat gives guttural two-note call and, like other robin-chats, its whistled notes do not sound as human. The Chorister Robin-Chat also mimics far more extensively than other robin-chats.

Red-capped Robin-Chat *Cossypha natalensis* Nataljanfrederik

309 Track detail 0:03–1:34 (song*) * Listen for mimicry of Bokmakierie, Common Myna, Red-chested Cuckoo and Fork-tailed Drongo

Song Comprises mainly **mimicked** sounds, not all of them bird calls. May, for instance, mimic dogs barking or telephones ringing. Mimicry regularly punctuated by a guttural and repetitive two-note *terrrr-terrrrr* whistle, which is helpful in distinguishing the song.
Other sounds Alarm and contact calls are variations of the guttural whistle in song.

Regional variation Extensive mimicry means that local species and noises determine how song sounds.
Habitat Forests and other lushly vegetated habitats, as well as very well-wooded gardens.
Similar sounding Chorister Robin-Chat (308). The guttural, repetitive whistled phrase is not given by Chorister Robin-Chat.

Cape Robin-Chat *Cossypha caffra* Gewone Janfrederik

310 Track detail 0:03–1:10 (song*) * Listen for mimicry of African Paradise Flycatcher, Dark-capped Bulbul, African Dusky Flycatcher and Karoo Thrush

Song Short, varying phrases, with extensive **mimicry**. *Every* phrase starts with a slurred, descending whistle, which, in combination with other phrases, is unique.
Other sounds A distinctive guttual *ki-ra-rirr* in alarm and when gathering to settle at a roost. Newly fledged birds give a shrill descending *pppeeeeeuuuuuu* shared by the young of many species in the region.
Regional variation Uncertain. Descending whistle starting each phrase is constant, but individuals

vary the remainder of their phrases widely, which is suggestive of regional differences. Mimicry of local species and other noises also result in variation.
Habitat Mixed habitat with large trees, dense cover and nearby water. Abundant in gardens.
Similar sounding Grey Cuckooshrike (266) and White-throated Robin-Chat (311). Alarm call is similar to that of the cuckooshrike. The White-throated Robin-Chat lacks the introductory whistle.

White-throated Robin-Chat *Cossypha humeralis* Witkeeljanfrederik

311 Track detail 0:03–0:28 (song)

Song A beautiful mix of tuneful notes. May mimic other birds. Each phrase up to 10 notes long.
Other sounds Alarm call gives either a deep, guttural croak or mimics the alarm call of another bird. Also a piercing, two-note, trilled whistle given in the evening, when settling down to roost.
Regional variation Phrases generally highly variable; also mimics those species present locally.

Habitat Thickets in coastal scrub, acacia and broad-leaved woodlands; also farms and gardens.
Similar sounding Dark-capped Bulbul (282), Kurrichane Thrush (288), Bearded (304) and White-browed (305) scrub robins and Cape Robin-Chat (310). Very slightly resembles Dark-capped Bulbul. More bulbul-like than Kurrichane Thrush. Less scratchy than any of the scrub robins. Lacks Cape Robin-Chat's slurred introductory whistle.

White-browed Robin-Chat *Cossypha heuglini* Heuglinjanfrederik

312 Track detail 0:03–0:36 (song*) * Mimics Dark-capped Bulbul

Song Phrases distinctive, comprising about 4–6 simple but beautiful whistles varying in pitch. On rare occasions mimics songs of other species.
Other sounds Sometimes mimics other birds' alarm calls, but this is uncommon. Gives shorter variation of song phrase as a contact call. Alarm call a single scratchy note.

Regional variation Some variation, particularly in contact call.
Habitat Riverine forests and forest margins, moist woodlands, lakesides and well-wooded gardens.
Similar sounding None.

NIGHTINGALES

The migratory Thrush Nightingale is the only representative of the nightingale family found in our region. Although it is vocal when present, it is secretive and easily missed, even in small bushes.

Thrush Nightingale *Luscinia luscinia* Lysternagtegaal

313 Track detail 0:03–1:07 (song)

Song Jumbled and warbled phrases. Unique and full-sounding, owing to distinctive deep churring with harsh clicks and chucks.
Other sounds A rasping rattling *trrrrrrrr* note, given in alarm.
Regional variation None.

Habitat Dense thickets in acacia and broad-leaved woodlands. Also found in densely vegetated gardens.
Similar sounding Eastern Nicator (285), Bush Blackcap (278) and Chestnut-vented Tit-babbler (321). Similar tone to nicator, but gives longer note sequences. Both blackcap and tit-babbler lack Thrush Nightingale's deep churring notes and intermittent clicks.

ATYPICAL WARBLERS

The warblers grouped together here for the purposes of this guide are all members of the so-called Sylviidae group, and do not fit cleanly into the prinia, cisticola or true warbler categories. Their songs always consist of distinctive, fairly complex, almost jumbled phrases that incorporate trills and other rapid notes. These songs tend to be piercing and to carry well. Phrases are generally constant throughout a species' range.

Rockrunner *Achaetops pycnopygius*   Rotsvoël

Track detail 0:02–0:23 (song)

Song A short, sharp, scratchy lead-in note, followed by a rapid jumble of rich liquid trills and warbles, decelerating and ending with a short whistle.
Other sounds Gives single drawn-out note if alarmed.
Regional variation Unknown. Range is limited so variation unlikely.

Habitat Rocky slopes and hillsides. Avoids rivers.
Similar sounding African Golden (267) and Black-headed (268) orioles and Eastern Nicator (285). May recall an oriole singing rapidly; however, confusion with any oriole is quite unlikely. Phrase is longer, with fewer harsh notes than is typical of the nicator.

Cape Grassbird *Sphenoeacus afer*   Grasvoël

Track detail 0:03–0:55 (song)

Song Shrill. Consists of a few scratchy lead-in whistles, followed by a rapid jumble of warbled notes; often ends on short trill.
Other sounds Cat-like mewing, presumably in alarm.
Regional variation None.
Habitat Rank grass, preferably close to a stream. Sometimes also among bracken or reeds.

Similar sounding Fawn-coloured Lark (234), Little Rush Warbler (326) and Lazy Cisticola (346). Differs from lark in sounding fuller, more jumbled and frantic; also listen for final trilled whistle. Alarm call may resemble that of Cape Little Rush Warbler and is almost identical to song of Lazy Cisticola. Take care when attempting to separate these species on call alone.

Victorin's Warbler *Cryptillas victorini*   Rooiborsruigtesanger

Track detail 0:04–1:06 (song*)
* Note that churring in track is another bird's contact call

Song A basic, very rhythmical phrase of two or three soft lead-in whistles, followed by a piercing, bubbly *tsip tsipy-steep, tsip tsipy-tsep* and variations on this theme.
Other sounds Alarm and contact calls comprise soft rasping *chur* notes.
Regional variation Song phrase varies considerably, despite this warbler's narrow distribution.

Habitat Moist bracken and fynbos, preferably close to a river.
Similar sounding Long-billed Crombec (317). Long-billed Crombec's song is bisyllabic, more repetitive, with a slower rhythm. Easy to hear the repetitive bisyllabic phrasing of crombec, whereas Victorin's Warbler sounds more rapid and jumbled.

Long-billed Crombec *Sylvietta rufescens* Bosveldstompstert

317 Track detail 0:33 (total length) = 0:03–0:26 (song); 0:26–0:33 (contact call)

Song One or two short, soft lead-in whistles, followed by a repetitive rhythmical phrase comprising bisyllabic *chirit* notes.
Other sounds A short, sharp, rattled *prrrrp* as alarm and contact call, like other small finches and waxbills.
Regional variation None.

Habitat Woodlands and open savanna with undergrowth. Favours drier areas.
Similar sounding Victorin's Warbler (316). Song is slower and lacks the one-and-two-syllable rhythm of Victorin's. Easier to discern the bisyllabic rhythm in Long-billed Crombec.

PENDULINE-TITS

Small woodland birds known for their loud, buzzing alarm calls and beautiful, full, warbled song phrases. Penduline-tits give very high-pitched metallic notes and their phrases remind one of a sunbird's song.

Cape Penduline-Tit *Anthoscopus minutus* Kaapse Kapokvoël

318 Track detail 0:02–0:14 (song)

Song A very high-pitched metallic *tseep* and a *tchip-tchip*, both reminiscent of a sunbird.
Other sounds Buzzing alarm and contact calls like those of a sunbird.
Regional variation None.

Habitat Acacia savanna and some drier habitats; requires shrubs or small trees in which to forage.
Similar sounding Amethyst Sunbird (434). Confusion unlikely as *tseep* and *tchip-tchip* sounds should help to separate them.

EREMOMELAS

Eremomelas are a unique group in that they display behaviour similar to that of the tree-dwelling warblers, but move around in groups and often sing together. Their songs are frequently repetitive and very high pitched. Separating eremomela songs is a relatively simple task.

Burnt-necked Eremomela *Eremomela usticollis* Bruinkeelbossanger

319 Track detail 0:02–0:38 (song)

Song A highly distinctive series of rapid, high-pitched, single-note whistles; ascends then descends, ending on a trilled whistle. Also slower *tsee-tsee-tsee-tsee-tsee* notes.
Other sounds Piercing trilled phrases, given in alarm and to maintain group contact.
Regional variation None.
Habitat Acacia and mixed woodlands.

Similar sounding Common Sandpiper (117), Little Swift (181), Red-faced Cisticola (347), Karoo (357) and Drakensberg (358) prinias and Namaqua Warbler (359). Vaguely like Common Sandpiper and the prinias. Less twittering and pitch variation than the swift. Slower song is like that of Red-faced Cisticola, but that species calls alone. Gives far fewer trills than Namaqua Warbler.

Green-capped Eremomela   *Eremomela scotops*   Donkerwangbossanger

320   Track detail 0:02–0:54 (alarm and contact calls)

Song A series of *tsip* notes.
Other sounds A churring, agitated, slightly rasping *trrip-trrip-trrip*, given as contact and alarm calls.
Regional variation None.
Habitat Dwells almost exclusively in broad-leaved woodlands.

Similar sounding Karoo (357) and Drakensberg (358) prinias and Cape Weaver (452). Resemblance to the prinias is superficial. Agitated alarm call and *tsip* notes are distinctive, but the *tsi* song on its own bears some resemblance to song of Cape Weaver.

TIT-BABBLERS

Tit-babblers are fairly drab, well-camouflaged birds known for their churring songs. One species mimics and the other does not, but both have a similar distinctive tone.

Chestnut-vented Tit-babbler   *Sylvia subcaeruleum*   Bosveldtjeriktik

321   Track detail 0:03–0:54 (song)

Song One member of a breeding pair initiates counter-singing **duet** with a *cheera-tik-tik-tik-tik* phrase; the other responds with a mix of sounds, incorporating the same main phrase.
Other sounds Juveniles **mimic** many species in their subsong.
Regional variation Only notable variation is in mimicry, which varies depending on local species.

Habitat Acacia woodlands, tree lines in open areas, and gardens.
Similar sounding Ashy (272) and Grey (273) tits, Bush Blackcap (278), Layard's Tit-babbler (322) and Thrush Nightingale (313). May mimic some tits. Bush Blackcap sounds more bulbul-like and, like Layard's, it doesn't give *cheera-tik-tik-tik-tik* phrase. Thrush Nightingale gives deeper churring notes.

Layard's Tit-babbler   *Sylvia layardi*   Grystjeriktik

322   Track detail 0:02–0:35 (song)

Song A bubbly mix of very short, sharp whistles and rasping *tjip* sounds. Does not mimic other species.
Other sounds None.
Regional variation None.
Habitat Favours arid rocky habitat, including scrub vegetation and fynbos.

Similar sounding Ashy (272) and Grey (273) tits, Bush Blackcap (278), Chestnut-vented Tit-babbler (321) and Amethyst Sunbird (434). Take care when attempting to separate it from the two tit species. Bush Blackcap sounds far more bulbul-like. Layard's song lacks the *cheera-tik-tik-tik-tik* phrase. Superficially resembles Amethyst Sunbird, but confusion is unlikely.

TRUE WARBLERS

This group comprises a number of related genera like the rush and woodland warblers and others whose members' calls sound similar. These species are known to most birders simply as 'warblers'. Strictly speaking cisticolas and prinias are warblers, but their songs sound quite different and so, for the purposes of this book, they are dealt with separately. True warblers, as their name suggests, sing trilled, warbling notes that are often given in a hurried jumble and may or may not follow a pattern, depending on the species. Some warblers also mimic other birds. Distinguishing warblers on appearance can be tricky, so call is a particularly useful aid to identification. To learn the subtle differences in calls, refer to *LBJs Made Simple* (Struik Nature), which provides a highly detailed treatment and many more comparative tracks for this challenging group.

Common Whitethroat   *Sylvia communis*   Witkeelsanger

323 Track detail **0:02–0:22 (song*)** * Similar to subsong; supplied for comparison

Song Not heard in the region, although subsong similar (see **Other sounds**).
Other sounds In alarm gives a single, rasping, warbler-like note. Subsong given by young birds from a secluded location and comprises a protracted soft warble similar to song given by adult birds in northern hemisphere.
Regional variation None.

Habitat Dry woodlands with thickets from which to sing.
Similar sounding Garden (324) and Marsh (339) warblers. Subsong sounds very similar to the songs of these warblers and care should be taken in separating the species by ear. Also sounds more sunbird-like than Marsh Warbler.

Garden Warbler   *Sylvia borin*   Tuinsanger

324 Track detail **0:02–0:24 (song)**

Song A sustained series of full, rapid, warbling notes running into one another; has slight sunbird-like quality. Phrases separated by pauses of under a second. Does not mimic other species.
Other sounds Alarm call is a short, sharp *tik*.
Regional variation None.

Habitat Very dense vegetation in woodland habitats, on forest margins, in lush gardens and in savanna.
Similar sounding Common Whitethroat (323), Marsh Warbler (339) and Red-backed Shrike (399). Very similar to subsong of Common Whitethroat. Separated from Marsh Warbler and Red-backed Shrike by the sunbird-like quality of its song.

Broad-tailed Warbler (Fan-tailed Grassbird)
Schoenicola brevirostris   Breëstertsanger

325 Track detail **0:03–0:37 (song)**

Song A high-pitched metallic *tseep*, something like a frog or a ship's sonar.
Other sounds Typical warbler-like grating alarm calls.

Regional variation None.
Habitat Rank grass on hillsides and in drainage channels.
Similar sounding None.

Little Rush Warbler · *Bradypterus baboecala* · Kaapse Vleisanger

326 Track detail 0:02–1:17 (song)

Song A gradually accelerating series of chirps, with a distinctive tone; recalls the sound of a playing card flapping against the spokes of a bicycle wheel as it speeds up.
Other sounds Alarm call reminiscent of a cat mewing.
Regional variation None.

Habitat Reed beds along rivers and in wetlands.
Similar sounding Cape Grassbird (315) and Cape Longclaw (389). Although song is distinctive, alarm call resembles that of Cape Grassbird and song of Cape Longclaw. Hard to distinguish but may be separated on basis of preferred habitat.

Knysna Warbler · *Bradypterus sylvaticus* · Knysnaruigtesanger

327 Track detail 0:02–0:50 (song)

Song A slowly accelerating series of *cheep* notes, culminating in a metallic rattle.
Other sounds As is typical of many warblers, alarm call comprises soft grating or churring sounds.
Regional variation None.

Habitat Dense undergrowth along rivers. Will temporarily avoid an area if frost kills the undergrowth.
Similar sounding Barratt's Warbler (328) and White-bellied Sunbird (441). Rattle is preceded by a longer series of chirps than in either Barratt's Warbler or White-bellied Sunbird.

Barratt's Warbler · *Bradypterus barratti* · Ruigtesanger

328 Track detail 0:02–0:26 (song)

Song A few metallic chirps precede a long metallic rattle.
Other sounds Like other warblers, gives grating or churring sounds when alarmed.
Regional variation Uncertain. Basic song structure remains constant, but some variations observed. Variations may or may not be geographical.

Habitat Tangled undergrowth in escarpment forests and along streams.
Similar sounding Knysna Warbler (327) and White-bellied (441) and other sunbirds. Shorter introduction to metallic trill than in Knysna Warbler. Fuller and less metallic than White-bellied and other similar-sounding sunbirds.

River Warbler · *Locustella fluviatilis* · Sprinkaansanger

329 Track detail 0:02–0:23 (song)

Song A few very soft scratchy notes reminiscent of an insect buzzing or the sound of a shaken tambourine. Culminates in a metallic rattle.
Other sounds In alarm gives short, sharp, insect-like clicks.
Regional variation None.
Habitat Dense vegetation in acacia and broad-leaved woodlands.

Similar sounding White-backed Mousebird (185), White-winged Widowbird (465) and Brown-backed Honeybird (not included). Buzzing, harsh, rhythmical rattling of River Warbler separates it from these others. Buzzing resembles *zrik* of the mousebird, but warbler sings alone, not in groups. Widowbird gives shorter rattle and no introductory notes. More metallic and rhythmical than the honeybird.

113

Yellow-throated Woodland Warbler *Phylloscopus ruficapilla* Geelkeelsanger

 Track detail 0:03–0:46 (song)

Song Beautiful, high-pitched, whistled phrases, comprising a single or double note repeated after a gap of a few seconds. Typical notes include *tseep*, *tweety* and *cheeu*, among others. A **duet** has been noted, but not fully described.
Other sounds None.
Regional variation Uncertain. Some variations recorded, but none formally described.

Habitat Forests along the escarpment and in other mountainous areas.
Similar sounding African Pied Wagtail (388), Striped Pipit (396) and Golden-breasted Bunting (500). May sound similar to these species, so take care when separating them on call alone; note the tone and phrasing. Wagtail is most distinctive, with more piercing, less tuneful tone.

Willow Warbler *Phylloscopus trochilus* Hofsanger

331 **Track detail 0:39 (total length) = 0:00–0:31 (song); 0:31–0:39 (contact or alarm call)**

Song A beautiful series of soft whistles that rise and fall in pitch, but always ends lower than initial whistle.
Other sounds Contact call is a soft *tooit* sound.
Regional variation None.

Habitat Wide ranging. Includes acacia, broad-leaved and riverine woodland habitats. Avoids forests, gardens and parks.
Similar sounding None.

Olive-tree Warbler *Hippolais olivetorum* Olyfboomsanger

332 **Track detail 0:03–0:47 (song)**

Song Very full, bold and deep. Includes some grating sounds.
Other sounds When alarmed, gives the churring call typical of most warblers.
Regional variation None.
Habitat Acacia thickets in dry areas; avoids damp regions. Intolerant of habitat change; avoids degraded woodlands.

Similar sounding Great Reed Warbler (336) and Lesser Swamp Warbler (337). Great Reed Warbler sounds scratchier and lacks the churring notes. Tone superficially like that of swamp warblers like Lesser Swamp Warbler, but confusion highly unlikely. Listen carefully for the bubblier components in Olive-tree Warbler's song.

Icterine Warbler *Hippolais icterina* Spotsanger

333 **Track detail 0:02–0:27 (song)**

Song A sustained medley of typical warbler notes, as well as some short whistles reminiscent of kisses; also **mimics** other species.
Other sounds Contact call a short, sharp *tick* sound. Gives extracts of song, when alarmed.
Regional variation None.

Habitat Woodlands and riverine bush.
Similar sounding Cape Glossy (416) and Greater Blue-eared (417) starlings. Subsong given by juvenile and non-breeding starlings similar to song of Icterine Warbler, but more piercing, while being deeper, harsher and more metallic than warbler songs.

Dark-capped Yellow Warbler   *Iduna natalensis*   Geelsanger

334 Track detail 0:03–0:31 (song)

Song A short, bubbling *tiku-tiku-tree-tree-tree* phrase, given repeatedly, with many variations, and punctuated by brief pauses. Alternates rapidly between high and low notes, bringing to mind a yodel.
Other sounds When alarmed, gives the churring call typical of most warblers.
Regional variation None.

Habitat Sometimes strays into rank vegetation and forests mainly along watercourses. Avoids major rivers.
Similar sounding Greater (not included) and Lesser Swamp (337) warblers. Dark-capped Warbler's song has more piercing whistles and bubbly yodelled notes, reminiscent of a canary.

Sedge Warbler   *Acrocephalus schoenobaenus*   Europese Vleisanger

335 Track detail 0:03–1:02 (song)

Song A series of agitated scratchy notes. Phrases given repetitively and follow vague three-note pattern, but not highly structured. Also mimics other birds.
Other sounds As is usual for a warbler, gives rasping and churring sounds when alarmed.
Regional variation A migrant species; may mimic birds not occurring locally.

Habitat Favours reed beds on margins of wetlands and streams, but may stray from water, particularly on migration.
Similar sounding African (338) and Eurasian (not included) reed warblers. Sounds harsher and scratchier than African and Eurasian reed warblers and repetitive three-note song structure less clearly defined.

Great Reed Warbler   *Acrocephalus arundinaceus*   Grootrietsanger

336 Track detail 0:03–0:27 (song)

Song A typical warbler's song, but far-carrying, deeper and far scratchier than any other warbler; includes many grating sounds such as *kraak* and *keek*.
Other sounds Alarm call a harsh croak. As with song, sounds much deeper than calls of other warblers.
Regional variation None.

Habitat Prefers moist areas including reed beds, wetlands with rank vegetation, farm lands and gardens. Often found quite far from water.
Similar sounding Olive-tree Warbler (332). Olive-tree Warbler gives more churring notes and lacks the Great Reed Warbler's scratchy tone.

Lesser Swamp Warbler   *Acrocephalus gracilirostris*   Kaapse Rietsanger

337 Track detail 0:03–0:22 (song)

Song Very full, bubbly and musical, with tuneful notes and yodels including a *dzu ti-you-you* phrase.
Other sounds Loud *tjuk* notes, given both to maintain group contact and as alarm call.
Regional variation None described, but a complex and varied song.
Habitat Reed beds along margins of rivers, dams and wetlands.

Similar sounding Greater Swamp (not included), Olive-tree (332) and Dark-capped Yellow (334) warblers and Collared Sunbird (439). Softer and higher-pitched than Greater Swamp Warbler. Lacks the full churring quality of Olive-tree Warbler. Dark-capped Yellow Warbler gives more one-note piercing whistles and fewer yodelled notes. Collared Sunbird's song is higher pitched.

African Reed Warbler *Acrocephalus baeticatus*

Kleinrietsanger

338 Track detail 0:03–0:32 (song)

Song A patterned and rhythmical *chip-chip-chip turra-turra-turra dzeet dzeet dzeet*; repeats one note 3–5 times, then switches to another note. Often **mimics** other birds.
Other sounds Like other warblers, gives rasping and churring sounds when alarmed.
Regional variation A migrant species. May mimic birds not found locally.

Habitat Mainly reed beds; also rank tangled vegetation along rivers.
Similar sounding Eurasian Reed (not included) and Sedge (335) warblers. Inseparable from Eurasian Reed Warbler (a rare vagrant in our region), even on call. Less scratchy than Sedge Warbler, with more repetitive phrase structure.

Marsh Warbler *Acrocephalus palustris*

Europese Rietsanger

339 Track detail 0:02–0:32 (song*) * Mimics South African Cliff Swallow at 0:10

Song Rapid notes that run into each other, with infrequent pauses. **Mimics** other birds extensively.
Other sounds Like other warblers, gives rasping and churring sounds in alarm. Subsong similar to song, but with less mimicry.
Regional variation A migrant species. May mimic birds not present locally.

Habitat Dense tangled vegetation types, often quite far from water.
Similar sounding Garden Warbler (324), Common Whitethroat (323) and Red-backed Shrike (399). Garden Warbler sounds fuller, with more pauses, and does not mimic other species. Song lacks the deeper sunbird-like quality of the whitethroat and shrike.

CISTICOLAS AND CISTICOLA-LIKE WARBLERS

Song is crucial when identifying cisticolas and cisticola-like warblers in the field. Their songs vary, with some giving just a short repetitive note, and others giving more elaborate phrases. Generally it is the male that displays and proclaims territory. Most songs given by members of this group are unique, but there are some more challenging cases. For detailed guidance in detecting the subtle differences between similar-sounding cisticolas, refer to *Southern African LBJs Made Simple* (Struik Nature).

Ayres' (Wing-snapping) Cisticola *Cisticola ayresii*

Kleinste Klopkloppie

340 Track detail 0:03–0:31 (display song)

Song In display flight gives two-pitched *I'm Ayres Ayres Ayres Ayres* phrase; the monosyllabic lead-in is lower pitched than later notes.
Other sounds Contact and alarm calls comprise same rapid clicking heard in display flight.
Regional variation None.
Habitat Short grasslands with bare patches. (At lower altitudes, Cloud Cisticola replaces Ayres' in this habitat.)

Similar sounding Cloud (341), Zitting (342) and Desert (343) cisticolas and Neddicky (345). All four species give the clicking sound, so in isolation this is not a useful distinguishing feature. Cloud Cisticola lacks the Ayres' Cisticola's inflection, although both songs vary in pitch.

Cloud Cisticola · Cisticola textrix · Gevlekte Klopkloppie

341 Track detail 0:02–0:17 (display song)

Song Male sings 3–4 ascending single-syllable notes. May substitute a series of two or three clicks for last (highest) note. No inflection on any of the notes (unlike Ayres').
Other sounds Rapid clicking sounds given in alarm and contact situations, but no wing-snapping in song or in calls.
Regional variation None.
Habitat Short grasslands, with some bare patches.

Similar sounding Ayres' (340), Zitting (342) and Desert (343) cisticolas and Neddicky (345). Three pitch changes distinguish song from those of Desert Cisticola, which maintains a steady pitch, and Ayres', which has just two pitches. Neddicky lacks clicks characteristic of Cloud Cisticola's song. Many small cisticolas, including the Zitting and Desert cisticolas, give identical clicking alarm calls, so in isolation this is not an identifying feature.

Zitting Cisticola · Cisticola juncidis · Landeryklopkloppie

342 Track detail 0:02–0:24 (song)

Song Male emits a metallic, ringing *tink-tink-tink-tink-tink*, as part of aerial breeding display.
Other sounds Alarm and contact calls a harsh rapid *tiktiktiktik*, given repeatedly.
Regional variation None.

Habitat Grasslands, particularly longer grass.
Similar sounding Ayres' (340), Cloud (341) and Desert (343) cisticolas. Display song is unique, but *tiktiktiktik* call resembles alarm and contact calls of Ayres', Cloud and Desert cisticolas and shouldn't be used in isolation as a distinguishing feature.

Desert Cisticola · Cisticola aridulus · Woestynklopkloppie

343 Track detail 0:03–0:36 (display song)

Song Phrase comprises a series of piercing, even *tee-tee-tee-tee-tee* notes. May change pitch between phrases, but does not vary notes within a single phrase.
Other sounds Staccato notes mixed with wing clicks given as both contact and alarm call.
Regional variation None.
Habitat Dry grasslands with scattered trees and bushes.

Similar sounding Ayres' (340), Cloud (341) and Zitting (342) cisticolas and Neddicky (345). Lack of pitch changes within phrase distinguish song from those of Ayres' and Cloud cisticolas. Cloud Cisticola sometimes also replaces last note of call with clicks. Alarm call nearly identical to that of Cloud and Desert cisticolas. Neddicky has similarly staccato call, but also lacks clicks.

Pale-crowned Cisticola · Cisticola cinnamomeus · Bleekkopklopkloppie

344 Track detail 0:02–0:18 (song)

Song Gives two main phrases – a shrill but soft cricket-like *srrree-srrreee-srrreee* and a gradually descending, laughing *tsee-tsee-tsee-tsee* whistle.
Other sounds Alarm call an agitated variation of whistle in song.
Regional variation None.

Habitat Moist grasslands around rivers, pans and wetlands.
Similar sounding Orange-breasted Waxbill (481). Waxbill gives some similar-sounding notes, but they are mixed with notes not heard in cisticola's song and have a less marked cricket-like tone.

117

Neddicky · *Cisticola fulvicapilla* · Neddikie

345 Track detail 0:02–0:37 (song)

Song A staccato *stuk-stuk-stuk-stuk*, repeated for long periods, with very short pauses between phrases.
Other sounds In alarm gives rattling call and a piercing whistle.
Regional variation None.
Habitat Understorey of broad-leaved and acacia woodlands. Also occurs on forest margins and in gardens.

Similar sounding Red-crested Korhaan (89) and Ayres' (340), Cloud (341) and Desert (343) cisticolas. Piercing alarm whistle may resemble that of Red-crested Korhaan, but lacks the click in that bird's call. Song superficially resembles those of Ayres', Cloud and Desert cisticolas, but is far more staccato; only their clicking alarm or contact calls could cause confusion.

Lazy Cisticola · *Cisticola aberrans* · Luitinktinkie

346 Track detail 0:03–0:33 (song)

Song A shrill squeal, like a rubber toy being squeezed. May also include buzzing and clicking notes.
Other sounds A harsh, rasping variation of the song is given as an alarm call. Contact call is a series of soft churring sounds mixed with chip notes.
Regional variation Some variation noted in

Zimbabwe, but variation minimal in South Africa.
Habitat Rocky habitat with grass or scattered bushes.
Similar sounding Spike-heeled Lark (232) and Cape Grassbird (315). Churring contact call resembles song and calls of the Spike-heeled Lark, but in lark no chip notes punctuate the churring. The song is nearly identical to the grassbird's alarm call.

Red-faced Cisticola · *Cisticola erythrops* · Rooiwangtinktinkie

347 Track detail 0:03–0:48 (song)

Song An excited series of whistles, generally rising in pitch. Sometimes also gives a series of descending whistles.
Other sounds In alarm gives long, drawn-out, plaintive whistles similar in tone to main song.
Regional variation None.

Habitat Riverine habitats including reed beds, riverine woodlands and, sometimes, forests.
Similar sounding Burnt-necked Eremomela (319). The occasional series of descending whistles *very* similar to descending whistled song given by Burnt-necked Eremomela, but slower.

Rattling Cisticola · *Cisticola chiniana* · Bosveldtinktinkie

348 Track detail 0:03–1:23 (song)

Song Highly variable, but basic song structure comprises 2–3 nasal, piercing *tjip tjip* notes, followed by a *turaurauraura* rattle.
Other sounds When alarmed, gives harsh, agitated variation of song's introductory note, repeatedly.
Regional variation Many variations occur over short distances and even neighbouring birds may differ, but may simply have evolved to distinguish

individual birds. Familiarity with basic song structure may assist with identification.
Habitat Acacia woodlands, patches of thornveld and, occasionally, gardens.
Similar sounding Sickle-winged Chat (296). Pattern and tone are distinctive, but notes bear superficial resemblance to some sounds given by Sickle-winged Chat.

Croaking Cisticola *Cisticola natalensis* Groottinktinkie

349 Track detail 0:03–0:28 (song*)
* Note that Black-headed Oriole is also prominent in this track

Song A *tzuuur-dzip* or *dzuu prrrrrreee* phrase incorporating a range of frog-like croaks and buzzes. **Other sounds** Shorter, harsher croaks, given as alarm and contact calls.

Regional variation None.
Habitat Moist grasslands with scattered bushes, particularly around pans.
Similar sounding None.

Levaillant's Cisticola *Cisticola tinniens* Vleitinktinkie

350 Track detail 0:58 (total length) = 0:04–0:32 (contact and confrontational calls); 0:32–0:48 (song); 0:48–0:58 (alarm call)

Song A highly distinctive and easily recognised *chip-tooralooralip.* **Other sounds** An agitated *dzeee-dzeee-dzeee* given in alarm and confrontations.

Regional variation None.
Habitat Reed beds and rank grasslands. Also rank vegetation along rivers.
Similar sounding None.

Chirping Cisticola *Cisticola pipiens* Piepende Tinktinkie

351 Track detail 0:02–0:20 (song)

Song Gives 2–3 *tik* notes, followed by a cicada-like buzz. Sometimes ends off with a series of plaintive whistles. **Other sounds** A buzzing contact call, similar to song. **Regional variation** None. **Habitat** Restricted to papyrus swamps mainly in northern Botswana.

Similar sounding Gabar Goshawk (49), Wailing (353), Grey-backed (354) and Tinkling (not included) cisticolas. Plaintive whistled song phrase vaguely resembles song of Gabar Goshawk. Concluding whistle of song similar to that given by Wailing Cisticola, but descends. Most closely resembles Grey-backed Cisticola, but separated on distribution. Tinkling Cisticola's whistled phrase is agitated and piercing.

Rufous-winged Cisticola *Cisticola galactotes* Swartrugtinktinkie

352 Track detail 0:03–0:51 (song)

Song A series of closely spaced petronia-like *chip-chip-chip…* chirps. **Other sounds** Harsher rising *zweee-zweee* alarm call. Also a machine gun-like rattle. **Regional variation** None.

Habitat Reed beds and rank growth along rivers and around dams and wetlands.
Similar sounding Singing Cisticola (not included). Unlike Singing Cisticola, Rufous-winged's tone slightly reminiscent of a House Sparrow.

Wailing Cisticola *Cisticola lais*   Huiltinktinkie

353 Track detail 0:03–0:48 (song)

Song A *dze-zee whee-wheet* comprising trilled, whistling and rasping notes. Each note has upward lilt. Sometimes punctuated by a buzzing rattle.
Other sounds Contact call made up of rasping notes like those in song.
Regional variation None.
Habitat Fynbos, karoo scrub, shrub lands and, in the northeast, grassy patches in rocky areas.

Similar sounding Chirping (351), Grey-backed (354) and Tinkling (not included) cisticolas and Cinnamon-breasted Warbler (365). Chirping Cisticola more plaintive (more like Gabar Goshawk than Wailing Cisticola). Grey-backed Cisticola's phrase flatter in pitch. Tinkling Cisticola's whistled phrase is agitated and piercing. Male Cinnamon-breasted Warbler's duet very like Wailing Cisticola's song, but separated by female warbler's response.

Grey-backed Cisticola *Cisticola subruficapilla*   Grysrugtinktinkie

354 Track detail 0:03–1:29 (mixed song and alarm calls*)
＊ Listen for song phrase at 0:39

Song A bubbly, trilled whistle followed by a series of piercing *tee-tee-tee-tee* notes.
Other sounds A metallic, trilled contact call.
Regional variation None.
Habitat Fynbos, karoo scrub, shrub lands and, in the northeast of its range, grassy patches in rocky areas.
Similar sounding Chirping (351), Wailing (353) and Tinkling (not included) cisticolas and Cinnamon-

breasted Warbler (365). Chirping has the most plaintive whistled phrase (resembles Gabar Goshawk). Tinkling has an agitated and piercing whistled phrase that is faster. Whistled note in Wailing Cisticola's phrase rises more in pitch. Male Cinnamon-breasted Warbler's duet similar to song of Grey-backed Cisticola, but separated by female warbler's response.

PRINIAS AND PRINIA-LIKE WARBLERS

Birds in this group tend to find a prominent perch near the top of a bush and then cock their tails while singing energetically. Songs are simple, comprising short piercing or rasping notes. The only exception is the Namaqua Warbler, which gives longer trilled notes. Members of this group are distinguished from many similar-sized species by their small round bodies and very long tails.

Black-chested Prinia *Prinia flavicans*   Swartbandlangstertjie

355 Track detail 0:47 (total length) = 0:02–0:20 (song); 0:20–0:33 (contact call);
0:33–0:47 (alarm call)

Song Gives repetitive *dzeeeep* notes and other variations, all with a distinct buzzing tone.
Other sounds Harsh, buzzing *dzzzt dzzzt dzzzt* alarm and contact call.
Regional variation None.
Habitat Occurs in dry habitats with scattered bush, in rank vegetation and along drainage lines

in grassland and savanna habitats. Also found in uncultivated crop lands.
Similar sounding Tawny-flanked (356), Karoo (357) and Drakensberg (358) prinias. Song bears some resemblance to those of other prinias, but sounds more buzzing. Alarm notes also harsher and more buzzing. Scratchy tone makes confusion unlikely.

Tawny-flanked Prinia *Prinia subflava*   Bruinsylangstertjie

356 Track detail 0:54 (total length) = 0:03–0:35 (song); 0:35–0:54 (contact call)

Song A deliberate piercing *chip-chip-chip* or a repeated *dzeep-dzeep-dzeep*.
Other sounds Metallic and piercing *dzeet* alarm and contact calls.
Regional variation None.
Habitat Grass and bushes along streams and in clearings. Avoids dense forests.

Similar sounding Black-chested (355), Karoo (357) and Drakensberg (358) prinias and Namaqua Warbler (359). Song sounds most like that of Black-chested Prinia, but Tawny-flanked sounds more piercing and metallic than this and other prinias. Drakensberg has a far more scratchy trilled quality.

Karoo Prinia *Prinia maculosa*   Karoolangstertjie

357 Track detail 0:38 (total length) = 0:02–0:06 (contact call); 0:06–0:38 (contact call mixed with song)

Song Gives excited introductory *pree-pree-pree* phrase, followed by *dzeeep* notes like those given by other prinias.
Other sounds Alarm and contact calls comprise strange churring and buzzing.
Regional variation None.
Habitat Shrub lands of various types; also fynbos.

Similar sounding Burnt-necked (319) and Green-capped (320) eremomelas and Black-chested (355), Tawny-flanked (356) and Drakensberg (358) prinias. Resemblance to eremomelas is superficial. Song scratchier than that of Tawny-flanked and less buzzing than Black-chested. Lower pitched and scratchier than Drakensberg Prinia.

Drakensberg Prinia *Prinia hypoxantha*   Drakensberglangstertjie

358 Track detail 0:23 (total length) = 0:02–0:08 (song); 0:08–0:23 (contact calls)

Song A high-pitched *dzeep dzeep dzeep dzeep* with a piercing whistled tone.
Other sounds Scratchy, high-pitched and rapid *dzip-dzip-dzip-dzip* sounds.
Regional variation None.
Habitat Rank grass along road edges and on the escarpment; also occurs along grassy river margins.

Similar sounding Burnt-necked (319) and Green-capped (320) eremomelas and Black-chested (355), Tawny-flanked (356), Karoo (357) and most other prinias. Resemblance to eremomelas is superficial. Song and calls resemble those of other prinias, especially the Black-chested and Karoo prinias, but softer and less rasping.

Namaqua Warbler *Phragmacia substriata*   Namakwalangstertjie

359 Track detail 0:02–0:22 (song)

Song A distinctive metallic *chi-chi-chi-trrrrrrrr*.
Other sounds Contact and alarm calls comprise two-note buzzing and *chit* calls.
Regional variation None.
Habitat Found near streams in arid areas, among thick bushes and reeds.

Similar sounding Little Swift (181), Burnt-necked Eremomela (319) and Tawny-flanked Prinia (356). Not as shrill and chittering as swift. Eremomela's trills lack structured repetitive phrasing of Namaqua Warbler.

Rufous-eared Warbler *Malcorus pectoralis* Rooioorlangstertjie

360 Track detail 0:02–0:19 (song)

Song A fast *teeteeteeteeteeteetee*, with a distinctive agitated tone.
Other sounds Alarm call a drawn-out plaintive-sounding *teeeeeeeee*.
Regional variation None.
Habitat Shrub lands on plains and low slopes.

Similar sounding Drakensberg (294) and Cape (not included) rockjumpers. Bears superficial resemblance to piercing whistles of rockjumpers, but their songs are slower, less repetitive and include other sounds not heard in songs and calls of Rufous-eared Warbler.

WREN-WARBLERS

Members of this warbler group are difficult to locate, as they sing from the tree canopy or from among densely tangled vegetation. Calls and songs comprise full, rapid, trilled notes and short, sharp gurgles, generally given by male birds. Individuals seldom call in a group, since the male sings from within his own territory, some distance from the nearest other male. They are differentiated from true warblers both by their chocolate brown barred plumage and by their simple, repetitive staccato calls.

Barred Wren-Warbler *Calamonastes fasciolatus* Gebande Sanger

361 Track detail 0:03–0:32 (song)

Song Has two main songs. In spring, male gives drawn-out *terrrrrrrrrrrrr* as part of display flight. Territorial proclamation song, heard throughout summer, comprises repetitive *pree-pree-pree-pree* phrases, punctuated with brief pauses; reminiscent of a ringing telephone.
Other sounds Not yet described.

Regional variation None.
Habitat Semi-arid acacia and broad-leaved woodlands; favours areas with dense cover.
Similar sounding Stierling's Wren-Warbler (362). Territorial call fairly distinctive, although Stierling's Wren-Warbler gives similar, softer, less repetitive call.

Stierling's Wren-Warbler *Calamonastes stierlingi* Stierlingsanger

362 Track detail 0:04–0:46 (song)

Song A bubbly, repetitive *piririt-piririt-piririt* phrase, with a cartoonish galloping rhythm.
Other sounds Alarm and contact calls comprise muted *preeee* sounds and soft sheep-like bleating.
Regional variation None.
Habitat Dense thickets in broad-leaved woodlands.

Similar sounding Barred Wren-Warbler (361), Green- (363) and Grey-backed (364) camaropteras. The bubbly sound and galloping rhythm of song are distinctive, but softer contact and alarm calls may recall Barred Wren-Warbler and some camaropteras, notably the Grey-backed and Green-backed.

CAMAROPTERAS

Some authorities consider Green- and Grey-backed camaropteras to be two forms of a single species. These species or 'races' have some distinctive plumage and are thus treated separately here. Both give some high-pitched, sheep-like sounds that have earned them the name bleating-warblers. They are secretive birds and call from within dense bush.

Green-backed Camaroptera *Camaroptera brachyura* Groenrugkwêkwêvoël

363 Track detail 0:03–0:33 (song variations)

Song A repetitive staccato *krit-krit-krit* note, reminiscent of static discharge.
Other sounds Alarm call a sheep-like bleat, but higher pitched. Mimics other birds, but context and particular species mimicked not yet described.
Regional variation None.
Habitat Dense vegetation in riverine, thicket, savanna and woodland habitats. Also occurs in lush gardens.

Similar sounding Stierling's Wren-Warbler (362), Grey-backed Camaroptera (364), Bar-throated (366) and Yellow-breasted (367) apalises. Stierling's Wren-Warbler also has soft bleating alarm call. Song so similar to that of Grey-backed Camaroptera that, without viewing plumage, species only separable on distribution. Bar-throated Apalis' song sounds fuller and lacks electric clicking notes.

Grey-backed Camaroptera *Camaroptera brevicaudata* Grysrugkwêkwêvoël

364 Track detail 0:03–1:31 (song variations)

Song A repetitive, staccato, electric-sounding *krit-krit-krit* note.
Other sounds Alarm call like a high-pitched version of a sheep's bleating. Mimics other species, but context and particular species mimicked have not been described.
Regional variation None.
Habitat Dense vegetation in riverine, thicket, savanna and woodland habitats; also occurs in evergreen forests and lush gardens.

Similar sounding Stierling's Wren-Warbler (362), Green-backed Camaroptera (363), Bar-throated (366) and Yellow-breasted (367) apalises. Stierling's Wren-Warbler also gives soft bleating alarm call that is difficult to separate. Song so similar to that of Green-backed Camaroptera that without viewing plumage, species only separable on distribution. Bar-throated Apalis' song sounds fuller and lacks electric clicking notes.

CINNAMON-BREASTED WARBLER

This warbler is treated separately as its vocalisations, behaviour and habitat are quite different from those of most prinias and of other warblers. It prefers calling from dense habitat, but in arid regions will also frequent rocky areas. It sounds similar to a cisticola, which is unique for a warbler.

Cinnamon-breasted Warbler   *Euryptila subcinnamomea*   Kaneelborssanger

365 Track detail 0:02–0:32 (duet)

Song Male sings 2–3 plaintive *phwee-phwee-phwee* notes; female responds with a rising whistle. This **duet** is frequently heard.
Other sounds A clear, plaintive, gradually descending whistle given in alarm.
Regional variation None.
Habitat Bushes on rocky hillside slopes in arid areas.

Similar sounding Eastern Clapper Lark (243) and Wailing (353), Grey-backed (354) and Tinkling (not included) cisticolas. Female's rising whistle in duet similar to that of Eastern Clapper Lark, but lacks the wing rattle. Wailing, Grey-backed and Tinkling cisticolas can resemble male's part of duet, but combined sound of male and female warblers is unique.

APALISES

Apalises give simple songs and calls – often just a single, staccato, churring note given repeatedly. All apalises duet. The male sings from a secluded perch, and the female responds.

Bar-throated Apalis   *Apalis thoracica*   Bandkeelkleinjantjie

366 Track detail 0:42 (total length) = 0:02–0:21 (duet with male more prominent); 0:21–0:38 (duet with female more prominent); 0:38–0:42 (alarm call)

Song A distinctive staccato **duet**. Male sings a *tlip-tlip-tlip-tlip* phrase (sometimes also a double-note *tilip-tilip;* female responds with a rapid *titititititititititi.*
Other sounds Gives squeaky sound in alarm, or a rapid ticking call, similar to female's part in duet.
Regional variation Some song variations noted among the 13 subspecies found in the region; more variations may well be described in future.

Habitat Favours riverine and evergreen forests. Also occurs in woodlands and dense karoo scrub.
Similar sounding Green-backed (363) and Grey-backed (364) camaropteras. Lacks the electric clicking sounds given by these camaropteras.

Yellow-breasted Apalis   *Apalis flavida*   Geelborskleinjantjie

367 Track detail 0:03–0:40 (duet*) * Listen for female's scratchy note among background calls

Song Male initiates **duet** with series of churring bisyllabic *kurra-kurra-kurra* notes to which female responds with single rasping *trrrk.*
Other sounds Buzzing churring notes, given as contact and alarm calls.
Regional variation Variations in duet most likely to be pair-specific rather than geographical.

Habitat Woodlands; avoids evergreen forests.
Similar sounding Green- (363) and Grey-backed (364) camaropteras. Male's churring note is distinctive, more so when female responds with her scratchy *trrrk*. Without a responding female, song sounds similar to those of the camaropteras, but is fuller, more liquid, and lacks clicking tone.

LARGE FLYCATCHERS

A group of flycatchers referred to here as large flycatchers to differentiate them from the warbler flycatcher and the crested flycatcher (including African Paradise Flycatcher) families. Large flycatchers generally sing piercing, metallic or scratchy songs and most phrases tend not to be musical. Birds are generally solitary and sing alone. These are comparatively quiet birds that do not sing as often as other flycatcher groups.

Fiscal Flycatcher *Sigelus silens* Fiskaalvlieëvanger

368 Track detail 0:03–1:19 (song)

Song Long phrases of about 20–25 seconds each, comprising mixed shrill *tsee, seeoooo* and metallic trilling *trrrrpp* notes.
Other sounds Wheezing contact calls and short, sharp, grating alarm calls. Does **mimic**, but context for this is poorly understood.
Regional variation Mimicry will depend on species present locally. Song's variations not described.

Habitat Wide ranging, but favours open habitats with clumps of large trees. Also occurs in parks and gardens.
Similar sounding Southern Black (369) and Fairy (377) flycatchers. Resemblance superficial; phrases are far longer and more complex than any of the calls given by these two species.

Southern Black Flycatcher *Melaenornis pammelaina* Swartvlieëvanger

369 Track detail 0:03–0:32 (song)

Song A high-pitched, piercing, three-note *tsee-tsooo-tsooo* phrase, given repetitively. Descends in pitch.
Other sounds Rapid repeated phrases, similar to the *tsee* note from song, given in alarm. Some **mimicry**, but context not understood. Like most flycatchers gives settling call at dusk that is soft but grating.
Regional variation Mimicry will be influenced by local species.

Habitat Both acacia and broad-leaved woodlands. Like most flycatchers, favours a treed environment with a clear open understorey.
Similar sounding Fiscal Flycatcher (368). Gives repetitive three-note phrase and clear *tsooo* notes, whereas Fiscal's song lacks *tsooo* notes and is complex and repetitive.

Chat Flycatcher *Bradornis infuscatus* Grootvlieëvanger

370 Track detail 0:02–0:10 (song)

Song A series of slightly thrush-like, scratchy *pree-pree-pruu-pree-prruu* notes.
Other sounds Largely silent outside breeding season. Alarm and contact calls resemble main song, but more agitated.
Regional variation None.

Habitat Open areas in dry acacia savanna. Also found in karoo vegetation provided there are large bushes and trees.
Similar sounding Familiar (295) and Sickle-winged (296) chats. Difficult to separate from Familiar and Sickle-winged on call alone, although sounds more thrush-like than either of these chats.

SMALL FLYCATCHERS

These birds are grouped together primarily owing to their similar plumage, behaviour and vocalisations. All four species give high-pitched piercing alarm calls. The grey members of the group (Grey Tit-Flycatcher and Ashy Flycatcher) give simple, but musical whistled phrases, comprising a few short notes repeated in sequence. The brown members of this group (Spotted and African Dusky) give short, sharp repetitive notes and soft metallic trills.

African Dusky Flycatcher *Muscicapa adusta* Donkervlieëvanger

371 Track detail 0:03–0:21 (alarm or contact call)

Song Seldom heard. A series of about seven short, sharp, varied notes, all with the sibilant scratchy tone typical of a flycatcher.
Other sounds Two main alarm and contact sounds are more common. A high-pitched descending *tsseeep*, similar to call of a Spotted Flycatcher, and a more distinctive ratchety *tsip-ree-ree-ree*. Context for these calls unclear.

Regional variation None.
Habitat Margins of dense evergreen forests and woodlands; avoids dark forest interior. Also occurs in well-wooded parks and gardens.
Similar sounding Grey Cuckooshrike (266). The high-pitched *tsseeep* is shared by the cuckooshrike and by 30 or more species and is not distinctive; however, the four-note ratchety call is unique.

Spotted Flycatcher *Muscicapa striata* Europese Vlieëvanger

372 Track detail 0:03–0:23 (alarm call)

Song Song rarely heard, as this species does not breed in our region.
Other sounds In our region most often gives 2–3-note *tchik-tchik* in alarm, and sometimes a long high-pitched *tsseeepp*, but the latter is shared by many birds.
Regional variation None.
Habitat Acacia and broad-leaved woodlands. Favours an open understorey. Camping and picnic sites may offer prime habitat.

Similar sounding Grey Cuckooshrike (266) and Familiar Chat (295). Grey Cuckooshrike's call sounds very similar to the high-pitched whistle of a Spotted Flycatcher. Two-note alarm call slightly resembles that of Familiar Chat, but is not as full; rhythm and tone quite distinctive. However, high-pitched *tsseeepp* alarm call is not distinguishing as it is shared by many species.

Ashy Flycatcher *Muscicapa caerulescens* Blougrysvlieëvanger

373 Track detail 0:03–0:33 (song)

Song An irregular, trilled, metallic *tsip tsip tsip tsip*, very occasionally ending with a *tsiptsiptsiptsiptsiptsiptsip*. Gives slight variation in courtship display.
Other sounds A more regular series of descending staccato *whit whit whit whit* notes. Phrases comprise about four notes with a bright, almost wagtail-like tone.

Regional variation None.
Habitat Open woodlands along rivers, but also ventures into some evergreen forests and dense woodlands.
Similar sounding None.

Grey Tit-Flycatcher *Myioparus plumbeus* Waaierstertvlieëvanger

374 Track detail 0:03–0:27 (song)

Song A mournful liquid *pree-yeer*, descending on second note.
Other sounds Gives a drawn-out *yeeeeerrrrr*, but the context for this call not yet known.
Regional variation None.

Habitat Bushveld, savanna, woodlands and riverine bush.
Similar sounding Bokmakierie (411). Very superficial resemblance as its song and calls are far softer than those of Bokmakierie and it does not duet.

CRESTED FLYCATCHERS

Grouped together both taxonomically and on call, paradise and crested flycatchers give similar buzzing *dzzzeee* alarm notes and high-pitched bubbly songs. Males often accompany songs with energetic displays of their flashy tail plumes.

Blue-mantled Crested Flycatcher *Trochocercus cyanomelas*
Bloukuifvlieëvanger

375 Track detail 0:57 (total length) = 0:03–0:37 (alarm or contact call); 0:37–0:57 (song)

Song A musical *tsee-zoo-zoo-zoo-zoo-zoo* given rapidly with only brief pauses.
Other sounds A rasping nasal *dzee*, repeated at varying intervals, given both as an alarm and contact call.
Regional variation None.

Habitat A wide variety of forest types within its range.
Similar sounding African Paradise Flycatcher (376) and Orange-breasted Bushshrike (412). Alarm call similar to that of the paradise flycatcher, but lacks the two-note phrasing. Song much faster than that of Orange-breasted Bushshrike.

African Paradise Flycatcher *Terpsiphone viridis* Paradysvlieëvanger

376 Track detail 1:17 (total length) = 0:04–0:59 (alarm or contact call); 0:59–1:17 (song)

Song Bubbly whistled notes and a *zweety-zweet-zweet-zweet-zweet* phrase.
Other sounds Various scratchy alarm notes, often a bisyllabic *zee-zoo*, but phrase may include more notes.
Regional variation None.
Habitat Forests and woodlands; also common in well-wooded suburbs. May venture into exotic plantations.

Similar sounding Blue-mantled Crested Flycatcher (375). The alarm notes of African Paradise Flycatcher are very similar to those of the Blue-mantled Crested Flycatcher, but their songs are distinct.

127

FAIRY FLYCATCHERS

The Fairy Flycatcher is the only member of its genus in the world. It is a member of a larger group of genera together known as the fairy flycatchers, but this is the only member of that group to be found in our region. It is related to the penduline-tit family and does not behave like a typical flycatcher.

Fairy Flycatcher *Stenostira scita* Feevlieëvanger

377 Track detail 0:03–0:37 (song)

Song Largely silent, but in spring and summer sings clean *zee-zoo-zyeeoo-zoowee* phrase, repetitively, sometimes giving an additional scratchy *zee* note. Most phrases about four notes, separated by brief pauses, but may also double the phrase length. Sometimes punctuates song with high-pitched whistled, slurred or trilled notes.
Other sounds Contact and alarm calls include a sunbird-like *tssk-tssk-tssk-tssk* sound and similar short harsh sounds.

Regional variation Unknown. Vocalisation in this species poorly understood. Some variation likely over distance, as is typical of birds with a broad repertoire of phrases.
Habitat Spends breeding season in fynbos, karoo scrub or other arid bushy habitat. Moves into acacia woodlands and gardens in winter.
Similar sounding Fiscal Flycatcher (368). Has thinner, less piercing, almost sunbird-like tone, unlike Fiscal Flycatcher.

BATISES

All batises give clear whistled notes and some nasal buzzing alarm and contact calls. Although some unique phrases do stand out, be aware that the songs of certain species may overlap. For example, similarities in the whistling songs of Cape and Chinspot batises sometimes lead to confusion.

Cape Batis *Batis capensis* Kaapse Bosbontrokkie

378 Track detail 0:02–0:21 (song)

Song A distinctive *whee-whee-whee-whee-whee-whee* phrase given at a fairly constant pitch. Also gives varied range of whistled notes, as is typical for a batis (see **Similar sounding**) and may sometimes resemble the sounds of other batises.
Other sounds Some whistled phrases like those of Chinspot Batis given in contact and alarm. In alarm may also give the rasping *grrrr* notes typical of all batises.

Regional variation None.
Habitat Various types of forest throughout its range. Prefers woodlands in drier areas.
Similar sounding Chinspot Batis (379). The *whee-whee-whee-whee* phrase is unique, but rasping alarm and contact phrases sound similar to those of Chinspot Batis. Also gives a phrase very similar to song of Chinspot, but context of this call in Cape Batis is unclear.

Chinspot Batis *Batis molitor* Witliesbosbontrokkie

379 Track detail 0:03–1:00 (song)

Song A three-note *weep-woop-woop*. Initial note higher pitched than those that follow. May replace final *woop* with a rasping sound.
Other sounds Most alarm and contact calls are rasping or buzzing sounds.
Regional variation None.

Habitat Acacia and broad-leaved woodlands; avoids open habitat and true forests.
Similar sounding Cape Batis (378). A distinctive call, but the song sounds much like that of the Cape Batis – take care where their ranges overlap.

Pririt Batis *Batis pririt* Priritbosbontrokkie

380 Track detail 0:03–0:32 (song)

Song A series of whistles descending in pitch and slowing down. Sounds much higher pitched and more monotonous than other batises. Also gives a *zreet-zreet-zreet-zreet* courtship call.
Other sounds Rasping sounds given in alarm.

Regional variation None.
Habitat Ventures into some woodlands but prefers open acacia savanna and acacia thickets along rivers in very dry areas.
Similar sounding None.

SHRIKE AND WATTLE-EYE

Grouped together because they have a close taxonomic relationship, these species share similar short, buzzy notes, and are known for repetitive, distinctive phrasing. Identifying their songs in the field does not generally pose a problem.

White-tailed Shrike *Lanioturdus torquatus* Kortstertlaksman

381 Track detail 0:47 (total length) = 0:03–0:29 (song); 0:29–0:47 (alarm call)

Song A *grrr-reee* that is reminiscent of a small plover, but still easily identified as the song of a shrike.
Other sounds Variations of this song and harsher sounds, given as alarm and contact calls. Also faster versions of the song given when excited or agitated.

Regional variation Diversity in sounds not likely to be the result of regional variation, given small range.
Habitat Dry savanna, where it favours mopane and acacia trees.
Similar sounding None.

Black-throated Wattle-eye   *Platysteira peltata*   Beloogbosbontrokkie

382 Track detail 0:03–0:22 (alarm or contact call)

Song The main song is a repetitive rasping *choo-ee choo-ee choo-ee* sung repeatedly; a rasping *dzip dzip dzip* sometimes precedes main song.
Other sounds Similar harsh sounds given as alarm and contact calls.

Regional variation None.
Habitat Various forest types throughout its range as well as densely wooded gardens and thickets, generally close to water.
Similar sounding None.

BROADBILL

The African Broadbill is among the few species that may use mechanical sound to serve the purpose of a song, although the exact origin of this noise is not certain. Whatever its source, the sound is very distinctive.

African Broadbill   *Smithornis capensis*   Breëbek

383 Track detail 0:03–1:20 (song)

Song Male displays in tiny forest clearings, giving loud, purring rattle. Not yet known if this is a true song or a mechanical sound produced by the wing feathers.
Other sounds A long *twee-oo* given in alarm.

Regional variation None.
Habitat Forests and miombo woodlands; in winter may venture briefly out of deciduous forest habitat.
Similar sounding None.

WHITE-EYES

White-eyes give relatively similar, high-pitched twittering songs, almost like soft warbles. They also give soft, twittering contact calls. Because groups of birds are more common than pairs or lone individuals, their contact calls are heard more often than their songs.

Cape White-eye   *Zosterops capensis*   Kaapse Glasogie

384 Track detail 0:41 (total length) = 0:03–0:25 (song); 0:25–0:41 (contact call)

Song A beautiful, tuneful mix of clean whistles, rising and falling in pitch. Often mimics other birds.
Other sounds Noisy group chatter comprised of rapidly trilled *treeyyaa* contact calls.
Regional variation Mimics species present locally.
Habitat Woodland habitats, such as forests and gardens with trees.

Similar sounding Grey-backed Sparrow-Lark (255) and Orange River (385) and African Yellow (386) white-eyes. Shares some sounds with the sparrow-lark, but confusion is unlikely. Song less warbler-like and contact call faster and less bubbly than those of Orange River White-eye. Told from very similar song of African Yellow White-eye by inclusion of mimicked phrases.

130

Orange River White-eye *Zosterops pallidus* Gariepglasogie

385 Track detail 0:03–0:30 (contact calls)

Song A tuneful mix of jumbled twitters and whistles.
Other sounds Contact call is rapid and comprises short, sharp, bubbly notes.
Regional variation None.
Habitat Thornveld along rivers. Also found around large trees and in gardens.

Similar sounding Grey-backed Sparrow-Lark (255) and Cape (384) and African Yellow (386) white-eyes. Resemblance to sparrow-lark is superficial. Song is less piercing than those of Cape or African Yellow white-eyes; its muted sound is more reminiscent of a warbler. This is the only white-eye with a unique contact call

African Yellow White-eye *Zosterops senegalensis* Geelglasogie

386 Track detail 0:03–0:37 (song)

Song Gives sweet, piercing, whistled notes that rise and fall in pitch. Has slightly plaintive tone.
Other sounds Contact call a sneered *tseeyrrr*, as is typical for a white-eye.
Regional variation None.
Habitat Broad-leaved woodlands. Sometimes strays into parks and gardens.

Similar sounding Grey-backed Sparrow-Lark (255), Cape (384) and Orange River (385) white-eyes. Resemblance to sparrow-lark is superficial. Song not easily told from that of Cape White-eye, but does not include any mimicry. Told from Orange River White-eye by sneered, not trilled contact call, and piercing, plaintive, not warbler-like song.

WAGTAILS, LONGCLAWS AND PIPITS

Wagtails and pipits are quite distinct. Male wagtails sing beautiful, musical songs while prominently perched, whereas pipits generally give unremarkable sparrow-like phrases that are difficult to tell apart. Pipits also sing more frequently in the air than do wagtails. The call behaviour of the longclaws lies midway between these two groups, with most calls and songs being fairly simple, and given on the ground.

Cape Wagtail *Motacilla capensis* Gewone Kwikkie

387 Track detail 0:03–1:42 (song)

Song Jumbled sparrow-like twitters, tweets and piercing *tseep* notes. Also gives a distinctive, shrill, descending whistle.
Other sounds Simpler *teep* notes given as alarm, flight and contact calls.
Regional variation None.
Habitat Almost any habitat near water; has adapted well to lush lawns in parks and gardens.

Similar sounding Some long-billed larks, Striped Pipit (396), Collared Sunbird (439) and Cape (443), House (444) and Southern Grey-headed (446) sparrows. Jumbled twittering vaguely reminiscent of a sparrow, while descending whistle recalls a member of the long-billed lark complex, but the wagtail uniquely combines twitters and descending whistles . The resemblance to the sunbird is superficial.

African Pied Wagtail   *Motacilla aguimp*   Bontkwikkie

388   Track detail 0:03–0:38 (song)

Song A beautiful phrase made up of sweet piercing whistles, chirps and tweets, often incorporating a *teep* note. Phrase incorporates some **mimicked** phrases, lacks trilled notes and may show some variation.
Other sounds Simple *teep* notes given as alarm, flight and contact calls.
Regional variation None.

Habitat Favours margins of large rivers; also man-made habitats with water, like golf courses or gardens.
Similar sounding Yellow-throated Woodland Warbler (330), Striped Pipit (396), Yellow-fronted Canary (491) and Cape (499) and Golden-breasted (500) buntings. Wagtail gives more complex phrases than any of the similar-sounding species listed here.

Cape Longclaw   *Macronyx capensis*   Oranjekeelkalkoentjie

389   Track detail 0:03–0:30 (song)

Song Cat-like *meeuww* given from a perch or in flight.
Other sounds When alarmed takes off with rapid *di-rit* and a single plaintive whistle.
Regional variation None.
Habitat Short grass in grasslands, along vlei margins and on ploughed fields.

Similar sounding Ant-eating Chat (299), Arnot's Chat (300), Little Rush Warbler (326) and Long-tailed Widowbird (463). Shares high-pitched whistle with the Ant-eating Chat. The cat-like *meeuww* song sounds very like the alarm calls of many other species, particularly those listed here. Preferred habitat helps to separate.

Yellow-throated Longclaw   *Macronyx croceus*   Geelkeelkalkoentjie

390   Track detail 0:03–0:38 (song)

Song A plaintive *choo-weeya-chooo* with a distinctly trilled quality.
Other sounds A rapidly sounded *titititititi* alarm call.

Regional variation None.
Habitat Scattered bush at the margins of wetlands or within short grasslands.
Similar sounding None.

Plain-backed Pipit   *Anthus leucophrys*   Donkerkoester

391   Track detail 0:02–0:46 (song)

Song A *zeea-treeu-preeu*, with a high first note, descending second note, and slightly higher third note. Final note has sparrow-like quality.
Other sounds A two-note *zee-zeeeoot*, given both as flight and alarm calls.
Regional variation None.

Habitat Sandy or burnt areas in very short grasslands.
Similar sounding Long-billed (395) and other pipits, including Kimberley, Wood and Buffy pipits (not included). Very similar to these other pipits, so take extra care when trying to separate these species by ear.

African Rock Pipit   *Anthus crenatus*   Klipkoester

392 Track detail 0:03–0:46 (song)

Song A shrill descending whistle often followed by a single or double-note trill, like a sound effect in an electronic game.
Other sounds None.

Regional variation Some regional variation noted in pitch and phrasing, but details of variation unclear.
Habitat Rocky outcrops above 1 000 m.
Similar sounding None.

African Pipit   *Anthus cinnamomeus*   Gewone Koester

393 Track detail 0:48 (total length) = 0:03–0:40 (song*); 0:40–0:48 (flight call)
          * Listen for flourish at 0:35

Song In display, gives sequence of *chit* notes, starting with two and adding another at the end of each phrase, with a long final flourish.
Other sounds Gives typical pipit's *ti-chik* in flight and when alarmed.
Regional variation None.

Habitat Grasslands and savanna, usually near water. Prefers areas of short or burnt grass, below 2 000 m.
Similar sounding Mountain Pipit (394) and Yellow-throated Petronia (445). Mountain Pipit's call does not follow the same structured pattern. Song is superficially like the display song of the petronia.

Mountain Pipit   *Anthus hoeschi*   Bergkoester

394 Track detail 0:27 (total length) = 0:02–0:20 (song); 0:20–0:27 (flight call)

Song In aerial display, gives series of widely spaced *chirit* notes with brief pauses and a flurry at the end.
Other sounds Flight and alarm calls comprise a *ti-chik*, as is usual for a pipit.
Regional variation None.

Habitat Montane grasslands above 2 000 m.
Similar sounding African Pipit (393). Bears a superficial resemblance to African Pipit, but single notes in phrase more widely spaced.

Long-billed Pipit   *Anthus similis*   Nicholsonkoester

395 Track detail 0:02–0:14 (song)

Song A series of single-note sparrow-like chirps, descending in pitch.
Other sounds As is typical for a pipit, gives a *ti-chik* call in flight and when alarmed.
Regional variation None.

Habitat Rock-strewn slopes in dry and grassy areas. Also occurs in most types of woodland habitat.
Similar sounding Plain-backed (391) and Kimberley, Wood, and Buffy (not included) pipits. Sounds less monotonous than these other pipits

Striped Pipit   *Anthus lineiventris*

Gestreepte Koester

396 Track detail 0:03–0:21 (song)

Song Vocal only in breeding season, when it gives beautiful, tuneful, wagtail-like song with some trilled notes. Phrases vary.
Other sounds None.
Regional variation Song varies widely.
Habitat Rocky areas with broad-leaved woodlands.

Similar sounding Yellow-throated Woodland Warbler (330), Cape (387) and African Pied (388) wagtails, Cape (499) and Golden-breasted (500) buntings. Difficult to distinguish from the species listed here, although the trilled notes are helpful in distinguishing the song from that of the Cape Wagtail.

SHRIKES AND FISCALS

The songs and calls of shrikes and fiscals are usually fairly complex, incorporating trilled, scratchy and squeaky notes. Typically they are easy to identify by their high-pitched and harsh tone. However, the Red-backed Shrike's song is more melodious and recalls that of a warbler.

Magpie Shrike   *Corvinella melanoleuca*

Langstertlaksman

397 Track detail 0:35 (total length) = 0:03–0:13 (song); 0:13–0:35 (alarm call)

Song Male gives a 2–3-note *tsee-leeoooo*. Female may respond with similar but higher-pitched note.
Other sounds Gives a distinctive scratchy *dzzreeeeoo* when alarmed.

Regional variation None.
Habitat Mainly open acacia savanna, but sometimes also found in parks and gardens.
Similar sounding Red-necked Falcon (55). Superficially resembles this falcon's song.

Southern White-crowned Shrike   *Eurocephalus anguitimens*
Kremetartlaksman

398 Track detail 0:04–0:47 (group contact calls)

Song Unknown.
Other sounds Group contact calls consist of nasal scratchy *dzee* notes, used to keep the group together.
Regional variation None.
Habitat Favours broad-leaved woodlands, but sometimes also occurs in acacia woodlands.

Similar sounding Acacia Pied Barbet (217), Red-throated Wryneck (229), Terrestrial Brownbul (279) and Yellow-bellied Greenbul (284). Calls are higher, quieter, thinner and more nasal than those of the barbet or wryneck. Terrestrial Brownbul sounds lower pitched and more churring. Yellow-bellied Greenbul sounds significantly more nasal and sneering.

Red-backed Shrike *Lanius collurio*   Rooiruglaksman

399 Track detail 0:02–0:15 (alarm call)

Song Gives warbler-like, jumbled, musical notes.
Heard only briefly towards end of summer, when the
shrike prepares to return to Europe.
Other sounds Alarm call a scratchy *tik-tik-tik*, as
is typical for a shrike.
Regional variation None.
Habitat Open, arid, acacia savanna. Females prefer
denser habitat than males.

Similar sounding Garden (324) and Marsh (339)
warblers, Lesser Grey Shrike (400) and Common Fiscal
(401). Song difficult to separate from those of these
warblers, but sounds slightly scratchier. Alarm call
similar to that of Lesser Grey Shrike, but a bit harsher
and more staccato. Common Fiscal sounds louder
and scratchier, with a less warbler-like tone.

Lesser Grey Shrike *Lanius minor*   Gryslaksman

400 Track detail 0:02–0:27 (alarm call)

Song Not heard in our region.
Other sounds A scratchy *tik-tik-tik* alarm call,
as is usual for a shrike.
Regional variation None.

Habitat Mainly open savanna. Avoids woodlands
as it needs open space with suitable perches from
which to scan and hunt for prey.
Similar sounding Red-backed Shrike (399) and
Common Fiscal (401). Lesser Grey's harsh, piercing
alarm call separates these species.

Common Fiscal *Lanius collaris*   Fiskaallaksman

401 Track detail 0:03–0:31 (song)

Song Jumbled scratchy noises typical of a shrike.
Has warbler-like feel, but more piercing. Known to
mimic many other birds.
Other sounds A long, grating *kherr-kherr kherr* given
in aggressive interactions and when alarmed.
Regional variation None.

Habitat Woodlands, grasslands and arid areas;
requires scattered perches from which to hunt.
Similar sounding Red-backed (399) and Lesser Grey
(400) shrikes. Song easily told from those of shrikes
by scratchy notes and inclusion of mimicked phrases.
Alarm call also longer and more grating than staccato
alarm notes of Red-backed and Lesser Grey shrikes.

HELMETSHRIKES

As a family, helmetshrikes are easily distinguished from shrikes and fiscals by their gregarious nature. They also move around in small groups, are more secretive and nomadic, and their songs and calls comprise strange squeaking or churring sounds.

White-crested Helmetshrike *Prionops plumatus* Withelmlaksman

 Track detail 0:03–0:35 (group song)

Song A mix of bill clicks and electric *zree-yow* notes, given by groups of birds.
Other sounds Contact call a rasping shrill *treeeuu*, given by individual birds when the family group is relocating.

Regional variation None.
Habitat Breeds in broad-leaved woodlands. Out of breeding season ranges further into acacia woodlands and even gardens.
Similar sounding None.

BRUBRU AND PUFFBACK

A small group of shrike-like birds whose vocalisations have two main features: their calls are trilled and piercing, and both species are known to duet.

Brubru *Nilaus afer* Bontroklaksman

 Track detail 0:02–0:36 duet (male with very distant female)

Song One or two lead-in *ti-brrrruuuuu* or *whi-ti-bruuuuuu* sounds often precede a drawn-out, liquid *pur*. Female sometimes **duets** with male, giving similar sounds.
Other sounds Nasal rasping and a piercing *titititititiiti* given both as alarm and contact calls.

Regional variation None.
Habitat Acacia, savanna and broad-leaved woodlands.
Similar sounding Olive Bushshrike (415). Drawn-out piercing *brrrrruuuuuuu* bears superficial resemblance to *prrrrrr* of the bushshrike, but distinctive enough not to be confused.

Black-backed Puffback *Dryoscopus cubla* Sneeubal

 Track detail 0:31 (total length) = 0:02–0:20 (song); 0:20–0:31 (alarm call)

Song A variety of click-and-whistle songs, of which *tik-wheeuu* is most often heard; frequently **duets** with a female.
Other sounds Alarm and contact calls comprise nasal rasping, clicking and whistled sounds.
Regional variation Some variations in phrasing and dialect have been described, which may suggest

the existence of different races or subspecies, or even that the species should be split. Further investigation is warranted.
Habitat Favours dense woodlands, riverine forests and forest margins.
Similar sounding None.

BOUBOUS AND CRIMSON-BREASTED SHRIKE

Boubous and the Crimson-breasted Shrike have similar plumage – with uniform underparts, black upperparts and a white bar in the folded wing. They also display similarly shy behaviour and require the same type of habitat. Most notably, they all duet with a similar call and response (synchronised duetting) style, and all give similarly nasal, buzzy and rasping song phrases.

Southern Boubou *Laniarius ferrugineus*

Suidelike Waterfiskaal

405 Track detail 0:41 (total length) = 0:02–0:22 (duet with distant female); 0:22–0:41 (song variations)

Song Highly variable **duet** in which the male sings whistled notes and the female responds with lower-pitched notes, somewhat like those of the Grey-headed Bushshrike.
Other sounds A broad range of whistles, hoots and rasps that are not easily told from the sounds made by other boubou species.
Regional variation A wide variety of sounds have been described and may be regional dialects or reflect the existence of races within the species.
Habitat Areas of dense bush in acacia thickets or woodlands, well-wooded gardens or in riverine vegetation, among others.

Similar sounding Tropical Boubou (406), Swamp Boubou (407), Crimson-breasted Shrike (408) and Grey-headed Bushshrike (414). The duet consists only of whistled notes, where Tropical Boubou duets with two rasping notes from male and lower rasping note from the female. Likewise, Swamp Boubou male gives one rasping note and female a lower-pitched, chittering, rasping note. Crimson-breasted Shrike also duets with a short, sharp *quip* from the male, a low-pitched rasping note from the female and a double-note *quip* from the male. The female Southern Boubou's note alone may resemble song of Grey-headed Bushshrike.

Tropical Boubou *Laniarius aethiopicus*

Tropiese Waterfiskaal

406 Track detail 1:00 (total length) = 0:03–0:37 (duet); 0:37–1:00 (song variations)

Song Male sings two grating *gherr* notes to which female responds with lower-pitched rasping *ghaaarr*. Territorial males do not react to **duet** playback, since they do not view paired birds as a threat, but playing just the male's part of the duet elicits aggression.
Other sounds A broad range of whistles, hoots and rasps that are not easily distinguished from the sounds of other boubous.
Regional variation A wide variety of sounds have been described, which may be geographical dialects or suggest the existence of different races within the species.

Habitat Various dense habitats. Favours miombo woodlands, riverine bush and well-wooded gardens.
Similar sounding Southern Boubou (405), Swamp Boubou (407) and Crimson-breasted Shrike (408). Duet told from that of Southern Boubou by rasping, not whistled, notes. Male Swamp Boubou sounds identical to male Tropical Boubou, but the pair duet is easily distinguished by the female Tropical Boubou's low-pitched rasping chitter. Tropical Boubou does not give short, sharp *quip* notes heard in Crimson-breasted Shrike's duet.

Swamp Boubou *Laniarius bicolor* Moeraswaterfiskaal

 Track detail 0:02–0:12 (duet)

Song Male initiates duet with a rasping whistled *ghaarrr*; female responds with a chittering *grr-grr-grr-grr-grr*.

Other sounds A wide range of whistles, hoots and rasps that are not easily told from the sounds made by other boubou species.

Regional variation Unknown, but variation unlikely in southern Africa, owing to limited distribution within region. Some regional variations almost certain across wider African range.

Habitat Restricted to dense thickets along rivers and around wetlands in the Okavango and northern Botswana region.

Similar sounding Southern Boubou (405), Tropical Boubou (406) and Crimson-breasted Shrike (408). Tropical Boubou duet comprises male's two-note rasping sound split by female's lower-pitched grating sounds, whereas Swamp Boubou's duet is a call-and-response. Female Southern Boubou's duet response comprises whistles of a lower pitch, not chittering. Crimson-breasted Shrike's duet comprises a *quip* from the male, a low-pitched rasping note from the female, and a double note from the male, whereas female Swamp Boubou does not interrupt male's part of duet.

Crimson-breasted Shrike *Laniarius atrococcineus* Rooiborslaksman

 Track detail 0:55 (total length) = 0:03–0:37 (duet); 0:37–0:55 (alarm call)

Song Taxonomically a boubou (not a shrike) and pairs therefore duet like boubous. Male initiates with a single sharp *dzoot* note. Female responds with lower-pitched *dzoo-doola*, and male concludes with another *dzoot* note.

Other sounds Short, sharp *quip* notes and boubou-like grating notes are also given.

Regional variation A wide range of vocalisations have been noted, but these may not be linked to location.

Habitat Acacia woodlands and savanna, as well as semi-arid areas with bushes.

Similar sounding Southern (405), Tropical (406) and Swamp (407) boubous. Swamp Boubou's duet comprises male's rasping whistle and female's chittering response. Tropical Boubou's duet similar in that female's song interrupts male's part, but he initiates with two-note rasping (not single sharp *dzoot*). Southern Boubou female response made up of whistles of variable pitches, not low-pitched rasping.

TCHAGRAS

Tchagras give a wide range of strong piercing whistles. Some tchagra species duet; others sing during aerial displays. Their songs are distinctive within the region.

Brown-crowned Tchagra *Tchagra australis*   Rooivlerktjagra

 409 Track detail 0:03–0:25 (display song)

Song In display, male flicks wings softly on takeoff, then drops into a bush uttering rapid *tiru-tiru-tiru-tiru-tiru-tiru* whistles that grow louder and deeper.
Other sounds Pair interaction sounds and alarm sounds include a nasal *ne-zerrrr* and other typical shrike-like clicks and hisses.

Regional variation None.
Habitat Much like Black-crowned Tchagra, prefers closed acacia woodlands, broad-leaved woodlands and forest margins.
Similar sounding None.

Black-crowned Tchagra *Tchagra senegalus*   Swartkroontjagra

410 Track detail 0:04–2:30 (duet)

Song Comprises a **duet** in which male gives floating whistled *zoo-dee-doo zoo-ee-doo* several times, rising and falling in pitch. This beautiful piercing song is preceded by a soft, rattling introduction, heard only at close range. Female responds with harsh vibrating notes.
Other sounds Excited versions of the bubbly whistled call given in territorial agression; rattles when alarmed.

Regional variation Some variations in the male's whistled phrase, but always recognisable as a Black-crowned Tchagra.
Habitat Acacia and broad-leaved woodlands; sometimes enters gardens.
Similar sounding None.

BUSHSHRIKES AND BOKMAKIERIE

Colourful and musical, the bushshrikes give easily recognisable strong, piercing, whistled phrases. All are secretive birds and although vocal, are rather difficult to spot. The Bokmakierie is the only bushshrike known to duet.

Bokmakierie *Telophorus zeylonus*   Bokmakierie

411 Track detail 0:36 (total length) = 0:03–0:13 (song variations); 0:13–0:36 (duet variations)

Song Highly variable, as is the **duet**, which often includes a *bok-bok-bok* phrase that gives this species its common name. Duet repertoire may include trills, rapid piercing whistles and grating sounds.
Other sounds When alarmed, gives some of the grating notes from its song.
Regional variation Great variation in phrasing, both locally and regionally, as is typical of bushshrikes.

Habitat One of the few bushshrikes to favour open areas. Found in karoo scrub, fynbos and grasslands with scattered trees and bushes.
Similar sounding Olive Bushshrike (415) and Grey Tit-Flycatcher (374). Olive Bushshrike and Grey Tit-Flycatcher sound similar to Bokmakierie, but neither duets, and Grey Tit-Flycatcher's song is more timid. Bokmakierie is only bushshrike that duets.

139

Orange-breasted Bushshrike *Chlorophoneus sulfureopectus*
Oranjeborslaksman

 Track detail 0:03–0:29 (two song variations)

Song A wide range of rapidly repeated piercing whistles, often with a single, higher-pitched, lead-in *dee-do-do-do-do-do*.
Other sounds Harsh shrike-like sounds given in alarm and confrontation.
Regional variation Much variation in the phrasing, locally and regionally, as is typical of bushshrikes.

Habitat Most often found in dense bush along rivers or near to water, but also occurs in dense acacia and broad-leaved woodlands.
Similar sounding Blue-mantled Crested Flycatcher (375). Song bears some resemblance to song of Blue-mantled Crested Flycatcher, but is much fuller and deeper. Song is unique among bushshrikes.

Gorgeous Bushshrike *Chlorophoneus viridis*   Konkoit

 Track detail 0:03–0:31 (song)

Song Many variations of *kon-koweet-koweet* or *koweet-koweet* (hence its Afrikaans common name).
Other sounds Harsh grating and hissing, given as alarm and contact calls. Male's calls are more tuneful than those of the female.
Regional variation Many variations across the range, but always with the same basic song structure.

Habitat Restricted to dense growth, for example in well-wooded areas along rivers, along forest margins and in coastal forest.
Similar sounding None.

Grey-headed Bushshrike *Malaconotus blanchoti*   Spookvoël

Track detail 0:03–0:27 (song)

Song Distinctive hooting as well as a ghostly *ooooooooooooooopp*.
Other sounds Bill clicking, followed by a short descending *piuuu* and two-note *ooooooooooooooopp-grr* variations on the ghostly *ooooooooooooooopp* sound. Also an eerie grating *geeerrrrr*.
Regional variation Some variations, but the differences are not marked as the song structure is very simple.

Habitat Well-established acacia and broad-leaved woodlands and well-wooded suburbs. Avoids true forests.
Similar sounding Southern Boubou (405). The eerie *ooooooooooopp* is unique, but beware of confusion with the song of a lone female Southern Boubou. Without the male's response her call sounds similar to that of Grey-headed Bushshrike, but shorter and less eerie.

Olive Bushshrike *Chlorophoneus olivaceus* Olyfboslaksman

415 Track detail 1:38 (total length)= 0:02–1:32 (song variations); 1:33–1:38 (alarm call)

Song A wide range of songs, including a piercing *ti-tiu-tiu-tiu-tiu*, a ringing rapidly repeated *tutututututututu* and a rolling *prrrrrrrrr*.
Other sounds Faster variants of main songs, given in territorial and alarm situations.
Regional variation Many variations throughout the region, as is typical of a bushshrike.

Habitat Forests and forested patches; sometimes also in heavily wooded ravines and along escarpments.
Similar sounding Brubru (403) and Bokmakierie (411). Easy to identify song as that of a bushshrike. The *prrrrrr* call is somewhat reminiscent of a Brubru, but fuller and less harsh. Superficially like song of Bokmakierie, but unlike that species it does not duet.

STARLINGS AND MYNAS

Sounds vary widely among starlings and mynas. Most starlings give warbler-like trills and whistles, but with a deeper, fuller, less piercing sound. They seldom if ever mimic other birds. The Common Myna is unique in the group. It has a very wide repertoire, a highly distinctive tone and the ability to mimic a broad range of sounds. Captive mynas have even been trained to mimic human speech. Starlings and mynas sing from exposed perches and group chatter is common.

Cape Glossy Starling *Lamprotornis nitens* Kleinglansspreeu

416 Track detail 0:03–0:39 (contact call)

Song Soft, sustained warbles, trills and scratchy notes.
Other sounds Contact and flight calls consist of a soft *spree-reeu*. When mobbing predators, sometimes imitates Dark-capped Bulbul's alarm calls, but is not a recognised mimic.
Regional variation None.

Habitat Trees in savanna, riverine bush, parks, gardens and even plantations.
Similar sounding Icterine Warbler (333), Red-winged (423) and Pale-winged (424) starlings. The song is hard to separate from those of the species listed here, but Cape Glossy is told apart by its *spree-reeu* contact call.

Greater Blue-eared Starling *Lamprotornis chalybaeus* Groot-blouoorglansspreeu

417 Track detail 0:03–0:35 (song)

Song Like other starlings gives sustained trilled and warbled notes, but includes some strikingly scratchy, nasal and sneering sounds.
Other sounds Alarm and contact calls like nasal sneer in song, but longer.
Regional variation None.

Habitat Broad-leaved and acacia woodlands. Prefers established undergrowth.
Similar sounding Icterine Warbler (333) and Common Myna (426). Superficially like Icterine Warbler, but more sneering; warbler lacks the starling's tone. Song also has vaguely myna-like quality, but again the nasal sneer is distinctive.

Black-bellied Starling *Notopholia corruscus* Swartpensglansspreeu

 Track detail 0:03–0:40 (song*)
* Listen for mimicry of Black-backed Puffback

Song A harsh series of warbles, trills and piercing whistles. Song, while still recognisably that of a starling, has thrush-like feel. Unlike other indigenous starlings **mimics** a number of bird species.
Other sounds Unknown. Although no other sounds described, presumably gives contact and alarm calls.

Regional variation Mimicry varies according to species present locally.
Habitat Dense coastal forests and bush. Also well-wooded coastal gardens.
Similar sounding None.

Meves's Starling *Lamprotornis mevesii* Langstertglansspreeu

 Track detail 0:03–0:34 (song)

Song A series of churring and nasal sneers. Some notes have parrot-like tone.
Other sounds Gives variations of nasal sneer from song as alarm and contact calls.
Regional variation None.

Habitat Open areas with tall trees, including both broad-leaved and acacia woodlands.
Similar sounding Burchell's Starling (420). Song more parrot-like and not as harsh as song of Burchell's.

Burchell's Starling *Lamprotornis australis* Grootglansspreeu

420 **Track detail** 0:03–0:27 (song)

Song A harsh, scratchy, vibrating song. Easily recognised by its very grating tone and vaguely parrot-like feel.
Other sounds Gives screechy extracts of main song as both alarm and contact calls.

Regional variation None.
Habitat Acacia woodland and savanna. Avoids broad-leaved woodlands and very open habitats.
Similar sounding Meves's Starling (419). Song harsher than, and not quite as parrot-like as that of Meves's.

Pied Starling *Lamprotornis bicolor* Witgatspreeu

421 **Track detail** 0:02–0:10 (song)

Song A loud, nasal *wheek* note, repeated several times, with a distinctive, easily recognised tone.
Other sounds Variations of the main song given in alarm and contact situations.

Regional variation None.
Habitat Mainly a grassland species, but may venture into parks, golf courses and rural settlements.
Similar sounding None.

Violet-backed Starling *Cinnyricinclus leucogaster* — Witborsspreeu

422 Track detail 0:03–0:15 (song*) * Note dual use of syrinx throughout

Song Gives some typical starling's notes and a rising three-note whistled phrase. Phrases are strangely discordant, owing to dual use of the syrinx, which allows this bird to sing unique odd harmonics simultaneously.

Other sounds Gives variations of the discordant whistle to maintain group contact.
Regional variation None.
Habitat Savanna woodlands and riverine forests. Also regularly found in mopane woodlands.
Similar sounding None.

Red-winged Starling *Onychognathus morio* — Rooivlerkspreeu

423 Track detail 0:03–0:28 (contact call)

Song A rambling series of warbles, whistles and metallic trills, with an overall soft feel to the song.
Other sounds A range of one- and two-note descending whistles, given in flight and in contact situations.
Regional variation None.
Habitat Rocky areas, as it nests on hills and cliffs. Also ventures into urban settlements where tall buildings provide nesting sites.

Similar sounding Steppe (44) and Forest (45) buzzards and Cape Glossy (416) and Pale-winged (424) starlings. Descending whistle superficially resembles calls of Steppe and Forest buzzards. Song is difficult to separate from those of Cape Glossy or Pale-winged starlings and their ranges overlap, but their contact calls differ.

Pale-winged Starling *Onychognathus nabouroup* — Bleekvlerkspreeu

424 Track detail 0:03–0:21 (song)

Song A series of rambling whistles and metallic notes as well as some trills and squeaks.
Other sounds Gives descending *preeeuuuu* whistle in flight.
Regional variation None.
Habitat Rocky hills, valleys and surrounding habitats.

Similar sounding Steppe Buzzard (44) and Cape Glossy (416) and Red-winged (423) starlings. Descending whistle resembles that of Steppe Buzzard, but more piercing. Song is very hard to separate from those of Cape Glossy or Red-winged starlings, but their contact calls differ.

Wattled Starling *Creatophora cinerea* — Lelspreeu

425 Track detail 0:03–0:34 (group song)

Song A soft, rasping, almost wheezing song with some distinctive, piercing, metallic trills. Phrases may last 15 seconds or more.
Other sounds A very metallic squeak given as alarm and flight calls. Group chatter similar to main song.
Regional variation None.

Habitat Open and lightly treed habitat, crop lands and gardens.
Similar sounding Common Starling (427) and Cape Weaver (452). Lacks the shrill squeaky sounds of Common Starling. Chatters like Cape Weaver, but still quite clearly identifiable as a starling.

143

INVASIVE MYNAS AND STARLINGS

The Common Myna and the Common Starling, although both members of the previous family, are in fact invasive alien species. Both birds give complex songs and calls and both are mimics.

Common Myna *Acridotheres tristis* Indiese Spreeu

426 Track detail 0:03–0:39 (song)

Song Highly distinctive, loud, clear *tiirrr-trrruup-trruup-trruup*. This skilful **mimic** can imitate many sounds including those of birds, mammals, insects and humans.
Other sounds Difficult to differentiate song from other sounds, owing to very large call repertoire. Sounds similar to those in main song presumably given in wide range of situations.

Regional variation Mimicry varies according to species present locally.
Habitat An introduced species and usually associated with humans, but may venture slightly into habitats adjoining both rural and urban settlements.
Similar sounding Greater Blue-eared Starling (417). Gives fewer sneered notes than this starling.

Common Starling *Sturnus vulgaris* Europese Spreeu

427 Track detail 0:03–0:35 (song)

Song Highly distinctive. Chattering and scratchy, with some mimicry of other species. Includes a unique rising and falling see-saw whistle that is generally very high pitched.
Other sounds A wide range of very high-pitched sounds given in alarm and to maintain group contact.

Regional variation Mimics local species.
Habitat Closely associated with human settlements.
Similar sounding Wattled Starling (425). Sounds more metallic and chattering and less weaver-like than Wattled Starling. See-saw whistles vaguely reminiscent of a long-billed lark, but unique when mixed with group chatter.

OXPECKERS

There are two species of oxpecker, of which the Red-billed is more often encountered. These species' songs and calls sound identical and incorporate rudimentary hisses and scratchy sounds. Both may include soft trills and whistles in their songs, but this is rare.

Red-billed Oxpecker *Buphagus erythrorhynchus* Rooibekrenostervoël

428 Track detail 0:03–1:03 (contact or alarm calls)

Song Seldom heard. A *tzeep tzeep dzrrrrrr* comprising soft hisses and trilled whistles.
Other sounds Alarm and contact calls consist of grating and cackling sounds, with occasional hisses.
Regional variation None.

Habitat Open savanna, where it is almost always associated with large ungulates.
Similar sounding Yellow-billed Oxpecker (not included). The oxpeckers cannot be separated on song or call as they give identical hissing notes.

SUGARBIRDS AND SUNBIRDS

Sugarbirds sing muted, jumbled phrases with a few scratchy notes, while sunbirds are known for the beautiful, metallic, high-pitched songs that males give while prominently perched. These songs are heard regularly in summer, but less often in winter. They consist of fast trills and whistles that have an almost warbler-like quality. While in some sunbirds the song phrases are short and distinctive, in others they are more jumbled and sustained. However, the very high-pitched metallic tone is what identifies their calls and it is relatively easy to distinguish between sugarbirds and sunbirds.

Cape Sugarbird *Promerops cafer*   Kaapse Suikervoël

429 Track detail 0:03–0:23 (song)

Song A slow jumbled phrase of about six scratchy nasal notes that descend, then ascend. Phrases are punctuated by long pauses.
Other sounds A harsh, hissing, scratchy note given as alarm and contact calls.
Regional variation None.

Habitat Stands of proteas on mountain slopes. May venture into gardens adjoining suitable habitat.
Similar sounding Gurney's Sugarbird (430). These sugarbirds have the same distinctive tone, but Gurney's sings faster.

Gurney's Sugarbird *Promerops gurneyi*   Rooiborssuikervoël

430 Track detail 0:03–0:29 (song)

Song Rapid jumbled phrases consisting of about six scratchy nasal notes that drop, then rise in pitch. Short pauses punctuate the phrases. The tone is typical for a sugarbird.
Other sounds A harsh, hissing, scratchy note given in alarm and contact situations.
Regional variation None.

Habitat Primarily montane slopes with protea stands but may venture into gardens adjoining suitable habitat.
Similar sounding Cape Sugarbird (429). These sugarbirds have the same distinctive tone, but Gurney's sings faster.

Malachite Sunbird *Nectarinia famosa*   Jangroentjie

431 Track detail 0:03–0:49 (song)

Song Short phrases comprising a few metallic *tseep* notes, followed by a slightly faster series of jumbled notes. Brief pauses punctuate the phrases. Tone reminiscent of a weaver.
Other sounds Alarm and contact calls are typical for a sunbird, featuring short, sharp, harsh, metallic chirps.

Regional variation None.
Habitat Wide ranging. Occurs among bushes on hillsides and in montane grasslands, in fynbos, arid scrub and even in parks and gardens.
Similar sounding Southern Masked Weaver (455). Song's tone recalls that of this weaver, but confusion is unlikely.

Orange-breasted Sunbird *Anthobaphes violacea* Oranjeborssuikerbekkie

432 Track detail 0:03–0:27 (song*)
* Listen for mimicry of Cape Robin-Chat

Song Male gives beautiful soft warbling reminiscent of a warbler, but higher pitched and more metallic. Juvenile subsong includes some mimicry.
Other sounds Both sexes give a fairly distinctive sunbird-like *tseeep* as alarm and contact calls.
Regional variation None.
Habitat Occurs almost exclusively in fynbos, but may occasionally venture into parks and gardens within this habitat.

Similar sounding Marico (438) and Dusky (442) sunbirds. Warbling song includes some mimicry that sets it apart from all other sunbirds, except Marico, which also mimics, but tends to sing in shorter phrases. Superficial resemblance to Dusky Sunbird, but mimicry separates them.

Scarlet-chested Sunbird *Chalcomitra senegalensis* Rooiborssuikerbekkie

433 Track detail 0:03–0:32 (song)

Song A series of short piercing whistles with a typical sunbird's tone, but slightly fuller, like a fast version of the Southern Grey-headed Sparrow's song. Most often gives three notes, with the second note pitched lowest.
Other sounds Alarm and contact calls comprise short, sharp, harsh, metallic chirps, as is typical of a sunbird.
Regional variation None.

Habitat Wide-ranging. Occurs in open savanna, broad-leaved and acacia woodlands as well as parks and gardens.
Similar sounding Amethyst Sunbird (434) and Southern Grey-headed Sparrow (446). Amethyst Sunbird sometimes give series of single whistles with a similar tone to those of Scarlet-chested, but the phrasing differs. Southern Grey-headed Sparrow's song is lower pitched with a more typical sparrow's chirp and slower phrasing.

Amethyst Sunbird *Chalcomitra amethystina* Swartsuikerbekkie

434 Track detail 0:43 (total length) = 0:03–0:24 (song); 0:24–0:44 (contact call)

Song Continuous twitterings with very few pauses. Has a canary- or warbler-like tone.
Other sounds Alarm and contact calls comprise a short, sharp, metallic *tjip* note that is shared by other sunbirds, but heard most often in this species.
Regional variation None.
Habitat Open woodlands and gardens. Targets flowering aloes for their nectar in spring and summer. Avoids closed habitats.

Similar sounding Layard's Tit-babbler (322), Cape Penduline-Tit (318), Scarlet-chested Sunbird (433), Black-throated (492) and other canaries. Bears a superficial resemblance to songs and calls of these species. Amethyst Sunbird's can be identified by frequency of the *tjip* note.

Grey Sunbird *Cyanomitra veroxii* Gryssuikerbekkie

435 Track detail 1:41 (total length) = 0:03–0:13 (alarm call); 0:13–1:41 (song)

Song Phrase is an accelerating *chip chip chip chee-tee-tir*, comprising 4–6 beautiful, sweet, high-pitched whistles that rise and fall in pitch. Short pauses separate phrases. Juveniles' subsong consists of soft continuous twittering.
Other sounds A very typical short, sharp, rasping sunbird alarm and contact call.

Regional variation None.
Habitat Most often found in tree canopy of coastal evergreen forests. May venture into woodlands.
Similar sounding None.

Greater Double-collared Sunbird *Cinnyris afer* Groot-rooibandsuikerbekkie

436 Track detail 0:03–0:46 (song)

Song Short, piercing, metallic *tseeep* notes, followed by ringing jumbled twittering. Phrases last a few seconds, separated by brief pauses.
Other sounds As is usual for a sunbird gives harsh alarm and contact calls comprising short, sharp, metallic chirps.
Regional variation None.
Habitat Montane, coastal and dune forests, acacia savanna and woodlands adjacent to rivers.

Similar sounding Southern (437) and Miombo (not included) double-collared sunbirds and Marico (438), Variable (440) and White-bellied (441) sunbirds. Songs of Southern and Miombo double-collared sunbirds almost identical to that of Greater Double-collared and cannot be separated by ear. Marico Sunbird's song also similar, but gives more introductory notes at a slower pace. Variable Sunbird has distinctive rhythm and less jumbled ending to its phrases. White-bellied Sunbird's tone and phrasing fairly distinctive.

Southern Double-collared Sunbird *Cinnyris chalybeus*
Klein-rooibandsuikerbekkie

437 Track detail 0:03–0:23 (song)

Song Short, piercing introductory *tseep* notes followed by jumbled twittering. Brief pauses separate phrases.
Other sounds Typical sunbird's alarm and contact calls, comprising short, sharp, harsh, metallic chirps.
Regional variation None.
Habitat Fynbos, arid scrub, coastal dune scrub, gardens and parks.
Similar sounding Greater (436) and Miombo (not included) double-collared sunbirds and Marico (438), Variable (440) and White-bellied (441) sunbirds.

Greater and Miombo double-collared sunbird songs best not separated from that of Southern Double-collared by sound alone. Marico has a similar song but the increased number of introductory notes are given at slower pace. Variable Sunbird has distinctive rhythm and less jumbled ending to its phrase. White-bellied Sunbird's tone and phrasing are fairly distinctive.

Marico Sunbird *Cinnyris mariquensis* Maricosuikerbekkie

438 Track detail 0:03–0:52 (song)

Song Like the double-collared sunbirds, gives series of about 4–6 *tseeep* notes, followed by a jumbled phrase. **Other sounds** As is typical for a sunbird gives short, sharp, metallic chirps as alarm and contact calls. **Regional variation** None. **Habitat** Acacia and mixed acacia and broad-leaved woodlands. Sometimes ventures into parks and gardens.

Similar sounding Orange-breasted (432), Greater Double-collared (436), Southern Double-collared (437), Variable (440) and White-bellied (441) sunbirds. Orange-breasted Sunbird includes mimicry. Song is similar to that of both double-collared sunbirds, but has more lead-in notes and these notes have a less rasping tone. Jumbled twitter ending song is less structured than that of Variable Sunbird.

Collared Sunbird *Hedydipna collaris* Kortbeksuikerbekkie

439 Track detail 0:31 (total length) = 0:03–0:26 (song); 0:26–0:31 (alarm or contact call)

Song A series of short piercing whistles. **Other sounds** A fairly distinctive rasping *chi-chi-tsrr*, given both as alarm and contact call. **Regional variation** None. **Habitat** Confined mainly to lowveld forests, but sometimes ventures into gardens close to well-wooded habitats.

Similar sounding Lesser Swamp Warbler (337) and Cape Wagtail (387). Whistles vaguely recall high-pitched tones of a Lesser Swamp Warbler or Cape Wagtail, but different enough not to be confused.

Variable Sunbird *Cinnyris venustus* Geelpenssuikerbekkie

440 Track detail 0:03–0:41 (song)

Song Rapid *tseep* notes, followed by a jumbled phrase. **Other sounds** The harsh metallic contact and alarm call that is shared by most sunbirds. **Regional variation** None. **Habitat** Rank vegetation along rivers and in broad-leaved woodlands, savannas and forest margins.

Similar sounding Greater Double-collared (436), Southern Double-collared (437), Marico (438) and White-bellied (441) sunbirds. Less rapid, jumbled and twittering than the double-collared sunbirds. Marico's song is slower, with more twittering. Song is tricky to separate from that of White-bellied Sunbird.

White-bellied Sunbird *Cinnyris talatala* Witpenssuikerbekkie

441 Track detail 0:03–0:35 (song)

Song Gives *dzeeep* notes, then jumbled twittering. **Other sounds** Contact and alarm calls comprise the harsh metallic notes given by many other sunbirds. **Regional variation** None. **Habitat** Some types of broad-leaved savanna but favours acacia savanna and open woodlands; sometimes ventures into parks and gardens.

Similar sounding Knysna (327) and Barratt's (328) warblers and Greater Double-collared (436), Southern double-collared (437), Marico (438) and Variable (440) sunbirds. Knysna Warbler's song starts more slowly. Song closely resembles that of Barratt's Warbler, but more jumbled. Sounds somewhat like the sunbirds listed here, but listen for the lead-in *dzeeep* notes.

Dusky Sunbird   *Cinnyris fuscus*   Namakwasuikerbekkie

442   Track detail 0:02–0:29 (song)

Song A near-constant stream of warbled trills and
sunbird-like squeaks, with few breaks and very
little structure.
Other sounds Both contact and alarm calls comprise
the harsh metallic notes given by many other sunbirds.
Regional variation None.

Habitat Tall vegetation along drainage lines and
succulent coastal scrub in the arid Karoo and Namib.
Similar sounding Orange-breasted Sunbird (432).
Constant stream of warbled sunbird's notes much like
those of Orange-breasted, but Dusky does not include
mimicry in its song.

SPARROWS AND PETRONIAS

The chirps of sparrows and petronias are so widely recognised that bird call descriptions
frequently make use of the phrase 'sparrow-like chirp'. Males give a series of chirps with a
distinctive pattern, while prominently perched. The notes and phrase patterns are often so
similar that it can be difficult to separate species, particularly the sparrows, on song alone.
However, contact and group calls are generally unique to each species.

Cape Sparrow   *Passer melanurus*   Gewone Mossie

443   Track detail 0:02–0:39 (song with background contact call)

Song A series of *chree-chiu-chip-cheep* chirps,
repeated regularly at dawn. Calls most actively in
spring and summer.
Other sounds A rattled two-note contact call.
Regional variation None formally recorded, but
variations have been noted in the tone and phrasing of
the contact call and in the phrasing of the song.
Habitat Includes some dry habitats, woodlands,
plantations, crop lands and human settlements.

Similar sounding Red-faced Mousebird (186),
Cape Wagtail (387), House Sparrow (444) and Scaly-
feathered Finch (474). Song superficially resembles
that of mousebird and wagtail, but confusion is
unlikely. Song differs from that of House Sparrow
by being deeper and fuller, with more repetition
of phrases, while contact call also sounds also less
ratchety. Contact call also vaguely resembles that of
Scaly-feathered Finch.

House Sparrow   *Passer domesticus*   Huismossie

444   Track detail 0:37 (total length) = 0:02–0:15 (territorial chirp); 0:15–0:37 (song)

Song Male's main song comprises *deeu, chiru*
and *preeuuu* notes given in series, but with no
specific pattern. Also a rasping *de-zip* chirp, to
proclaim territory.
Other sounds Contact call made up of ratchety
rattles. Female also chirps, but context uncertain.
Regional variation None.
Habitat Mostly associated with human habitation.

Similar sounding Sanderling (118), Red-faced
Mousebird (186), Black-eared Sparrow-Lark (254),
White-throated Swallow (257), Rock Martin (262), Cape
Wagtail (387), Cape Sparrow (443) and Scaly-feathered
Finch (474). Male's territorial chirp superficially like
flight call of Sanderling. Song most resembles that
of Cape Sparrow, but higher pitched and thinner.
Resemblance of song to that of Scaly-feathered Finch
and the other species listed is superficial.

149

Yellow-throated Petronia   *Gymnoris superciliaris*   Geelvlekmossie

445 Track detail 0:02–0:16 (song)

Song Phrases, each comprising 3–4 rapid *chirp* notes, are separated by short pauses. Tone and rhythm distinctive.
Other sounds More rapid versions of song. Context unclear, but presumably given as contact and alarm calls.

Regional variation None.
Habitat Acacia savanna woodlands.
Similar sounding African Pipit (393). Song superficially resembles that of this pipit, but sufficiently sparrow-like to be easily distinguished.

Southern Grey-headed Sparrow   *Passer diffusus*   Gryskopmossie

446 Track detail 0:03–0:32 (song)

Song A series of *cheeuu* notes given in sequence with very little variation.
Other sounds A single territorial *chirp*, much like the song note. Contact call is a rattling series of rapid *ti-ru-rup* notes.
Regional variation None.
Habitat Woodlands.

Similar sounding Cape Wagtail (387), Northern Grey-headed Sparrow (not included), Scarlet-chested Sunbird (433) and Scaly-feathered Finch (474). Bears superficial resemblance to wagtail. The single repetitive *cheeuu* makes song easy to distinguish from that of most other sparrows, except Northern Grey-headed, which sounds nearly identical. Song vaguely like that of Scaly-feathered Finch, but far slower.

TRUE WEAVERS, BUFFALO WEAVERS AND SPARROW-WEAVERS

In most cases it is easy to identify a true weaver by its swizzling, rasping song, often given by a male as he hangs upside-down displaying from his nest. Buffalo weavers and sparrow-weavers are similiarly easy to identify to group level. Their songs are much more piercing than those of true weavers, and consist of very short, sharp chirps and shrill whistles, generally given from a perch close to the nest.

White-browed Sparrow-Weaver   *Plocepasser mahali*   Koringvoël

447 Track detail 0:32 (total length) = 0:03–0:18 (song); 0:18–0:32 (alarm call)

Song Male gives jumbled warbles, trills and short, sharp chirps with a distinctive shrill tone. Proclaims territory with rasping whistles that rise and fall in pitch.
Other sounds Alarm call a short, sharp *tuk*. A wide range of other sounds has also been described, but their context is uncertain.

Regional variation None.
Habitat Acacia woodlands and dry savanna.
Similar sounding None.

Sociable Weaver *Philetarius socius* Versamelvoël

448 Track detail 0:02–0:46 (group song at nest colony)

Song Varied, short, staccato chirps with a readily identifiable tone.
Other sounds Rapidly sounded high-pitched notes given in alarm. Group chatter similar to main song. It is not always possible to distinguish the purpose of group chatter as these are colonial nesting birds that are seldom alone.

Regional variation None.
Habitat Arid areas with large trees or artificial structures upon which to build a massive communal nest.
Similar sounding Red-billed Buffalo Weaver (449). Buffalo Weaver's song is less shrill.

Red-billed Buffalo Weaver *Bubalornis niger* Buffelwewer

449 Track detail 0:03–0:44 (group song at nest colony)

Song Male gives rapid *witta-witta-witta-witta* phrase, repeatedly.
Other sounds Female gives short descending whistle, presumed to be a contact call.
Regional variation None.
Habitat Acacia woodlands and thornveld. Prefers grazed habitats disturbed by animals so often associated with wild and farm animals and human settlements in rural areas. Avoids broad-leaved woodlands.

Similar sounding African Red-eyed (281) and Dark-capped (282) bulbuls and Sociable Weaver (448). Male's song bears superficial resemblance to group chatter of Dark-capped and African Red-eyed bulbuls, but more piercing. Song also similar to that of Sociable Weaver, but much louder, fuller and more piercing.

Thick-billed Weaver *Amblyospiza albifrons* Dikbekwewer

450 Track detail 0:02–0:17 (song)

Song Unique, rapid, high-pitched, metallic chirps lead into bubbling phrases.
Other sounds A range of short metallic chirps and swizzles, similar to main song, presumed to be alarm and contact calls. Largely silent away from the nest.
Regional variation None.
Habitat Confined to reed beds during breeding season, but ventures into forest margins and clearings at other times.

Similar sounding Fan-tailed Widowbird (464). Vaguely recalls this widowbird, but tone as well as unique combination of rapid chips and bubbling phrases make Thick-billed Weaver's song easy to identify.

151

Dark-backed Weaver *Ploceus bicolor*   Bosmusikant

 451 Track detail 0:33 (total length) = 0:03–0:08 (song);
0:08–0:33 (alarm and contact calls)

Song Very uncharacteristic for a true weaver; a distinctive combination of beautiful musical whistles and almost shrike-like vibrating notes.
Other sounds A short, sharp *dzeet* given both as an alarm and contact call.

Regional variation Whistled notes in song may vary.
Habitat Forests and dense riverine bush.
Similar sounding None.

Cape Weaver *Ploceus capensis*   Kaapse Wewer

 452 Track detail 0:02–0:45 (song)

Song A series of typical swizzling notes, but this is the only weaver whose song accelerates and decelerates while also rising and falling in pitch. Recalls sound of a propeller plane starting up.
Other sounds Individual weaver-like chirps given in both contact and alarm situations.
Regional variation None.

Habitat Parks, gardens and even areas of arid vegetation, provided there are suitable trees in which to build a nest overhanging water.
Similar sounding Sickle-winged Chat (296), Green-capped Eremomela (320), Wattled Starling (425) and Red-headed Weaver (458). Resemblances are slight. Confusion unlikely.

Yellow Weaver *Ploceus subaureus*   Geelwewer

453 Track detail 0:02–0:41 (song)

Song Soft for a weaver. A unique combination of one or two sparrow-like chirps interspersed with metallic swizzles. Recalls sound of a dial on an old-fashioned telephone.
Other sounds Single weaver-like chirp given in contact and alarm situations.

Regional variation None.
Habitat Restricted to reed beds in breeding season (summer), but ventures further afield at other times of the year.
Similar sounding None.

Village Weaver *Ploceus cucullatus*   Bontrugwewer

454 Track detail 0:02–0:23 (song)

Song Typical weaver-like swizzles interspersed with distinctive, rapid, staccato notes resembling machine-gun fire.
Other sounds Like most weavers, a single rasping chirp serves as both alarm and contact calls.
Regional variation None.

Habitat Favours woodlands, forest margins, parks and gardens close to water, but ventures further afield outside of breeding season.
Similar sounding Red-billed Quelea (460). Although the staccato song is distinctive among weavers, similar chattering is given by Red-billed Quelea. However, quelea also emits some high-pitched whistles not heard in Village Weaver.

Southern Masked Weaver *Ploceus velatus*   Swartkeelgeelvink

455 Track detail 0:03–0:36 (song)

Song Main phrase comprises unique combination of ascending swizzling notes, followed by a drawn-out descending sigh. Also randomly includes various other swizzling notes typical of a weaver.
Other sounds Like other true weavers, a single chirp serves as both contact and alarm call. Also some short, high-pitched, metallic *tseep* notes, but context uncertain.

Regional variation None.
Habitat Most wooded habitats, but avoids dense forests, as well as deserts and other very arid environments.
Similar sounding Malachite Sunbird (431). Confusion is unlikely.

Lesser Masked Weaver *Ploceus intermedius*   Kleingeelvink

456 Track detail 0:03–0:44 (song*) * Note Monotonous Lark in the background

Song A typical weaver's swizzling, but distinctive for its high speed and slightly liquid tone.
Other sounds As is usual for a weaver, gives a single chirp both as an alarm and contact call.

Regional variation None.
Habitat Acacia savanna and woodlands, often near water.
Similar sounding None.

Spectacled Weaver *Ploceus ocularis*   Brilwewer

457 Track detail 0:02–0:10 (song)

Song Male gives brief, swizzling, typically weaver-like notes.
Other sounds Both sexes give highly distinctive descending *too-too-too-too-too-too* whistles. This call is more frequently heard than the song, but context uncertain.

Regional variation None.
Habitat Dense vegetation in woodlands, riverine bush, parks and gardens.
Similar sounding None.

Red-headed Weaver *Anaplectes melanotis*   Rooikopwewer

458 Track detail 0:03–0:33 (song)

Song A combination of nasal *zeep* and *chirup* notes reminiscent of those of a pipit or weaver, but higher pitched.
Other sounds Contact calls comprise typical weaver-like chirps and swizzling notes.
Regional variation None.
Habitat Favours broad-leaved woodlands, but also ventures into acacia woodlands.

Similar sounding Bushveld Pipit (not included), Cape Weaver (452) and Purple (471) and Village (472) indigobirds. Strictly speaking no similar sounding species, since combination of weaver-like swizzling and high-pitched *tseep* is unique. However, nasal notes in song recall Bushveld Pipit and swizzling notes recall a high-pitched Cape Weaver. Tone is somewhat reminiscent of an indigobird.

153

Chestnut Weaver *Ploceus rubiginosus*

Bruinwewer

459 Track detail 0:03–0:27 (song at nest colony)

Song A unique combination of well-spaced wader-like *cheeuu* notes mixed with the usual rolling swizzles given by most weavers.
Other sounds Rapid chattering *tip* notes.

Regional variation None.
Habitat Thornveld and riverine woodlands.
Similar sounding None.

BISHOPS AND WIDOWBIRDS

The songs of the birds in this group are complex, with a distinctive rhythm that can be recognised with some practice. However, certain members of the group do have unique, more easily identifiable songs. Bishops tend to nest in close proximity with one another and are often heard calling together. Widowbirds are known for the males' display flights and songs and for their very diverse plumage.

Red-billed Quelea *Quelea quelea*

Rooibekkwelea

460 Track detail 0:02–0:28 (song at nest colony)

Song Nondescript swizzling, as is typical for a weaver, but punctuated with soft whistles.
Other sounds Gives nondescript weaver-like swizzles as contact and alarm calls.
Regional variation None.

Habitat Grasslands, savanna and crop lands, but never strays too far from water.
Similar sounding Village Weaver (454). These species give the same staccato chattering call, but quelea's soft whistles separate it from the weavers.

Yellow-crowned Bishop *Euplectes afer*

Goudgeelvink

461 Track detail 0:02–0:28 (display song)

Song Brightly coloured male flits around his territory giving distinctive, insect-like, churring display song. High-pitched and metallic, yet soft.
Other sounds Nondescript swizzles and chirps, typical of both weavers and bishops.

Regional variation None.
Habitat In breeding season occurs in reed beds in wetlands or in rank or flooded grasslands. May venture into drier grasslands in winter.
Similar sounding None.

154

Southern Red Bishop *Euplectes orix* Rooivink

462 Track detail 0:03–0:29 (song)

Song A unique combination of three distinct sounds – a weaver-like swizzle repeated rapidly, a churring, bubbly gargle, also repeated rapidly, and a distinctive rising or falling, soft, nasal whistle that punctuates everything.
Other sounds Typical bishop or weaver-like chirps and swizzles.

Regional variation None.
Habitat Closely associated with wetlands during breeding season, but in winter ranges further afield into grasslands and crop lands to feed.
Similar sounding None.

Long-tailed Widowbird *Eucplectes progne* Langstertflap

463 Track detail 0:02–0:30 (display song)

Song Male sings excited *chip-chip-chip* before taking off into display flight and giving repetitive *churra-churra-churra* notes.
Other sounds General bishop-like chirps and swizzles given as contact call. Alarm call comprises cat-like mewing.

Regional variation None.
Habitat Almost exclusively a grassland species, but may feed in crop lands.
Similar sounding Cape Longclaw (389). Display song is distinctive, but cat-like mewing resembles high-pitched, less nasal version of Cape Longclaw's song.

Fan-tailed Widowbird *Euplectes axillaris* Kortstertflap

464 Track detail 0:03–0:30 (song)

Song A rapidly sounded phrase beginning with one or two soft liquid trills and followed by three rapid *zeep-zeep-zeep* notes.
Other sounds Contact and alarm calls comprise chirps and swizzling notes, as is typical for a bishop or weaver.

Regional variation None.
Habitat Reed beds and flooded and rank grasslands.
Similar sounding Thick-billed Weaver (450). Resemblance to weaver superficial. Structure and rhythm of male Fan-tailed Widowbird's song is unique and easily identified.

White-winged Widowbird *Euplectes albonotatus* Witvlerkflap

465 Track detail 0:03–0:41 (display song)

Song Male gives insect-like metallic rattle.
Other sounds A soft sound, like something rustling in grass, or a short *zrik*. Context uncertain.
Regional variation None.
Habitat Rank grasslands, often with scattered bushes. Also occurs in wetlands.

Similar sounding White-backed Mousebird (185) and River Warbler (329). Rapid *zrik* like that of White-backed Mousebird, but given by a lone individual, not by groups of birds. Song like that of River Warbler, but less harsh and piercing and is given in display flight by the brightly coloured male, whereas River Warbler sings from a dense thicket.

Red-collared Widowbird   *Euplectes ardens*   Rooikeelflap

466 Track detail 0:02–0:09 (display song)

Song A series of very piercing metallic chirps, often followed by a very high-pitched metallic rattle.
Other sounds General chirps, like those of a widowbird, given as both contact and alarm calls.
Regional variation None.

Habitat Wide-ranging. Includes montane grasslands, savanna and wetlands.
Similar sounding Pin-tailed Whydah (467). Sounds higher pitched, softer and more metallic than the whydah.

WHYDAHS, INDIGOBIRDS AND ALLIES

With the exception of the Pin-tailed Whydah, all of these seed-eating parasitic birds mimic the sounds of the species in whose nests they lay their eggs. Their own songs are typical for seedeaters and include high-pitched metallic trills, warbles and whistles.

Pin-tailed Whydah   *Vidua macroura*   Koningrooibekkie

467 Track detail 0:02–0:25 (display song)

Song Male's display flight involves bobbing up and down in the air before a potential mate, singing a series of short, high-pitched, ringing *chip* notes, followed by rapid, metallic twittering notes.
Other sounds Contact and alarm calls are variations of the metallic chirps and twittering from the song.

Regional variation None.
Habitat Grasslands with scattered bushes, woodlands and savanna, as well as wetlands and their surrounds.
Similar sounding Red-collared Widowbird (466). Whydah's song is fuller and lower pitched than that of this widowbird.

Shaft-tailed Whydah   *Vidua regia*   Pylstertrooibekkie

468 Track detail 0:03–0:50 (song)

Song A unique series of metallic twittering notes, combined with mimicry of a Violet-eared Waxbill's whistled song.
Other sounds Some short, simple, ringing alarm and contact calls. Gives soft rattle with tail or wings in response to playback of its own song.

Regional variation Local variations observed.
Habitat Acacia woodlands and savanna with higher rainfall than is average for these types of vegetation. Avoids broad-leaved woodlands.
Similar sounding None.

Long-tailed Paradise Whydah *Vidua paradisaea* Gewone Paradysvink

469 Track detail 0:03–0:18 (song*) * Listen for mimicry of Green-winged Pytilia at 0:12

Song Combines its own jumbled metallic twittering notes with a rising and falling whistle that it **mimics** from its host species, the Green-winged Pytilia.
Other sounds Alarm and contact calls are short, sharp, metallic notes. Also softly rattles its tail or wings in response to playback of its own song.

Regional variation Variation in mimicked phrase matches regional variation in its host's songs.
Habitat Open savanna and acacia woodlands; favours dry habitats.
Similar sounding Green-winged Pytilia (480). Mimics the song of this pytilia, but the combination of mimicked and non-mimicked sounds is distinctive.

Dusky Indigobird *Vidua funerea* Gewone Blouvinkie

470 Track detail 0:03–0:46 (song*) * Listen for mimicry of African Firefinch at 0:22

Song It **mimics** the popping rattles given by its host, the African Firefinch, combining them with its own jumbled, metallic, twittering notes.
Other sounds Contact and alarm calls comprise variations of metallic chirps and twitterings from song.
Regional variation None.

Habitat Woodlands, riverine and montane forest and crop lands.
Similar sounding African Firefinch (482). Mimics the firefinch's song, but combination of mimicked and non-micked sounds helps to distinguish it.

Purple Indigobird *Vidua purpurascens* Witpootblouvinkie

471 Track detail 0:02–0:56 (song*) * Listen for mimicry of Jameson's Firefinch at 0:48

Song A unique blend of its own metallic chirps and twitterings and a bubbling phrase that it **mimics** from its host, Jameson's Firefinch.
Other sounds Variations of metallic chirps and twitterings from song, given in contact and alarm.
Regional variation None.

Habitat Dry woodlands, riverine forests and crop lands.
Similar sounding Red-headed Weaver (458) and Jameson's Firefinch (483). Red-headed Weaver doesn't mimic Jameson's Firefinch. Indigobird told from Jameson's Firefinch by combination of mimicked and non-mimicked sounds.

Village Indigobird *Vidua chalybeata* Staalblouvinkie

472 Track detail 0:02–0:25 (song*) * Listen for mimicry of Red-billed Firefinch at 0:07

Song A unique mix of its own jumbled twittering notes with a *tik* alarm and two-note *pee-ya* song that it **mimics** from the Red-billed Firefinch.
Other sounds Gives variations of the metallic chirps and twittering in song as contact and alarm calls.
Regional variation None.

Habitat Acacia savanna and thickets near rivers and farm lands. Also some broad-leaved woodlands.
Similar sounding Red-billed Firefinch (484) and Red-headed Weaver (458). Mimics the song of Red-billed Firefinch, but the combination of mimicked and non-mimicked sounds separates these species. Red-headed Weaver doesn't mimic the Red-billed Firefinch

Cuckoo Finch *Anomalospiza imberbis* Koekoekvink

473 Track detail 0:03–0:38 (song)

Song Bubbly, rising and falling trills, with a softly nasal, slightly ringing quality.
Other sounds Flight call is a short, sharp, nasal *tjip*.
Regional variation None.

Habitat Rank grass in moist valleys, provided several potential host species occur in the area.
Similar sounding Cinnamon-breasted Bunting (498). Cuckoo Finch's song is softer and more nasal.

SCALY-FEATHERED FINCH

This finch is the only member of its family. A distinctive and gregarious little seedeater, its calls are very simple and it often calls from within a group of other seedeaters.

Scaly-feathered Finch *Sporopipes squamifrons* Baardmannetjie

474 Track detail 0:03–0:31 (contact calls)

Song Chirps like a sparrow, but sounds higher pitched and more liquid.
Other sounds Variations of main song, given in various situations. Told from song mainly by context.
Regional variation None.

Habitat Dry acacia woodlands.
Similar sounding Cape (443), House (444) and Southern Grey-headed (446) sparrows. Superficial resemblances only; confusion is unlikely.

WAXBILLS, FINCHES AND ALLIES

A large family the members of which generally all sound similar. Their songs are basic, usually comprising high-pitched but soft notes. Certain species do, however, have a metallic tone or a more distinctive song. The most familiar sound given by members of this family is group chatter, although, more rarely, individual birds may sing from a prominent perch.

Bronze Mannikin *Spermestes cucullatus* Gewone Fret

475 Track detail 0:02–0:14 (song)

Song Rapid, jumbled, metallic *chree* and *chit* notes.
Other sounds Contact call is a short sharp *trit* note, with a slightly liquid tone.
Regional variation None.
Habitat Lush ground cover in grasslands, savanna, woodlands, parks and gardens.

Similar sounding Orange-breasted Waxbill (481), Jameson's (483) and other firefinches and Pink-throated (486) and other twinspots. The waxbill sounds less harsh and gives a more trilled whistle. Most firefinches and twinspots give very similar songs that are extremely difficult to separate.

Red-headed Finch *Amadina erythrocephala*   Rooikopvink

476 Track detail 0:03–0:38 (group contact calls)

Song Male displays by puffing up throat and
giving churring and buzzing sounds, usually from a
prominent perch.
Other sounds Agitated chattering and chirps, with
slight sparrow-like tone.

Regional variation None.
Habitat Grasslands with scattered shrubs, as well as
crop lands and gardens adjoining suitable habitat.
Similar sounding None.

Blue Waxbill *Uraeginthus angolensis*   Gewone Blousysie

477 Track detail 0:03–0:35 (contact call)

Song Seldom heard, but comprises a series of
distinctive, rapid, high-pitched, metallic notes.
Other sounds Alarm and contact calls, heard
far more frequently than song, comprise a highly
distinctive, soft, nasal, high-pitched *dzee-dzeei*.
Regional variation None.

Habitat Moist to semi-arid savanna, particularly
where large trees provide shaded cover. Ventures into
acacia and some broad-leaved woodlands.
Similar sounding None.

Common Waxbill *Estrilda astrild*   Rooibeksysie

478 Track detail 0:03–0:40 (contact and alarm calls)

Song A distinctive, seldom heard *chi-chi-chi-zweee*.
Other sounds Contact call is given by groups of
birds; comprises nondescript chirps with the soft
metallic tone typical of a waxbill.
Regional variation None.
Habitat Rank grasslands, wetland margins and, in
more arid areas, riverine scrub.

Similar sounding Orange-breasted (481) and
other waxbills. The nondescript group chatter is
recognisable with practice. Male's song most closely
resembles that of Orange-breasted Waxbill but not as
high-pitched or cleanly metallic.

Grey Waxbill *Estrilda perreini*   Gryssysie

479 Track detail 0:02–0:11 (song)

Song A scratchy, almost swift-like *zeeerrr zeeerr* along
with other rasping sounds.
Other sounds Short, sharp, high-pitched whistles,
given as both group and alarm calls.
Regional variation None.

Habitat Dense vegetation including coastal forests
and thick riverine bush.
Similar sounding African Palm Swift (not included)
and White-rumped Swift (183). Some resemblance to
the scratchy sounds of a swift, but confusion unlikely.

Green-winged Pytilia · *Pytilia melba* · Gewone Melba

480 Track detail 0:02–0:16 (contact call)

Song A distinctive series of very high-pitched, rising and falling, metallic trills, interspersed with short, sharp *tink* notes.
Other sounds The *tink* note often given in isolation as a contact call.
Regional variation None.

Habitat Favours tall grass in dry habitats, but also ventures into rank grass in acacia woodlands.
Similar sounding Long-tailed Paradise Whydah (469) and African Firefinch (482). Whydah mimics pytilia, but includes non-mimicked sounds that distinguish it.

Orange-breasted Waxbill · *Sporaeginthus subflavus* · Rooiassie

481 Track detail 0:02–0:21 (contact calls)

Song No specific display song described, but the short, clean, sharp, metallic *chip* given in most contexts probably also serves as breeding song.
Other sounds The same high-pitched metallic *chip* notes given in alarm and contact situations.
Regional variation None.
Habitat Rank grasslands, reed beds and other damp habitat around wetlands.

Similar sounding Pale-crowned Cisticola (344), Bronze Mannikin (475) and Common Waxbill (478). Superficial resemblance to Pale-crowned Cisticola. Bronze Mannikin's calls similar in pitch but notes are vibrating and duller. Song is higher pitched than that of Common Waxbill, with cleaner, more metallic notes.

African (Blue-billed) Firefinch · *Lagonosticta rubricata* · Kaapse Vuurvinkie

482 Track detail 0:03–0:28 (song)

Song A drawn-out, high-pitched, metallic trill that rises and falls in pitch.
Other sounds Short, sharp *tik* given as alarm call.
Regional variation None.
Habitat Moist wooded areas, forest margins and grasslands with bracken and shrubs, and vegetation along river courses.

Similar sounding Dusky Indigobird (470) and Green-winged Pytilia (480). Confusion unlikely, as African Firefinch's song is distinctive, more trilled and more insect-like in tone than that of the pytilia. Dusky Indigobird mimics African Firefinch's song, but also includes non-mimicked sounds and this combination helps to separate these birds.

Jameson's Firefinch · *Lagonosticta rhodopareia* · Jamesonvuurvinkie

483 Track detail 0:41 (total length) = 0:02–0:34 (song); 0:34–0:41 (contact call)

Song High-pitched tweets punctuated by a distinctive gurgling trill that makes the song unique.
Other sounds Contact and alarm calls comprise sounds similar to those in song.
Regional variation None.
Habitat Long grass in well-wooded areas and along wooded streams.

Similar sounding Bronze Mannikin (475) and Purple Indigobird (471). Song bears superficial resemblance to that of the mannikin. Song mimicked by Purple Indigobird, but that species combines mimicked with distinctive non-mimicked sounds.

Red-billed Firefinch   *Lagonosticta senegala*   Rooibekvuurvinkie

484 Track detail 0:02–0:20 (song)

Song Short, metallic *tseep* notes that rise and fall in pitch.
Other sounds Rapidly sounded metallic *tseep* notes, given as both contact and alarm calls.
Regional variation None.

Habitat Feeds in patches of grass near bare ground in acacia woodlands and savanna.
Similar sounding Village Indigobird (472). Song is mimicked by indigobird, but that species also includes distinctive non-mimicked sounds.

Swee Waxbill   *Coccopygia melanotis*   Suidelike Swie

485 Track detail 0:02–0:38 (song and contact call)

Song A very high-pitched rising or descending *sweeee* note.
Other sounds Group and alarm calls consist of softer, shorter variations of song's *sweeee* note.
Regional variation None.

Habitat Thick vegetation along the escarpment and in coastal forests; also riverine bush and dense fynbos.
Similar sounding Yellow-bellied Waxbill (not included). Told from Swee Waxbill by range, which does not overlap.

Pink-throated Twinspot   *Hypargos margaritatus*   Rooskeelkolpensie

486 Track detail 0:03–0:36 (song)

Song A staccato series of high-pitched, cricket-like, metallic trills and *tseep* notes; recalls morse code.
Other sounds Contact and alarm calls comprise single cricket-like trill.
Regional variation None.
Habitat Thickets in dry savanna and along evergreen forest margins.

Similar sounding Bronze Mannikin (475), Red-throated (487) and other twinspots and Forest Canary (495). Resemblance of song to that of mannikin is superficial. Pink-throated Twinspot gives shorter phrase and slower trill than Red-throated. Twinspots all give very similar high-pitched songs and calls. Resemblance to Forest Canary is superficial.

Red-throated Twinspot   *Hypargos niveoguttatus*   Rooikeelkolpensie

487 Track detail 0:03–0:23 (song)

Song A series of rising and falling *teep* notes, followed by bubbly warbling.
Other sounds Short notes, similar to the *teep* given as contact and alarm calls.
Regional variation None.
Habitat Forest margins and densely wooded streams.

Similar sounding Pink-throated Twinspot (486) and Forest Canary (495). Fairly similar, but warbling concluding notes are slower than those in Pink-throated's song. Resemblance to canary is superficial.

161

CANARIES, SEEDEATERS AND BUNTINGS

Canaries and seedeaters have always been known for their beautiful sweet songs. The members of this group sing very tuneful, warbled and bubbly songs, often from an exposed perch. Some canary species also mimic other sounds. The buntings are equally musical, but their songs tend to sound a little more piercing or metallic.

White-throated Canary *Crithagra albogularis*   Witkeelkanarie

488 Track detail 0:03–0:33 (song)

Song May sing for long periods. Gives short phrases comprising jumbled trills and sweet melodious notes, separated by brief pauses. Also mimics other species.
Other sounds Flight call is a single *tleep* note.
Regional variation Mimics the local bird species.
Habitat Shrub lands and, occasionally, rocky slopes.

Similar sounding Streaky-headed Seedeater (489), Brimstone (490) and other canaries. The seedeater's flight call may punctuate its song, which aids in distinguishing these similar songs. Most canaries give similar twittering notes and experience is needed to separate species.

Streaky-headed Seedeater *Crithagra gularis*   Streepkopkanarie

489 Track detail 0:03–0:47 (song)

Song May sing for long periods. Gives lengthy phrases and, like other canaries, combines jumbled trills with some sweet notes, punctuated by brief pauses. Mimics other species.
Other sounds Flight call is a double-note *chirup* with the metallic tone typical for canaries.
Regional variation None.

Habitat Various woodland types, frequently on rocky hills but also in more open areas; may frequent forest margins.
Similar sounding White-throated (488) and other canaries and seedeaters. Most canaries give a stream of melodious twittering very like that of Streaky-headed Seedeater. However, listen for this seedeater's distinctive flight call, which may punctuate its song.

Brimstone Canary *Crithagra sulphurata*   Dikbekkanarie

490 Track detail 0:02–0:24 (song)

Song A typical jumbled series of canary-like trills and sweet notes. Short phrases are separated by longer pauses. May sing for extended periods.
Other sounds A single scratchy *tirup* given in flight.
Regional variation None.
Habitat Varying forest and thicket habitats as well as gardens, parks and plantations.

Similar sounding White-throated (488), Yellow (493) and other canaries and seedeaters. Most canary songs consist of melodious twittering. They can be difficult to separate, but try to listen out for the tone and the pattern of short phrases separated by longer pauses.

Yellow-fronted Canary   *Crithagra mozambica*   Geeloogkanarie

 Track detail 0:02–0:21 (song)

Song A series of sweet piercing whistles that rise and fall in pitch, with some markedly wagtail-like *tiru-ree* phrases. Sometimes mimics other birds.
Other sounds None.
Regional variation Mimicry varies according to species present locally.

Habitat Savanna, broad-leaved woodlands, some crop lands. Also parks and gardens.
Similar sounding African Pied Wagtail (388), Cape (499) and Golden-breasted (500) buntings. Song's resemblance to that of the bunting is superficial, but very like that of Pied Wagtail. Habitat helps to separate.

Black-throated Canary   *Crithagra atrogularis*   Bergkanarie

492 **Track detail 0:02–0:27 (song)**

Song Phrases comprise energetic notes with a typical canary-like tone, punctuated by piercing whistles, a *peeoooo* note and other notes reminiscent of those in the Cape Sparrow's song. Phrases are up to 15 seconds long, separated by brief pauses. Sometimes mimics other birds.
Other sounds A distinctive, sweet, whistled *peeoooo*, rising in pitch.
Regional variation Mimicry varies according to species present locally.

Habitat Woodlands, parks and gardens.
Similar sounding Amethyst Sunbird (434) and White-throated (488) and other canaries and seedeaters. Song bears superficial resemblance to that of the Amethyst Sunbird. Most canaries give a stream of melodious twittering notes and can be tricky to separate. The *peeoooo* note punctuating the song helps to identify this species.

Yellow Canary   *Crithagra flaviventris*   Geelkanarie

493 **Track detail 0:01–1:20 (song)**

Song May sing for an extended period. Notes are typical of a canary. Phrases last about 20 seconds, separated by brief pauses. Mimics other species.
Other sounds Like other canaries, gives single-note flight call.
Regional variation Mimicry varies according to species present locally.

Habitat Open shrub lands at a range of altitudes.
Similar sounding White-throated (488), Brimstone (490) and other canaries and seedeaters. The melodious twittering songs of canaries are difficult to tell apart. To distinguish the Yellow Canary's song from those of White-throated and other canaries, listen for the stop-start rhythm. The Brimstone Canary has a similar call structure, but with longer pauses.

Cape Canary *Serinus canicollis*　　　　　　　　Kaapse Kanarie

494 Track detail　0:34 (total length) = 0:03–0:28 (song); 0:28–0:34 (contact call)

Song A continuous stream of twittering and warbling notes, given for up to 30 seconds at a time, with a brief pause between phrases. Tone slightly reminiscent of a grassbird.
Other sounds A distinctive bubbly *pi-ri-ri-ri*, given as flight and contact calls. The same phrase is also often heard in the song.
Regional variation None.

Habitat Mainly grasslands with patches of trees and bushes, but also protea woodlands and, sometimes, parks and gardens.
Similar sounding White-throated (488) and other canaries and seedeaters. While the continuous twittering songs of canaries can be difficult to separate, the bubbly *pi-ri-ri-ri* often punctuating the Cape Canary's song helps to distinguish it.

Forest Canary *Crithagra scotops*　　　　　　Gestreepte Kanarie

495 Track detail　0:02–0:48 (song)

Song Gives jumbled, short, metallic notes at a more piercing pitch than is usual for a canary. This is the least canary-like song given by any member of this group; it is as high pitched as that of a twinspot.
Other sounds In flight and when foraging gives a sharp note like those in its song.
Regional variation None.

Habitat Primarily evergreen forests, but may venture into adjoining habitat and even into lush gardens.
Similar sounding Pink-throated (486) and Red-throated (487) twinspots. Song bears superficial resemblance to those of these twinspots.

Common Chaffinch *Fringilla coelebs*　　　　　Gryskoppie

496 Track detail　0:19 (total length) = 0:02–0:13 (song); 0:13–0:19 (alarm call)

Song A jumbled mix of melodic trills and chirps, given in descending phrases of 4–5 notes each, and ending in a trill. Phrasing is distinctive.
Other sounds A series of chirps alternating between a high-pitched wagtail-like chirp and a high-pitched sparrow-like chirp; context uncertain. Phrasing is distinctive.

Regional variation None.
Habitat Restricted to plantations, parks and gardens in Cape Town.
Similar sounding None.

Lark-like Bunting *Emberiza impetuani*　　　　Vaalstreepkoppie

497 Track detail　1:15 (total length) = 0:03–1:04 (song); 1:04–1:15 (alarm call)

Song Gives repeated series of short swizzling notes that speed up; phrases end distinctively with a soft metallic rattle, reminiscent of a very high-pitched thrush's song.
Other sounds Alarm and contact calls comprise a short, harsh *tuk*.

Regional variation Unknown. Variations noted may not be a result of geographical location.
Habitat Very short grasslands, as well as shrub lands and rocky outcrops in dry areas.
Similar sounding None.

Cinnamon-breasted Bunting *Emberiza tahapisi* Klipstreepkoppie

498 Track detail 0:03–0:28 (song)

Song A slightly rasping *dzee-ree-oo-ree* with a distinctive, monotonous, high-pitched tone.
Other sounds Soft whistled alarm and contact calls.
Regional variation None.
Habitat Mainly rocky slopes with scattered bushes. Also rocky and sandy areas in grasslands and broad-leaved woodlands.

Similar sounding Monotonous Lark (239) and Cuckoo Finch (473). Tone and phrase of song distinctive enough that vague resemblance to song of these similar species is unlikely to cause confusion.

Cape Bunting *Emberiza capensis* Rooivlerkstreepkoppie

499 Track detail 0:02–0:26 (song)

Song Gives short, sweet, whistled *chee chee chee chip chip chira ru ree* phrases that vary in pitch.
Other sounds Very soft contact and alarm calls, often heard only at close range, comprising a rising nasal *ree-ree-ree*.
Regional variation Unknown.
Habitat Rocky slopes with scrub and scattered bushes. May venture into dry woodlands.

Similar sounding African Pied Wagtail (388), Striped Pipit (396), Yellow-fronted Canary (491) and Golden-breasted Bunting (500). Tone and rhythm of song readily identifiable, so superficial resemblance to the songs of those species listed here shouldn't cause confusion.

Golden-breasted Bunting *Emberiza flaviventris* Rooirugstreepkoppie

500 Track detail 0:02–0:38 (song)

Song Comprises short phrases of rapid repetitive *teeu* notes; concludes with some note variations.
Other sounds Short, sharp alarm and contact calls.
Regional variation Unknown.
Habitat Both acacia and broad-leaved woodlands. Favours dry conditions.

Similar sounding Yellow-throated Woodland Warbler (330), African Pied Wagtail (388), Striped Pipit (396), Yellow-fronted Canary (491) and Cape Bunting (499). Resemblance to species listed is superficial. Tone and rhythm should be readily identifiable.

INDEX TO SCIENTIFIC NAMES AND TRACK NUMBERS

 Page number in bold

 Track number in blue column

Chlorophoneus olivaceus	141	415		*Cyanomitra veroxii*	147	435
sulfureopectus	140	412		*Dendrocygna bicolor*	25	29
viridis	140	413		*viduata*	25	28
Chroicocephalus cirrocephalus	52	121		*Dendroperdix sephaena*	35	66
hartlaubii	52	122		*Dendropicos fuscescens*	82	227
Chrysococcyx caprius	61	157		*namaquus*	82	226
cupreus	62	159		*Dicrurus adsimilis*	92	263
klaas	62	158		*ludwigii*	92	264
Ciconia episcopus	23	24		*Dryoscopus cubla*	136	404
Cinnyricinclus leucogaster	143	422		*Egretta ardesiaca*	22	20
Cinnyris afer	147	436		*garzetta*	21	17
chalybeus	147	437		*Elanus caeruleus*	30	46
fuscus	149	442		*Emberiza capensis*	165	499
mariquensis	148	438		*flaviventris*	165	500
talatala	148	441		*impetuani*	164	497
venustus	148	440		*tahapisi*	165	498
Circaetus fasciolatus	28	41		*Eremomela scotops*	111	320
Cisticola aberrans	118	346		*usticollis*	110	319
aridulus	117	343		*Eremopterix australis*	89	254
ayresii	116	340		*verticalis*	89	255
chiniana	118	348		*Estrilda astrild*	159	478
cinnamomeus	117	344		*perreini*	159	479
erythrops	118	347		*Euplectes afer*	154	461
fulvicapilla	118	345		*albonotatus*	155	465
galactotes	119	352		*ardens*	156	466
juncidis	117	342		*axillaris*	155	464
lais	120	353		*orix*	155	462
natalensis	119	349		*progne*	155	463
pipiens	119	351		*Eupodotis caerulescens*	43	93
subruficapilla	120	354		*rueppellii*	43	92
textrix	117	341		*Eurocephalus anguitimens*	134	398
tinniens	119	350		*Euryptila subcinnamomea*	124	365
Clamator glandarius	61	156		*Eurystomus glaucurus*	74	202
Coccopygia melanotis	161	485		*Falco biarmicus*	31	53
Colius colius	69	185		*chicquera*	32	55
striatus	69	184		*rupicolus*	32	56
Columba delegorguei	55	134		*subbuteo*	32	54
guinea	55	133		*Fringilla coelebs*	164	496
livea	56	135		*Fulica cristata*	38	76
Coracias caudatus	73	199		*Galerida magnirostris*	83	231
garrulus	74	200		*Gallinago nigripennis*	49	110
naevius	74	201		*Gallinula chloropus*	38	77
Coracina caesia	93	266		*Geocolaptes olivaceus*	82	228
Corvinella melanoleuca	134	397		*Glareola pratincola*	46	100
Corvus albicollis	94	269		*Glaucidium capense*	64	167
albus	94	270		*perlatum*	65	169
capensis	94	271		*Guttera pucherani*	33	60
Corythaixoides concolor	59	150		*Gymnoris superciliaris*	150	445
Cossypha caffra	107	310		*Gyps coprotheres*	27	35
dichroa	107	308		*Haematopus moquini*	45	97
heuglini	108	312		*Halcyon albiventris*	71	193
humeralis	108	311		*chelicuti*	72	194
natalensis	107	309		*senegalensis*	71	191
Coturnix coturnix	37	74		*senegaloides*	71	192
delegorguei	38	75		*Haliaeetus vocifer*	27	36
Creatophora cinerea	143	425		*Hedydipna collaris*	148	439
Crecopsis egregia	40	82		*Heteromirafra ruddi*	89	253
Crithagra albogularis	162	488		*Himantopus himantopus*	44	94
atrogularis	163	492		*Hippolais icterina*	114	333
flaviventris	163	493		*olivetorum*	114	332
gularis	162	489		*Hirundo albigularis*	90	257
mozambica	163	491		*rustica*	90	256
scotops	164	495		*Hydroprogne caspia*	53	123
sulphurata	162	490		*Hypargos margaritatus*	161	486
Cryptillas victorini	109	316		*niveoguttatus*	161	487
Cuculus clamosus	60	153		*Iduna natalensis*	115	334
gularis	60	151		*Indicator indicator*	80	221
solitarius	60	152		*minor*	81	222

Ixobrychus minutus	23	22
Jynx ruficollis	82	229
Kaupifalco monogrammicus	30	47
Lagonosticta senegala	161	484
rhodopareia	160	483
rubricata	160	482
Lamprotornis australis	142	420
bicolor	142	421
chalybaeus	141	417
mevesii	142	419
nitens	141	416
Laniarius aethiopicus	137	406
atrococineus	138	408
bicolor	138	407
ferrugineus	137	405
Lanioturdus torquatus	129	381
Lanius collaris	135	401
collurio	135	399
minor	135	400
Larus dominicanus	52	120
Limosa lapponica	50	113
Lioptilus nigricapillus	97	278
Locustella fluviatilis	113	329
Lophaetus occipitalis	28	40
Lophotis ruficrista	42	89
Luscinia luscinia	108	313
Lybius torquatus	78	214
Macronyx capensis	132	389
croceus	132	390
Malaconotus blanchoti	140	414
Malcorus pectoralis	122	360
Megaceryle maximus	70	188
Melaenornis pammelaina	125	369
Melierax canorus	30	48
Merops apiaster	72	195
bullockoides	72	196
nubicoides	73	197
pusillus	73	198
Micronisus gabar	30	49
Milvus parasitus	29	42
Mirafra africana	86	241
apiata	86	244
cheniana	85	240
fasciolata	86	243
passerina	85	239
rufocinnamomea	86	242
Monticola angolensis	101	292
explorator	102	293
rupestris	101	291
Morus capensis	16	3
Motacilla aguimp	132	388
capensis	131	387
Muscicapa adusta	126	371
caerulescens	126	373
striata	126	372
Myioparus plumbeus	127	374
Myrmecocichla arnoti	104	300
formicivora	104	299
Nectarinia famosa	145	431
Nicator gularis	99	285
Nilaus afer	136	403
Notopholia corruscus	142	418
Numenius arquata	50	112
phaeopus	49	111
Numida meleagris	33	59
Oena capensis	58	143
Oenanthe pileata	105	301
Onychognathus morio	143	423
nabouroup	143	424
Oriolus auratus	93	267
larvatus	93	268
Otus senegalensis	64	168
Oxylophus jacobinus	61	155
levaillantii	61	154
Parus afer	95	273
cinerascens	95	272
niger	95	274
Passer diffusus	150	446
domesticus	149	444
melanurus	149	443
Pavo cristatus	34	61
Pelecanus onocrolatus	17	4
Peliperdix coqui	37	73
Petrochelidon spilodera	91	261
Phalacrocorax capensis	18	7
lucidus	18	6
Philetarius socius	151	448
Phoenicopterus roseus	17	5
Phoeniculus damarensis	77	210
purpureus	77	209
Phragmacia substriata	121	359
Phyllastrephus terrestris	97	279
Phylloscopus ruficapilla	114	330
trochilus	114	331
Platysteira peltata	130	382
Plegadis falcinellus	19	11
Plocepasser mahali	150	447
Ploceus bicolor	152	451
capensis	152	452
cucullatus	152	454
intermedius	153	456
ocularis	153	457
rubiginosus	154	459
subaureus	152	453
velatus	153	455
Pluvialis squatarola	48	107
Podiceps cristatus	24	26
Pogoniulus bilineatus	80	220
chrysoconus	80	219
pusillus	79	218
Poicephalus cryptoxanthus	58	146
meyeri	59	147
robustus	58	145
rueppellii	59	148
Polemaetus bellicosus	28	38
Polihierax semitorquatus	32	57
Polyboroides typus	31	52
Porphyrio alleni	39	79
madagascariensis	39	78
Porzana pusilla	40	83
Prinia flavicans	120	355
hypoxantha	121	358
maculosa	121	357
subflava	121	356
Prionops plumatus	136	402
Procellaria aequinoctialis	16	2
Promerops cafer	145	429
gurneyi	145	430
Psophocichla litsitsirupa	101	290
Pternistis adspersus	36	67
afer	36	70
capensis	36	68
hartlaubi	37	72
natalensis	36	69
swainsonii	37	71
Pterocles bicinctus	55	132

gutturalis	55	131		*layardi*	111	322
namaqua	54	130		*subcaeruleum*	111	321
Ptilopsis granti	64	166		*Sylvietta rufescens*	110	317
Ptyonoprogne fuligula	91	262		*Tachybaptus ruficollis*	24	27
Pycnonotus capensis	98	280		*Tachymarptis melba*	68	180
nigricans	98	281		*Tadorna cana*	26	31
tricolor	98	282		*Tauraco porphyreolopha*	59	149
Pytilia melba	160	480		*Tchagra australis*	139	409
Quelea quelea	154	460		*senegalus*	139	410
Rallus caerulescens	39	81		*Telephorus zeylonus*	139	411
Recurvirostra avosetta	44	95		*Terathopius ecaudatus*	27	37
Rhinopomastus cyanomelas	77	211		*Terpsiphone viridis*	127	376
Rhinoptilus cinctus	46	101		*Thalasseus sandvicensis*	53	124
Sagittarius serpentarius	42	88		*Threskiornis aethiopicus*	19	9
Sarothrura elegans	41	85		*Tockus alboterminatus*	76	207
rufa	40	84		*erythrorhynchus*	76	208
Saxicola torquatus	105	302		*leucomelas*	76	206
Schoenicola brevirostris	112	325		*nasutus*	75	205
Scleroptila africanus	34	62		*Trachyphonus vaillantii*	79	216
levaillantii	35	63		*Treron calvus*	57	140
levaillantoides	35	65		*Tricholaema leucomelas*	79	217
shelleyi	35	64		*Tringa glareola*	51	116
Scopus umbretta	24	25		*nebularia*	50	114
Scotopelia peli	65	171		*stagnatilis*	51	115
Serinus canicollis	164	494		*Trochocercus cyanomelas*	127	375
Sigelus silens	125	368		*Turdoides bicolor*	96	277
Smithornis capensis	130	383		*hartlaubii*	96	276
Spermestes cucullatus	158	474		*jardineii*	96	275
Spheniscus demersus	16	1		*Turdus libonyanus*	100	288
Sphenoeacus afer	109	315		*olivaceus*	100	286
Spizocorys conirostris	88	250		*smithi*	100	287
fringillaris	88	251		*Turtur chalcospilos*	57	141
sclateri	88	252		*tympanistria*	57	142
Sporaeginthus subflavus	160	481		*Tyto alba*	66	174
Sporopipes squamifrons	158	476		*Upupa africana*	78	212
Stactolaema leucotis	79	215		*Uraeginthus angolensis*	159	477
olivacea	78	213		*Urocolius indicus*	69	186
Stenostira scita	128	377		*Vanellus albiceps*	47	103
Stephanoaetus coronatus	28	39		*armatus*	47	102
Sterna hirundo	53	125		*coronatus*	47	104
Sternula albifrons	53	126		*melanopterus*	48	105
balaenarum	54	127		*senegallus*	48	106
Streptopelia capicola	56	138		*Vidua chalybeata*	157	472
decipiens	56	136		*funerea*	157	470
semitorquata	56	137		*macroura*	156	467
senegalensis	57	139		*paradisaea*	157	469
Strix woodfordii	63	164		*purpurascens*	157	471
Struthio camelus	33	58		*regia*	156	468
Sturnus vulgaris	144	427		*Zoothera gurneyi*	101	289
Sylvia borin	112	324		*Zosterops capensis*	130	384
communis	112	323		*pallidus*	131	385
				senegalensis	131	386

INDEX TO AFRIKAANS COMMON NAMES AND TRACK NUMBERS

169

Bromvoël	75	203
Byvanger, Klein-	92	264
Mikstert-	92	263
Byvreter, Europese	72	195
Klein-	73	198
Rooibors-	73	197
Rooikeel-	72	196
Diederikkie	61	157
Dikkop, Gewone	45	98
Water-	45	99
Dobbertjie, Klein-	24	27
Kuifkop-	24	26
Draaihals	82	229
Drawwertjie, Drieband-	46	101
Duif, Gewone Tortel-	56	138
Grootring-	56	137
Krans-	55	133
Papegaai-	57	140
Rooioogtortel-	56	136
Tuin-	56	135
Witbors-	57	142
Withalsbos-	55	134
Duifie, Groenvlek-	57	141
Namakwa-	58	143
Rooibors-	57	139
Duiker, Trek-	18	7
Witbors-	18	6
Eend, Fluit-	25	29
Geelbek-	26	32
Koper-	26	31
Nonnetjie-	25	28
Swart-	26	33
Teel-	26	34
Elsie, Bont-	44	95
Rooipoot-	44	94
Fisant, Bosveld-	37	71
Kaapse	36	68
Natalse	36	69
Rooibek-	36	67
Rooikeel-	36	70
Klip-	37	72
Flamink, Groot-	17	5
Flap, Kortstert-	155	464
Langstert-	155	463
Rooikeel-	156	466
Witvlerk-	155	465
Fret, Gewone	158	474
Gans, Kol-	25	30
Glansspreeu, Groot-	142	420
Groot-blouoor-	141	417
Klein-	141	416
Langstert-	142	419
Swartpens-	142	418
Glasogie, Gariep-	131	385
Geel-	131	386
Kaapse	130	384
Grasvoël	109	315
Griet, Bandstert-	50	113
Gryskoppie	164	496
Hadeda	19	10
Hamerkop	24	25
Heuningwyser, Groot-	80	221
Klein-	81	222
Hoephoep	78	212
Houtkapper, Bont-	79	217
Groen-	78	213
Kuifkop-	79	216
Rooikop-	78	214
Witoor-	78	215
Ibis, Glans-	19	11
Jakkalsvoël, Bos-	29	45

Bruin-	29	44
Rooibors-	29	43
Janfrederik, Gewone	107	310
Heuglin-	108	312
Lawaaimaker-	107	308
Natal-	107	309
Witkeel-	108	311
Jangroentjie	145	431
Kakelaar, Pers-	77	210
Rooibek-	77	209
Swartbek-	77	211
Kalkoentjie, Geelkeel-	132	390
Oranjekeel-	132	389
Kanarie, Berg-	163	492
Dikbek-	162	490
Geel-	163	493
Geeloog-	163	491
Gestreepte	164	495
Kaapse	164	494
Streepkop-	162	489
Witkeel-	162	488
Kapokvoël, Kaapse	110	318
Katakoeroe, Blou-	93	266
Swart-	92	265
Katlagter, Pylvlek-	96	275
Wit-	96	277
Witkruis-	96	276
Kelkiewyn	54	130
Kiewiet, Bont-	47	102
Grootswartvlerk-	48	105
Kroon-	47	104
Lel-	48	106
Ringnekstrand-	48	108
Witkop-	47	103
Klappertjie, Hoëveld-	86	243
Kaapse	86	244
Laeveld-	86	242
Kleinjantjie, Bandkeel-	124	366
Geelbors-	124	367
Klipwagter, Berg-	104	298
Klopkloppie, Bleekkop-	117	344
Gevlekte	117	341
Kleinste	116	340
Landery-	117	342
Woestyn-	117	343
Koekoek, Afrikaanse	60	151
Gevlekte	61	156
Swart-	60	153
Koester, Berg-	133	394
Donker-	132	391
Gestreepte	134	396
Gewone	133	393
Klip-	133	392
Nicholson-	133	395
Kolpensie, Rooikeel-	161	487
Rooskeel-	161	486
Koningriethaan, Groot-	39	78
Klein-	39	79
Konkoit	140	413
Korhaan, Blou-	43	93
Bos-	42	89
Swartvlerk-	42	90
Witvlerk-	43	91
Woestyn-	43	92
Koringvoël	150	447
Kraai, Swart-	94	271
Witbors-	94	270
Withals-	94	269
Kraanvoël, Blou-	41	87
Kwartel, Afrikaanse	37	74
Bont-	38	75

Kwêkwêvoël, Groenrug-	123	363
Grysrug-	123	364
Kwelea, Rooibek-	154	460
Kwêvoël	59	150
Kwikkie, Bont-	132	388
Gewone	131	387
Laksman, Bontrok-	136	403
Fiskaal-	135	401
Grys-	135	400
Kortstert-	129	381
Kremetart-	134	398
Langstert-	134	397
Olyfbos-	141	415
Oranjeborsbos-	140	412
Rooibors-	138	408
Rooirug-	135	399
Withelm-	136	402
Langstertjie, Bruinsy-	121	356
Drakensberg-	121	358
Karoo-	121	357
Namakwa-	121	359
Rooioor-	122	360
Swartband-	120	355
Langtoon, Groot-	44	96
Lewerik, Barlow-	85	237
Bosveld-	85	239
Dikbek-	83	231
Drakensberg-	89	253
Duin-	84	236
Grasveldlangbek-	87	246
Grysrug-	89	255
Karoo-	84	235
Karoolangbek-	87	247
Kortklou-	87	245
Namakwa-	88	252
Overberg-	88	249
Pienkbek-	88	250
Rooi-	85	238
Rooikop-	83	230
Rooinek-	86	241
Sabota-	84	233
Spot-	85	240
Swartoor-	89	254
Vaalbruin-	84	234
Vaalrivier-	88	251
Vlakte-	83	232
Weskus	87	248
Loerie, Bloukuif-	59	149
Lyster, Angolaklip-	101	292
Geelbek-	100	287
Gevlekte	101	290
Kaapse Klip-	101	291
Langtoonklip-	102	293
Olyf-	100	286
Oranje-	101	289
Oranjeborsberg-	102	294
Rooibek-	100	288
Mahem	41	86
Malgas, Wit-	16	3
Mees, Akasiagrys-	95	272
Gewone Swart-	95	274
Piet-tjou-tjougrys-	95	273
Meeu, Gryskop-	52	121
Hartlaub-	52	122
Kelp-	52	120
Meitjie	62	158
Melba, Gewone	160	480
Mooimeisie	62	159
Mossie, Geelvlek-	150	445
Gewone	149	443

Gryskop-	150	446
Huis-	149	444
Muisvoël, Gevlekte	69	184
Rooiwang-	69	186
Witrug-	69	185
Nagtegaal, Lyster-	108	313
Naguil, Afrikaanse	67	176
Donker-	66	175
Laeveld-	67	179
Natalse	67	178
Rooiwang-	67	177
Neddikie	118	345
Neushoringvoël, Geelbek-	76	206
Gekroonde	76	207
Grys-	75	205
Rooibek-	76	208
Nikator, Geelvlek-	99	285
Nuwejaarsvoël, Bont-	61	155
Gestreepte	61	154
Ooievaar, Wolnek-	23	24
Papegaai, Bloupens-	59	148
Bosveld-	59	147
Bruinkop-	58	146
Woud-	58	145
Parkiet, Rooiwang-	58	144
Patrys, Berg-	34	62
Bos-	35	66
Kalahari-	35	65
Laeveld-	35	64
Rooivlerk-	35	63
Pelikaan, Wit-	17	4
Piek, Bont-	104	300
Swart-	104	299
Piet-my-vrou	60	152
Pikkewyn, Bril-	16	1
Pou, Mak-	34	61
Reier, Blou-	20	14
Groenrug-	23	23
Grootriet-	22	21
Grootwit-	21	16
Kleinriet-	23	22
Kleinwit-	21	17
Ral-	22	19
Reuse-	20	12
Rooi-	20	13
Swart-	22	20
Swartkop-	21	15
Vee-	22	18
Renostervoël, Rooibek-	144	428
Riethaan, Afrikaanse	40	82
Groot-	39	81
Klein-	40	83
Swart-	39	80
Rooibekkie, Koning-	156	467
Pylstert-	156	468
Rotsvoël	109	314
Ruiter, Bos	51	116
Gewone	51	117
Groenpoot-	50	114
Moeras-	51	115
Sandpatrys, Dubbelband-	55	132
Geelkeel-	55	131
Sanger, Breëstert-	112	325
Bruinkeelbos-	110	319
Donkerwangbos-	111	320
Europese Riet-	116	339
Europese Vlei-	115	335
Gebande	122	361
Geel-	115	334
Geelkeel-	114	330
Grootriet-	115	336

171

Hof-	114	331
Kaapse Riet-	115	337
Kaapse Vlei-	113	326
Kaneelbors-	124	365
Kleinriet-	116	338
Knysnaruigte-	113	327
Olyfboom-	114	332
Rooiborsruigte-	109	316
Ruigte-	113	328
Spot-	114	333
Sprinkaan-	113	329
Stierling-	122	362
Tuin-	112	324
Witkeel-	112	323
Sekretarisvoël	42	88
Skaapwagter, Hoëveld-	105	301
Skoorsteenveër	19	9
Slanghalsvoël	18	8
Slangverklikker	107	307
Sneeubal	136	404
Snip, Afrikaanse	49	110
Speg, Baard-	82	226
Bennett-	81	225
Goudstert-	81	223
Grond-	82	228
Kardinaal-	82	227
Knysna-	81	224
Spekvreter, Gewone	103	295
Vlakte-	103	296
Woestyn-	103	297
Sperwer, Afrikaanse	31	50
Gebande	31	51
Witkruis- (Kleinsingvalk)	30	49
Spookvoël	140	414
Spreeu, Bleekvlerk-	143	424
Europese	144	427
Indiese	144	426
Lel-	143	425
Rooivlerk-	143	423
Witbors-	143	422
Witgat-	142	421
Springkaanvoël, Rooivlerk-	46	100
Sterretjie, Damara-	54	127
Gewone	53	125
Groot-	53	124
Klein-	53	126
Reuse-	53	123
Witbaard-	54	128
Witvlerk-	54	129
Stompstert, Bosveld-	110	317
Strandkiewiet, Drieband-	49	109
Grys-	48	107
Strandloper, Drietoon-	51	118
Klein-	52	119
Streepkoppie, Klip-	165	498
Rooirug-	165	500
Rooivlerk-	165	499
Vaal-	164	497
Suikerbekkie, Geelpens-	148	440
Groot-rooiband-	147	436
Grys-	147	435
Klein-rooiband-	147	437
Kortbek-	148	439
Marico-	148	438
Namakwa-	149	442
Oranjebors-	146	432
Rooibors-	146	433
Swart-	146	434
Witpens-	148	441
Suikervoël, Kaapse	145	429
Rooibors	145	430

Swael, Witkeel-	90	257
Europese	90	256
Familie-	91	261
Grootstreep-	91	259
Kleinstreep-	90	258
Krans-	91	262
Rooibors-	91	260
Swempie	37	73
Swie, Suidelike	161	485
Sysie, Gewone Blou-	159	477
Grys-	159	479
Roobek-	159	478
Tarentaal, Gewone	33	59
Kuifkop-	33	60
Tinker, Geelbles-	80	219
Rooibles-	79	218
Tinktinkie, Bosveld-	118	348
Groot-	119	349
Grysrug-	120	354
Huil-	120	353
Lui-	118	346
Piepende	119	351
Rooiwang-	118	347
Swartrug-	119	352
Vlei-	119	350
Tiptol, Kaapse	98	280
Rooibek-	97	278
Rooioog-	98	281
Swartoog-	98	282
Tjagra, Rooivlerk-	139	409
Swartkroon-	139	410
Tjeriktik, Bosveld-	111	321
Grys-	111	322
Tobie, Swart-	45	97
Troupant, Europese	74	200
Geelbek-	74	202
Gewone	73	199
Groot-	74	201
Uil, Bos-	63	164
Gebande	64	167
Gevlekte Oor-	66	173
Kaapse Oor-	65	172
Nonnetjie-	66	174
Reeuse-oor-	65	170
Skops-	64	168
Vis-	65	171
Vlei-	64	165
Witkol-	65	169
Witwang-	64	166
Valk, Akkedis-	30	47
Bleeksing-	30	48
Blou-	30	46
Dwerg-	32	57
Edel-	31	53
Europese Boom-	32	54
Kaalwang-	31	52
Krans-	32	56
Rooinek-	32	55
Versamelvoël	151	448
Vink, Gewone Paradys-	157	469
Goudgeel-	154	461
Kleingeel-	153	456
Koekoek-	158	473
Rooi-	155	462
Rooikop-	158	475
Swartkeelgeel-	153	455
Visvanger, Bont-	70	189
Bosveld-	71	191
Bruinkop-	71	193
Gestreepte	72	194
Kuifkop-	71	190

172

Mangliet-	71	192		Waterhoender, Groot-	38	77
Reuse-	70	188		Wewer, Bontrug-	152	454
Vleikuiken, Gevlekte	41	85		Bril-	153	457
Rooibors-	40	84		Bruin-	154	459
Vleiloerie, Gewone	62	161		Buffel-	151	449
Groot-	62	160		Dikbek-	151	450
Senegal-	63	162		Geel-	152	453
Swart-	63	163		Kaapse	152	452
Vlieëvanger, Blougrys-	126	373		Rooikop-	153	458
Bloukuif-	127	375		Wielewaal, Afrikaanse	93	267
Donker-	126	371		Swartkop-	93	268
Europese	126	372		Willie, Geelbors-	99	284
Fee-	128	377		Gewone	99	283
Fiskaal-	125	368		Windswael, Horus-	68	182
Groot-	125	370		Klein-	68	181
Paradys-	127	376		Witkruis-	69	183
Swart-	125	369		Witpens-	68	180
Waaierstert-	127	374		Wipstert, Baard-	106	304
Volstruis	33	58		Bruin-	105	303
Vuurvinkie, Jameson-	160	483		Gestreepte	106	305
Kaapse	160	482		Kalahari-	106	306
Rooibek-	161	484		Wou, Geelbek-	29	42
Waterfiskaal, Moeras-	138	407		Wulp, Groot-	50	112
Suidelike	137	405		Klein-	49	111
Tropiese	137	406				

INDEX TO ENGLISH COMMON NAMES AND TRACK NUMBERS

Apalis, Bar-throated	124	366		Olive	141	415
Yellow-breasted	124	367		Orange-breasted	140	412
Avocet, Pied	44	95		Buzzard, Forest	29	45
Babbler, Arrow-marked	96	275		Jackal	29	43
Hartlaub's	96	276		Lizard	30	47
Southern Pied	96	277		Steppe	29	44
Barbet, Acacia Pied	79	217		Camaroptera, Green-backed	123	363
Black-collared	78	214		Grey-backed	123	364
Crested	79	216		Canary, Black-throated	163	492
Green	78	213		Brimstone	162	490
White-eared	79	215		Cape	164	494
Bateleur	27	37		Forest	164	495
Batis, Cape	128	378		White-throated	162	488
Chinspot	129	379		Yellow	163	493
Pririt	129	380		Yellow-fronted	163	491
Bee-eater, European	72	195		Chaffinch, Common	164	496
Little	73	198		Chat, Ant-eating	104	299
Southern Carmine	73	197		Arnot's	104	300
White-fronted	72	196		Buff-streaked	104	298
Bishop, Southern Red	155	462		Familiar	103	295
Yellow-crowned	154	461		Sickle-winged	103	296
Bittern, Eurasian	22	21		Tractrac	103	297
Little	23	22		Cisticola, Ayres' (Wing-snapping)	116	340
Blackcap, Bush	97	278		Chirping	119	351
Bokmakierie	139	411		Cloud	117	341
Boubou, Southern	137	405		Croaking	119	349
Swamp	138	407		Desert	117	343
Tropical	137	406		Grey-backed	120	354
Broadbill, African	130	383		Lazy	118	346
Brownbul, Terrestrial	97	279		Levaillant's	119	350
Brubru	136	403		Pale-crowned	117	344
Bulbul, African Red-eyed	98	281		Rattling	118	348
Cape	98	280		Red-faced	118	347
Dark-capped (Black-eyed)	98	282		Rufous-winged	119	352
Bunting, Cape	165	499		Wailing	120	353
Cinnamon-breasted	165	498		Zitting	117	342
Golden-breasted	165	500		Coot, Red-knobbed	38	76
Lark-like	164	497		Cormorant, Cape	18	7
Bushshrike, Gorgeous	140	413		White-breasted	18	6
Grey-headed	140	414		Coucal, Black	63	163

Burchell's	62	161	**Francolin**, Coqui	37	73
Coppery-tailed	62	160	Crested	35	66
Senegal	63	162	Grey-winged	34	62
Three-banded	46	101	Orange River	35	65
Crake, African	40	82	Red-winged	35	63
Baillon's	40	83	Shelley's	35	64
Black	39	80	**Gallinule**, Allen's	39	79
Crane, Blue	41	87	**Gannet**, Cape	16	3
Grey Crowned	41	86	**Go-away-bird (Lourie)**, Grey	59	150
Crombec, Long-billed	110	317	**Godwit**, Bar-tailed	50	113
Crow, Cape	94	271	**Goose**, Egyptian	25	30
Pied	94	270	**Goshawk**, African	31	50
Cuckoo, African	60	151	Gabar	30	49
African Emerald	62	159	Pale Chanting	30	48
Black	60	153	**Grassbird**, Cape	109	315
Dideric	61	157	**Grebe**, Great Crested	24	26
Great Spotted	61	156	Little (Dabchick)	24	27
Jacobin	61	155	**Greenbul**, Sombre	99	283
Klaas's	62	158	Yellow-bellied	99	284
Levaillant's	61	154	**Greenshank**, Common	50	114
Red-chested	60	152	**Guineafowl**, Crested	33	60
Cuckooshrike, Black	92	265	Helmeted	33	59
Grey	93	266	**Gull**, Grey-headed	52	121
Curlew, Eurasian	50	112	Hartlaub's	52	122
Darter, African	18	8	Kelp	52	120
Dove, African Mourning	56	136	**Hamerkop**	24	25
Cape Turtle	56	138	**Harrier-Hawk**, African (Gymnogene)	31	52
Emerald-spotted Wood	57	141	**Helmetshrike**, White-crested	136	402
Laughing	57	139	**Heron**, Black	22	20
Namaqua	58	143	Black-headed	21	15
Red-eyed	56	137	Goliath	20	12
Rock (Feral Pigeon)	56	135	Green-backed (Striated)	23	23
Tambourine	57	142	Grey	20	14
Drongo, Fork-tailed	92	263	Purple	20	13
Square-tailed	92	264	Squacco	22	19
Duck, African Black	26	33	**Hobby**, Eurasian	32	54
Fulvous Whistling	25	29	**Honeyguide**, Greater	80	221
White-faced Whistling	25	28	Lesser	81	222
Yellow-billed	26	32	**Hoopoe**, African	78	212
Eagle, African Fish	27	36	**Hornbill**, African Grey	75	205
Crowned	28	39	Crowned	76	207
Long-crested	28	40	Southern Ground-	75	203
Martial	28	38	Southern Red-billed	76	208
Southern Banded Snake	28	41	Southern Yellow-billed	76	206
Egret, Great	21	16	Trumpeter	75	204
Little	21	17	**Ibis**, African Sacred	19	9
Western Cattle	22	18	Glossy	19	11
Eremomela, Burnt-necked	110	319	Hadeda	19	10
Green-capped	111	320	**Indigobird**, Dusky	157	470
Falcon, Lanner	31	53	Purple	157	471
Pygmy	32	57	Village	157	472
Red-necked	32	55	**Jacana**, African	44	96
Finch, Cuckoo	158	473	**Kestrel**, Rock	32	56
Red-headed	158	476	**Kingfisher**, Brown-hooded	71	193
Scaly-feathered	158	474	Giant	70	188
Firefinch, African (Blue-billed)	160	482	Malachite	71	190
Jameson's	160	483	Mangrove	71	192
Red-billed	161	484	Pied	70	189
Fiscal, Common	135	401	Striped	72	194
Flamingo, Greater	17	5	Woodland	71	191
Flufftail, Buff-spotted	41	85	**Kite**, Black-shouldered	30	46
Red-chested	40	84	Yellow-billed	29	42
Flycatcher, African Dusky	126	371	**Korhaan**, Blue	43	93
African Paradise	127	376	Northern Black	43	91
Ashy	126	373	Red-crested	42	89
Blue-mantled Crested	127	375	Rüppell's	43	92
Chat	125	370	Southern Black	42	90
Fairy	128	377	**Lapwing (Plover)**, African Wattled	48	106
Fiscal	125	368	Black-winged	48	105
Southern Black	125	369	Blacksmith	47	102
Spotted	126	372	Crowned	47	104

White-crowned	47	103		**Pipit**, African	133	393
Lark, Agulhas Long-billed	88	249		African Rock	133	392
Barlow's	85	237		Long-billed	133	395
Botha's	88	251		Mountain	133	394
Cape Clapper	86	244		Plain-backed	132	391
Cape Long-billed	87	248		Striped	134	396
Dune	84	236		**Plover**, Common Ringed	48	108
Eastern Clapper	86	243		Grey	48	107
Eastern Long-billed	87	246		Three-banded	49	109
Fawn-coloured	84	234		**Pratincole**, Collared (Red-winged)	46	100
Flappet	86	242		**Prinia**, Black-chested	120	355
Karoo	84	235		Drakensberg	121	358
Karoo Long-billed	87	247		Karoo	121	357
Large-billed (Thick-billed)	83	231		Tawny-flanked	121	356
Melodious	85	240		**Puffback**, Black-backed	136	404
Monotonous	85	239		**Pytillia**, Green-winged	160	480
Pink-billed	88	250		**Quail**, Common	37	74
Red	85	238		Harlequin	38	75
Red-capped	83	230		**Quelea**, Red-billed	154	460
Rudd's	89	253		**Rail**, African	39	81
Rufous-naped	86	241		**Raven**, White-necked	94	269
Sabota	84	233		**Robin-Chat**, Cape	107	310
Sclater's	88	252		Chorister	107	308
Short-clawed	87	245		Red-capped	107	309
Spike-heeled	83	232		White-browed	108	312
Longclaw, Cape	132	389		White-throated	108	311
Yellow-throated	132	390		**Robin**, Bearded Scrub	106	304
Lovebird, Rosy-faced	58	144		Brown Scrub	105	303
Mannikin, Bronze	158	475		Kalahari Scrub	106	306
Martin, Rock	91	262		Karoo Scrub	107	307
Moorhen, Common	38	77		White-browed Scrub	106	305
Mousebird, Red-faced	69	186		**Rockjumper**, Drakensburg	102	294
Speckled	69	184		**Rockrunner**	109	314
White-backed	69	185		**Roller**, Broad-billed	74	202
Myna, Common	144	426		European	74	200
Neddicky	118	345		Lilac-breasted	73	199
Nicator, Eastern	99	285		Purple	74	201
Nightingale, Thrush	108	313		**Sanderling**	51	118
Nightjar, Fiery-necked	67	176		**Sandgrouse**, Double-banded	55	132
Freckled	66	175		Namaqua	54	130
Rufous-cheeked	67	177		Yellow-throated	55	131
Square-tailed (Mozambique)	67	179		**Sandpiper**, Common	51	117
Swamp (Natal)	67	178		Marsh	51	115
Oriole, African Golden	93	267		Wood	51	116
Black-headed	93	268		**Scimitarbill**, Common (Greater)	77	211
Ostrich, Common	33	58		**Secretarybird**	42	88
Owl, African Scops	64	168		**Seedeater**, Streaky-headed	162	489
African Wood	63	164		**Shelduck**, South African	26	31
Cape Eagle-	65	172		**Shikra**	31	51
Marsh	64	165		**Shrike**, Crimson-breasted	138	408
Pel's Fishing	65	171		Lesser Grey	135	400
Southern White-faced	64	166		Magpie	134	397
Spotted Eagle-	66	173		Red-backed	135	399
Verreaux's (Giant) Eagle-	65	170		Southern White-crowned	134	398
Western Barn	66	174		White-tailed	129	381
Owlet, African Barred	64	167		**Snipe**, African (Ethiopian)	49	110
Pearl-spotted	65	169		**Sparrow-Lark**, Black-eared	89	254
Oxpecker, Red-billed	144	428		Grey-backed	89	255
Oystercatcher, African (Black)	45	97		**Sparrow-Weaver**, White-browed	150	447
Parrot, Brown-headed	58	146		**Sparrow**, Cape	149	443
Cape	58	145		House	149	444
Meyer's	59	147		Southern Grey-headed	150	446
Rüppell's	59	148		**Spurfowl**, Cape	36	68
Peafowl, Indian	34	61		Hartlaub's	37	72
Pelican, Great White	17	4		Natal	36	69
Penduline-Tit, Cape	110	318		Red-billed	36	67
Penguin, African	16	1		Red-necked	36	70
Petrel, White-chinned	16	2		Swainson's	37	71
Petronia, Yellow-throated	150	445		**Starling**, Black-bellied	142	418
Pigeon, African Green	57	140		Burchell's	142	420
Eastern Bronze-naped (Delegorgue's)	55	134		Cape Glossy	141	416
Speckled	55	133		Common	144	427

176